Walter Schwarz

The Ideal Occupation

A memoir

Revel Barker
Publishing

First published 2011 by Revel Barker Publishing

By the same author:

The Arabs in Israel (Faber 1959)

Nigeria (Pall Mall 1968)

The New Dissenters – The nonconformist conscience in the age of Thatcher (Bedford Square Press 1989)

Breaking Through – theory and practice of holistic living (with Dorothy Schwarz, Green Books 1987)

Living Lightly – travels in post-consumer society (with Dorothy Schwarz, Jon Carpenter 1997)

The Ideal Occupation
ISBN: 978-1-907841-02-6

Revel Barker Publishing
66 Florence Road, Brighton, England BN2 6DJ
revelbarker@gmail.com

Contents

Introduction

When I was 13 we all had to write an essay called The Ideal Occupation. After dismissing rich bank manager on one hand and quiet life with lots of free time on the other, I opted for 'a life of travel, excitement, freedom: in short a journalist.'

I added that I didn't want to be controlled in an office by an editor, plagued with deadlines, but to 'visit places (ordinary places), and talk to people (ordinary people) and build up my articles from that.' The teacher wrote at the bottom: 'Pleasantly written. An interesting ambition, not easily realised.'

Decades later, as the *Guardian* man in Nigeria (1964-67), Israel (1970-72), India (1972-75) and France (1975-84), visiting ordinary places and talking to ordinary people, with or without a notebook in my hand, was as much fun as I had imagined.

I never became a roving commentator, free from the pressure of news. A friend in Delhi held that exalted position for the *Süd Deutsche Zeitung*. I envied him a little, but I fancy he sometimes envied me for the rush of adrenalin that comes with news and deadlines.

I never won a prize and was not promoted to the Washington bureau. I have written leaders and comment pieces but never became a pundit. Notebook in hand, I was a good listener – but only up to a point: the point where my angle, my story became apparent, and then my attention might wander a bit, perhaps missing another story that a subtler journalist might have picked up.

Did I matter? I was good at explaining. People tell me they gained insight into Nigeria, Israel, India, France and religious affairs through my pieces and my books. I might have mattered less if I had worked in the digital age where everyone has instant access to news, comment and background. Still, we will always need good correspondents on the spot to reveal, relate, explain and evaluate. We need them to discern and highlight the heroic, the pathetic, the shameful and the grotesque in what may look like a bland environment.

It was harder for us then, stumbling with our typewriters out of airplanes into the scene of a crisis, knowing only what we heard on the radio, desperate to update ourselves however we could. Dare I suggest that in those days our stories might have been sharper, leaner, fresher? Modern correspondents have so much information at their fingertips that they must often be tempted to cut-and-paste and paraphrase background information, anecdotes and opinion into their copy, making it a little flabbier, a little more like the story written by their rivals?

It was also easier. We filed our stories to a deadline and then we could relax, drink away the tension and enjoy the places and people we lived in and among. I know no finer taste than the first mouthful of beer in a hotel bar after filing my story. Today's correspondents serve a digital, round-the-clock, seven-days-a-week newsdesk. I am sorry for them, just as I used to be sorry for BBC colleagues who could never join us for a drink after a press conference because they had deadlines all the time.

I loved this profession from first to last, from precarious freelancing to the comfortable prestige of a foreign correspondent on the staff of a great newspaper which mostly let me do what I wanted. Now I want to write about why I loved it so much, how I got into it, the fun we had, and the scrapes we got into, with our children in Africa, the Middle East, Asia and Europe.

This is a career I could not have achieved and a life I could not have lived without Dorothy and the children – Habie, Ben, Tanya, Zoë and, at the last, little Zac, because they were all game for adventure. Their insights, friends and hobbies enriched both my reporting and my life. The children hated abrupt moves to yet another new country, and their Dad was too often absent on assignment. Still, I hope our travels enriched their lives. For a start, they are all fluent in French. And Ben found his Fréderique in his French lycée.

In this memoir I start with my early life, because I see that as not only a prelude but quite often, as will become apparent, a rehearsal.

7

From an early age I kept diaries and wrote letters to my parents, which they kept and returned to me, and they are available to me as I write now.

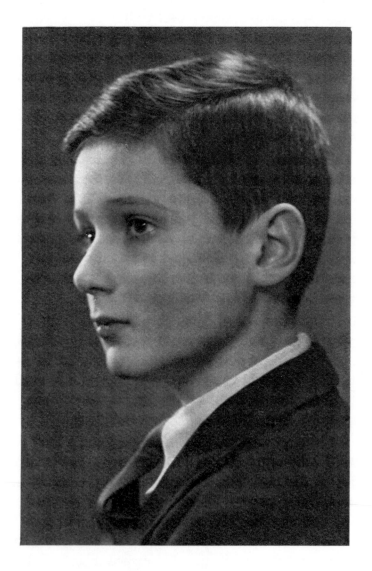

A dreamy boy in Vienna

A Viennese tram, single-deck, white above and red below, glides down the Boschstrasse. It has just passed Karl Marx Hof, the massive apartment block built as a fortress to house socialist workers and defend them from fascists. It is 1933. On the track in front of him the driver sees a small boy squatting, immobile, his back to the tram, rapt in contemplation of the gravelled ground. The tram stops; the driver rings his bell, keeps on ringing. The boy does not hear, does not move. Half a minute passes. A young woman pushing a pram rushes forward, grabs the child with her free hand and pulls him clear.

This is my first real memory, not just nanny's account, because Lina would not have cared to publicise her moment of inattention. In any case it fits in with my character, my bad habit of withdrawing from the external world even when someone is ringing a bell. Or talking to me. I was three.

My second memory, a year later, is hearing artillery fire. We were standing on the balcony of our Viennese flat in lofty Döbling, looking down on plumes of smoke. We were not scared because this conflict didn't concern us. It was February 12, 1934. Socialist workers had started a revolt; armed militants were barricaded in the Karl Marx Hof. The army opened fire. The revolt was swiftly crushed.

Cannon fire had nothing to do with our smooth and comfortable life. Yet for my parents, my elder brother Vicky and my little sister Marlene, the battle on February 12 was a portent: two years later we were preparing to sell our two-storey apartment at 3 Gallmeyergasse, leave our wider family and friends and move to England. There was no sense of crisis. Mother and Father still entertained friends, took us on excursions, laughed about our more eccentric relatives.

On September 14 in the year of my birth, 1930, Hitler's National Socialists won 107 seats in the German Reichstag. Most Viennese Jews considered Hitler a crazed windbag speaking to an envious rabble. Until 1938, when German troops marched in, the Jews of Austria refused to believe that Nazi fantasies could ever be enacted in a civilised country. But my father took Hitler at his word. As an importer and exporter of textiles, he had contacts in Manchester and in my seventh year he moved us peacefully and comfortably to England.

Even then, when we were safe in Manchester and Britain was at war, unease and worry were to return and grow into dread that Germany might win and that we might, after all, be at the mercy of the Nazis.

Chapter one:
A land of cockroaches and Maltesers

'Is this London?' I asked as we stepped off the train and I looked up at the immensity of Victoria station. I must have asked it in German.

But Vicky and I knew some English already, thanks to Miss Church who had been hired to teach us. We had spent our last month in Austria on holiday at Innsbruck in the Tyrol, where Father's family owned Bauer-Schwarz, the big department store which is still there, now known as *Kaufhaus Tyrol*. We stayed with Grandma Rosa at Igls, the pretty resort village just above the town.

Jennifer Church, a tall, slender, long-haired 20-year-old, had come to Austria to study singing. She had fallen in love with the country and when trouble arrived she volunteered to smuggle out the valuables of Jewish refugees; at the border she would cover her voluminous luggage with a cloth picture of Hitler to avoid searches. Later when she was carrying messages for the Resistance, she was arrested and spent the whole war in an Austrian prison.

> Before my arrest I had two charming little boys as pupils for English. Their father came from Innsbruck, where their family had the largest and best-known draper's shop. During the summer of 1937 I spent a most delightful holiday with the family, ostensibly as English teacher to three children, but actually Frau Lilly Schwarz treated me as her own elder daughter. She was the most charming woman imaginable ... and as for the children I have never met such delightfully natural and well-mannered small people.
>
> From an unpublished memoir by Jennifer Church, 1945.

Our block of flats in North End Road, Hammersmith, seemed to me even larger than Victoria station, but dismal after our leafy home in Vienna. Every night huge, bloated cockroaches crept out from somewhere. You could hear them in the dark if they passed over anything crackly like a newspaper. Turn on the light and you saw their shiny black backs. Even with the light on they were in no hurry to leave.

Vicky and I went to Colet Court, the St Paul's prep school, of which I remember nothing except lining up to go from one place to another and then sitting still. It was in the concrete playground around the Hammersmith flats that I slowly learnt how to be English. A big girl, at least nine years old, said to me in disgusted disbelief: 'You mean to say you don't even know what *Maltesers* are?' She relented and gave me one, confirming my growing belief that we had come to a good land and that I was a lucky boy.

We were in London, not yet Manchester, because Father had moved into a new business – rashly as it turned out. He had bought the patent for a brilliant new process for making artificial marble. Every day he went to his hired workshop to watch beautiful slabs come off the pilot production line. One day someone spilt some water over a finished tile. It left an indelible stain. The patent was worthless.

Father was resilient: he still had his contacts and his reputation in textiles. We moved to a house in the respectable Manchester suburb of West Didsbury where we stayed for 13 years. Our school, Vic's and mine, was the 400-year-old Manchester Grammar School. For the first two years I went to its prep school known as South, which was conveniently in West Didsbury.

South was a humane school without over-emphasis on sport. It allowed me to dream away much of the time and one day, at the end of summer term, I was only half aware when the teacher started writing our 20-odd names on the blackboard in order of academic merit. Mine was second. I was surprised, mildly pleased.

At South I had my first friend, Michael Grainger. I can't remember what we did together but I loved him. When Mother picked us both up from school and put him on his homeward bus, I was desolate and wanted to cry. Michael lived in another suburb and sometimes I went home with him on the bus and his Dad would drive me back through blacked-out streets without headlights. He seemed to me a genius because he could drive in pitch darkness without crashing.

Michael's Mum came to visit. Mother, pleased that I had an English friend, wanted to be correct and polite in this new country. Our guest had been complaining about her wartime domestic chores and Mother, inviting her to forget her troubles, said: 'Mrs Grainger, you are too much at home here.' Our friends had better refugee howlers than that to joke about.

> In a bus, refugee woman sits downstairs, man sits upstairs. Conductor asks woman for the fare. Woman (translating *der Herr Oben wird bezahlen*) says: 'The Lord Above will pay'.

The war was distant theatre whose sounds reached us kids intermittently. It gave us excitement, a shared yearning for victory, occasional fear when whistling bombs came down in a scream that pitched lower and lower until the explosion. We had been assured that if you heard a whistling bomb you were safe; when you didn't you had to worry.

But first there was the evacuation. Only two years after being uprooted, here I was again, aged nine, leaving home. Hundreds of us lined up on the platform at Piccadilly Station with cardboard name-plates and boxed gasmasks around our necks. 'Are we downhearted?' No, but we were utterly bewildered. Excited, too: I was on a journey, an adventure, something I already loved and have loved ever since.

We arrived at the small town of Uttoxeter in Staffordshire. We sat in a school hall as foster parents queued up to take us away in lots of two, three or four. Not many of us were left in the hall when a teacher said: 'And now we have a family who want to take only one child. Who wouldn't mind being alone?' Up went my hand. I have never minded being alone. That is my paradox: journalists are supposed to be gregarious but I like travelling alone, because then I have no shield against new people and places.

The second car in the garage was a Rolls-Royce. A grown-up daughter, Margaret, came to my room the first morning. I had wet my bed. 'Do you always do that?' she asked with dismay but no reproach. I said only sometimes. I was fitted with a rubber undersheet and the problem was solved. My hosts were cool and stiff, but kind, and took me on Sunday outings in the Rolls.

The evacuation must have been a logistic nightmare and the authorities put a huge effort into it. The local schools had to have double-shift classes and I remember grown-ups with clipboards checking roll calls, re-arranging timetables, trudging round to every evacuee's billet. They were cheerful and helpful and everything seemed to me to run like clockwork – another lesson in Britishness and further confirmation of how lucky I was to be here. In our first week, on a fine September morning, we were taken into an open space with a radio and a loudspeaker to hear Mr Chamberlain declare war.

The evacuation had only lasted a few months when it was abandoned and we came home just in time for the Blitz. Father had a room in our cellar reinforced and fitted with bunks. When the sirens sounded, usually at night, the routine was to take our bedding down to the shelter, stopping in the kitchen to grab a flask of tea and snacks. I enjoyed the adventure and the camaraderie. Fear was concentrated in the person of our grown-up cousin Hedi, a figure of fun who always got into a state when there was what she called a *veessling* bomb. One night a stick of bombs, not whistling, dropped nearby. A splinter blew in through the window of Vicky's bedroom and lodged in the wall above his bed. Vicky was proud of his splinter.

For boys big enough to know what was happening but too young to imagine death and mutilation, war was exciting. We collected fragments of shrapnel, took them to school, swapped and traded them. Just before Christmas, 1940, on the morning after Manchester's only air raid on the scale of a Blitz, we looked out of an upstairs window and saw fires blazing in the nearby Withington hospital. Then we all took a bus into town, just like tourists, to see the ruined buildings, many still burning. Manchester Cathedral, the Royal Exchange and the Free Trade Hall were all hit. Nearly 700 people had been killed, 2,000 injured.

One sunny afternoon, standing on our lawn with our heads tilted back, we children watched a dogfight. The sirens had sounded and

14

Mother and Father kept calling us to go down into the shelter, but the aerial battle was too exciting to miss. We didn't see its outcome.

With our gasmask cases slung over our shoulders Vicky and I took the bus at the end of our road to Rusholme. Separately in our respective gangs we walked down Old Hall Lane, through the gates and up the imposing drive to the massive red-brick school with its clock tower. One morning there was a crater in the playing fields where a landmine had parachuted down in the night and blown out the windows of houses in the lane.

Manchester Grammar School has long, echoing corridors; it can take weeks for a dreamy boy to learn how to get from English to maths, from French to history. For years after leaving school I had bad dreams of being late for class but unable to work out how to get there.

Our teachers were splendidly eccentric and seemed to us brilliant. Mr Lingard taught us French by talking mainly about himself, which worked because he had loved every moment of the years he spent in France, making the country and the language romantic for us. Few of us enjoyed Latin but it has helped me to survive in Spain, Portugal and Brazil, and given me a finer feel for English. Mr Mason, our excellent English teacher, didn't like me because I was dreamy and inattentive; he was visibly put out when I won the annual Shakespeare scholarship essay competition with its rich prize of £40.

My sixth-form master, Mr Bunn, was a socialist at least, perhaps even left of that – a new experience for me since Father was a conservative and Vicky was to follow his lead. In my end-of-year report Mr Bunn used only six words to describe me: 'A liberal of the old school.' I do not think it was meant as a compliment.

Peter Noble was my best friend. We both loved cycling and classical music. We learnt to play the recorder and played duets, he on the treble and I the descant.

25 February 1946
Half Term. Went for cycle ride with Noble – to Liverpool. Noble had his recorder mended and we spent a happy half hour rooting about among recorder music, and we bought quite a lot. So we

never even saw the docks or the Cathedral. We stopped on the way back and played some Purcell duets in a field.

Sometimes we took our bikes on the train to the Peak District. On one of those rides we were rolling downhill in torrential rain on a steep and twisty country lane. Peter was in front, out of sight round a sharp bend. I was heading for the bend, faster and faster. My brakes were wet: I could neither stop nor negotiate the bend. Straight ahead was a stone wall.

I hit the wall and bounced over it, bike and all, unconscious for a second yet quite unhurt. Lucky boy. We even found a shop in the nearby village that sold me a new front wheel and we continued on our way.

Peter when he grew up was not lucky at all: he caught polio and lived his last fifteen years in a wheelchair. I was abroad for most of that time, so I could do little to comfort my poor best friend.

My first political memory is a wartime fund-raising reception at our house. A cloth banner draped across the upstairs windows read: 'WE SHALL NEVER FORGET THAT AUSTRIA WAS THE FIRST VICTIM OF NAZI-AGGRESSION' – WINSTON CHURCHILL

This was hardly true, since most Austrians had supported the 1938 union with Nazi Germany. Right up to the war our parents had worked in networks trying to help people get out of Austria. After the *Anschluss* Austrian émigrés and refugees agitated for the eventual liberation of Austria from the Nazis. Father was prominent in the Free Austria movement. Gradually it was taken over by communists. Father hated communists and took a back seat.

During the war we Austrians were technically 'enemy aliens'. One day we were informed that Father was to be taken away to be interned. He packed his bags, a car came for him, and we did not expect to see him for the rest of the war. By evening he was back. They had diagnosed him – wrongly – as diabetic and decided they could not handle him in the internment camp.

We had a map on the sitting room wall and as the Germans retreated Father chalk-marked every Russian advance. On red-letter days – Smolensk, Kiev, Leningrad – we celebrated with cider, the first alcohol we kids ever tasted.

Churchill of course was our hero. We felt – and so did all our friends and relations – that this man, by his sangfroid and his quintessentially British leadership, was protecting his country from the Nazis and us Jews from death. As if this was not enough, he kept us in good cheer as we listened on the radio to his warm, stirring, defiant and funny speeches. Churchill remains my only hero. Except Beethoven.

Mother was lovely, lively, hospitable – still a Viennese. She knew Mozart's operas practically by heart: listening to records she often sang along in a good soprano voice. She cooked well, especially *strudels* and *torte*, loved entertaining though she was shy with English guests who struck her as sophisticated: she was no intellectual. Louise Fischbein, known as Lilly, the late child of an old mother, had been lovingly brought up by two of her older sisters, Emmy and Helene. Helene and the oldest sister, Adele, both perished in the Holocaust.

Mother was famous for her sighs. Was she thinking of Adele and Helene? She never agonised and rarely complained about wartime shortages and restrictions, though Manchester was drab and dull after peacetime Vienna. She managed the war well. She bought unrationed pork fat – which the British didn't appreciate, while we non-Kosher Jews rendered it down into *schmaltz* which was tasty and nutritious on bread: the first thing we did coming home from school was to ask for a *Schmaltzbrot*.

She often sent me, her dreamy boy, with our ration books to the shops in Burton Road and when I forgot some items and brought back some wrong ones she laughed. We had an allotment near the house, on the banks of the Mersey, where every Sunday we all, with our refugee friends, went 'digging for victory'. Only one of the friends, Liesl, knew anything about gardening so we followed her lead. Forty years later when Mum was old (in that new age we had started calling her Mum) Marlene recorded some of her memories in *Conversations with Lilly* (by Marlene Hobsbawm. Nassington Press 1998):

17

There was the story about Walter who had been sent to the allotment (about ten minutes away) to bring back a lettuce. He returned with all the little plants I had carefully put in the previous day. They were of course the easiest to get out. I had to laugh. It was so funny. Anyway it was impossible to be cross with Walter. He was such a lovely child – always solemn and always thinking.

Mother took us boys, with Father too when he was not working late or away on business, to almost every concert by the Hallé Orchestra. She used to laugh about John Barbirolli's sultry showmanship – his extravagant gestures and long frowning pauses to reprimand latecomers. But really she was grateful to Barbirolli. We immigrants in this drab city loved him for the colour and glamour as well as musicianship he offered us week in week out.

The Hallé was our cultural rendezvous. My schoolfriends, Peter Noble, Duncan Rutter and Michael Goldman, were often sitting with us. I started learning the piano and I've never stopped playing, although I lack the talent to perform. I listened to the long-playing records in our house until they were worn out; the classics were all there and Barbirolli inspired me to blow my pocket money on Sibelius. I learnt to read miniature scores, from which I would 'conduct', imitating Barbirolli's lush gestures and facial eloquence.

Duncan Rutter could imitate Mother's accent when she came out with Viennese cultural snobberies. When she was asked if she intended to go to the Covent Garden Opera when the company came to Manchester, she was alleged by Duncan to have replied: 'Bad concert – yes. Bad ballet – yes. Bad opera – No!' Thank you Duncan, now dead, for revealing to me that my parents had their funny side.

Father, however, was serious, preoccupied with the ups and downs of his business, often buried in the austere pages of the *Manchester Guardian*. He became approachable over cider after dinner, at weekends and on holiday. He took us on Sunday rambles in the Peak District which we reached in those splendid hikers' trains that still run from Piccadilly station to Edale, Bakewell, Chapel-en-le-Frith... He took us to North Wales and the Lake

District where we stayed on farms and went on mountain hikes. We all loved that except little Marlene who did not see the point of unnecessary walking. I owe to Mother my love of classical music and to Father my need for long country walks, my reverence for Paris and affection for all things French. And of course, it was Father's feeling for politics that saved us all from the Holocaust.

Theodor Schwarz, having only meagre prospects in the Bauer-Schwarz store at Innsbruck because he was the fourth son in a family of 10, bravely left home at 15 to take himself into the hotel business. He started as a waiter in Paris, a city he grew to love more even than Vienna. He had friends in Paris from the days of his first job to his death. I have his long letters still, written to me in Paris, Oxford, Malaya, typed single-space to save postage, switching even in mid-sentence between English, German and French. We mostly called him Father but his respect for everything English made him sign himself 'Daddy'.

He was not cuddly. My dreamy nature went down better with Mother and I think he preferred Vicky, his big boy, and Marlene, his little girl. To me he could be harsh and insensitive, his jokes crude. When I came home from school he was capable of asking, as a joke: 'What have you done stupid today, Walter?'

On my own in Paris

I was 17 when Father gave me a stupendous present. Ahead of my age group at school, I had a spare half-year before my Higher School Certificate exam. Father's fantastic idea was to arrange, through old French friends, for me to spend six months in Paris.

This was 1947. Food was rationed, Parisians queued for bread and beggars played their accordions. Mass tourism had not been invented and 17-year-olds were still children, yet here I was, venturing abroad alone – and to Paris! This was high adventure from the moment the train moved out of Piccadilly station.

I was to be under the protection of father's old friends the Hervés who lived in Montmartre; they had arranged for me to stay with Mademoiselle de Lessert, a genteel, impoverished old lady in the rue de la Faisanderie in the affluent 16e *arrondissement*, a few minutes' walk from the Bois de Boulogne. My family kept all my voluminous letters and I kept theirs.

'The truth of the matter is that I have settled down in Paris and become a Parisian,' I wrote at the end of my first week.

> 13 June 1947
> Speaking French to strangers has become part of the natural order of things... It is no longer a nightmarish adventure to take a ride in the metro or ask someone for information. I sit reading a newspaper without bothering to look up, for I know all the stations between Porte Dauphine and Jules-Joffrin. It does take some time for the smiling spaciousness of the streets to sink in... It is wonderful to live in a beautiful street. At one end are the Avenues Victor Hugo and Henri Martin – the one with its white, young trees on either side and the Arc de Triomphe visible at the end (about a mile away) and the other with its double line of trees in the centre, curving gracefully into the Bois and at its other end is the Avenue Foch... Just imagine me going out to do my shopping in the Ave Victor Hugo instead of Burton Road! There is no need to describe to my Parisian father the breathtaking beauty of such things as the view from the Place du Carousel to the Etoile, as the Jardin des Tuileries, as the Bois de Boulogne, as Notre Dame, as the view from the Trocadéro...

The Hervés had a big apartment just under the Sacré Coeur where they could not, in my eyes, have been more French.

> 16 June 1947
> The dinners are splendid affairs. Usually there are four different sorts of wine. One starts the evening with an aperitif, then one has two successive table wines (several glasses of each) and then some exquisite liqueur. I hope you don't mind me smoking occasionally now. It steadies me after all the wine and makes me feel much more sociable... To return to the dinners – I like particularly the vegetables, which are – as you know – eaten apart from the meat. The evenings are always very jolly affairs with all sorts of interesting people.

Madame Hervé was an expansive hostess even in those austere times.

Their two agreeable and clever sons were both older than me; their elder sister Rosine sighed a lot: she was becoming an old maid apparently because she could never think of leaving *maman*. Rosine was affectionate, modest, feminine, pretty and kind to me and I soon fell in love with her, secretly but I suppose it was obvious to all.

28 June 1947

Well now, let's come back to earth a bit and talk about such minor problems as food and money... Mlle de Lessert's figure of 100 francs for a minimum restaurant charge was very optimistic indeed – a meal nearly always comes to 120-130 francs. It is very difficult to control the price of your meal, for there are always mysterious scribbles on the bill for which they charge 20 or 30 francs! And by the time the bill comes I have usually made such a fool of myself (by ordering impossible combinations of things, as I don't know what most of the words on the menu mean) that I have not the moral courage to inquire into the mysterious scribbles.

The main trouble is bread. The ration is small and I cannot afford black market prices. However there are plenty of excellent vegetables and fruit, and Mlle gets some stuff sent from Switzerland... As for sending me some food, what I want is stuff that makes a good meal with vegetables but not with bread... because there is not enough bread. Besides, there are some excellent cheeses here.

I even have to pay 30 francs to have a bath, for there is none in this building. Don't worry, Mother, I promise to have one at least once a week and Paris is much cleaner than Manchester.

I evidently saw no irony in informing my father, a veteran francophile, that there were excellent cheeses in France. The restaurant problem was soon solved when I discovered Le Grand Cardinal on the corner of the Boulevard des Italiens and the Bouelvard Haussmann, where I ate well for 70 francs, with no squiggles on the bill.

Father wrote to me at length in his three languages: the one he loved was French.

2 July 1947

Your writing that you wish you could feel and act like an old Parisian pleased me a lot because I always fervently wished to do just that! My first address in Paris was 33 Avenue de Friedland – the Hotel Royal. That's where I started off, one April day in 1906, in the company of my dear Papa. How well I remember it! And when you wrote that you drank a lemonade in the Tuileries Gardens it brought me right to the last time I lived in Paris in 1914. Every morning, coming out of the Regina Hotel, where I was head of night reception, passing the Louvre's Pavilion de Flore, crossing the Place du Carousel gardens, then across the Pont Royale onto the Rue du Bac, across the Boulevard St Germain to the Rue de Varennes where I lived at number 35, not far from the magnificent old Austrian Embassy. And how many times in Russia during the 1914-18 war did I remember Paris with sickening nostalgia and determination to go back and live there again.

I went to concerts at the Salle Gaveau and wrote critiques to my family, who reciprocated with news of the latest recitals in Manchester.

15 July 1947

New friends: 1. One of the best-known young French pianists – called Wilfred Maggiar. Great friend of the Hervés, where I met him. A very nice chap, not conceited. He likes me, and we see each other a lot. He plays to me often in his studio at the Salle Gaveau (to me alone, and whatever I ask for.) He says I am *très musicien* and *très sympathique*. We also went to Versailles together to visit the Chateau. He is going to make a tour in England in November which will include Manchester and he'll probably play with the Hallé. He has 18 concertos in his repertoire including the Emperor, the Schumann, Brahms 2nd, Tchaikovsky, and the C. Franck Variations which he plays to me. But he plays mostly Chopin.

2. Another chap I met is a student called Bourguiba, nephew of the Tunisian nationalist leader. He hates the French and maintains that what the French do in Tunisia is just as bad as what the Nazis ever did, only it is concealed from the outside world. He lives for the day when the French will clear out, and belongs to a society with that object in view.

An interesting thing about this chap Bourguiba is where he lives. It's a big student hostel which, just six months ago, was an official brothel. Signs are still up on the walls of the rooms with instructions on precautions against disease. There is also a big hall lit up in red where the girls were on display for people to choose. I thought this was very funny – a bit of real Parisian life but don't worry, all that is gone. I go out with this young man quite a lot…

Wilfred Maggiar took a very great fancy to me indeed and we spent a lot of time together. He was a warm, frank, emotional man. The two of us stayed for a few days in a studio flat in the magnificent Place des Vosges, where I slept chastely on a mattress on the floor. Wilfred among other things was a gentleman.

1, Place des Vosges, Paris 4e

Saturday 11 September 1947

Dear Folks, Wilfred was here to receive me on Wednesday evening in this charming little 'studio' in this charming square which consists entirely of 17th Century buildings – similar huge blocks on each of the four sides which are today *exactly* as they were then. As we live on the sixth floor we have a splendid view of the square which has a park in the centre with a statute of Louis XIII. Over the roofs we have a view of the Sacré Coeur.

The life we lead here is bohemian in the extreme. The owner of the studio is a poet… The place has a kitchen and a sort of indoor balcony which is the bathroom, and a lavatory just outside. Instructions for use:

1. Remove electric bulb from place A to place B.

2. – 3. Spend five minutes trying to get the flushing system to work.

4. Give up in despair and get a saucepan (or rather the saucepan) full of water…

Wilfred is very charming with his 100% artist's temperament, his frank and simple manner – curiously combined with an immense conceit. When I am alone I spend a lot of the time in the Louvre, or just walking about, which is the best thing to do in Paris.

Wilfred took me to the Conservatoire where he was one of the judges in a piano competition – 'in the hall where Chopin and Liszt had played, with the very walls almost made of music.'

I wrote in my diary:

22 July 1947
...There were five candidates in the competition, three girls and two men, all of whom had come first in other competitions. Wilfred asked me to take notes of my opinions on each one, so that when I see him tomorrow we can compare notes.

23 July
...we were both delighted to find that not only had I chosen the winner but had grouped all five in the right order! Then we went over to the studio where he played to me for a long time. I got him to play some pre-romantic things which he had almost forgotten – Bach, Mozart etc. Then we talked of symphonies and he was very impressed by the amount of music I knew and especially so when I played the themes on the piano. He showed me how to hold my hands when playing and I am dying to practise this.

Too young at Oxford

After Paris I had to grow up. Back in the sixth form, Higher School Certificate was not a problem: I enjoyed revising, glorying in the use of Father's typewriter. I got good results except in maths, and went to The Queen's College, Oxford, to sit its entrance exam. Interviewed by a roomful of dons, I was so awed that I have blotted the occasion from my memory. To my astonishment I was awarded an Open Exhibition – one of three that year. Forty years later Marlene asked Mother, aged 89, what occasion had stood out in her life and she replied: Walter getting an Exhibition to Oxford.

But now I was 18 and awaited call-up for my two years in the army, like everybody else. Then a curt letter from the Ministry of Labour and National Service: because I had been naturalised as a child on my father's certificate I was not properly British until I was 21, and therefore not eligible for military service until then. So The Queen's College agreed to admit me forthwith – reluctantly because Oxford was full to capacity with ex-servicemen. I'd have to grow up faster than was good for me and faster than I properly managed.

Oxford catapulted me into an adult world of infinite beauty, knowledge and wisdom, a privileged place you go 'up' to, not just

24

from Manchester, from anywhere, and at the end of every term you go 'down'. Here was the freedom of dreams – fifty clubs to join or not join, dances, debates, sherry parties, punting on the Isis by moonlight with or without a girl, lectures you could attend or not as you pleased. The idyll was played out against the backdrop of dreaming spires and the magnificent High Street curving past the Palladian grandeur of The Queens College front.

I chose to read modern history – which doesn't really mean modern, it means post-classical – and opted for medieval because I thought there might be fewer books to read than for later periods, and that greater distance left more scope for imagination.

I was still an adolescent, writing every few days to the family who replied at length, sent me parcels because food was still rationed, and kept all my letters after proudly passing them round their circle of friends and relations.

113 Iffley Road
10 October 1948
Dear Folks, Oxford is as lovely as ever and I can still hardly believe I am here. Queen's is in the finest street – The High, which leaves one breathless... Dinner in the Hall is impressive with the rows of gowned students and the High Table with the Master, the Dean and all the Fellows also in gowns, and portraits of past Masters down the centuries...

I cannot yet report much success in making friends. I am the youngest member of the College, and cannot help feeling it: 90 per cent of the students are ex-servicemen

Our tutor is quite young and extremely sympathetic. I shall see him once a week in his rooms to read an essay to him. He has an awful habit of saying 'Why?' to everything you say. It is surprising how many things you can say in a few minutes that don't seem to have any reason at all when you try to find one!

Lectures are only in the mornings and there is no compulsion to attend them... the tutor just tells us who is good and who doesn't know what he's talking about. I have a deluge of letters from all sorts of clubs and societies – and this morning two representatives called in person – from the Labour Club and the Socialist Society... I have already got a second-hand gown for 10/- (I am unfortunately not entitled to a long scholar's gown). I shall have to buy a white bow tie for the matriculation ceremony, and also for exams.

But none of this was real. I was out of my depth. I could not hold my own with men who had served in the war as captains, majors: there was even a colonel. Still a dreamy boy, I lacked the discipline and concentration to tackle a world where everything you knew turned out to be only a theory, needing to be supported by facts that were elusive and contradicted by other facts.

I tried to read everything and finished up reading almost nothing. I could not sleep. With an Open Entrance Exhibition I was tacitly expected to get a First. But I could not study. To make it worse, the College put me in my first year in its hostel in Iffley Road – half a mile away. Without a room in college, I felt even more of an outsider.

John Prestwich was my tutor. This famous medievalist was kind and courteous, sympathetic when yet again I hadn't produced an essay. When I did, he could be disconcerting. A heavy smoker, he coughed incessantly and his notorious habit was to use his cough to interrupt his students as they read him their essays. 'Ahurrm. Let's have a look. Ahurrm.' Then he would get up and walk, still coughing, to his extensive bookshelves, take down a dusty edition of a medieval chronicle or monastic roll, flick its pages and cite some item in Latin which cast serious doubt on whatever had been asserted in the essay.

For my special subject I chose John of Gaunt. So unhappy were my studies in medieval history that today at the moment of this writing I can tell you absolutely nothing whatsoever about John of Gaunt unless I cheat and look him up in Google.

20 October 1948

I have not slept properly *once* since I came here, and the result is that I have been tired every day. I go to one or two lectures a day, sometimes less. I have a terrific amount of reading to do – in French and occasionally German as well as English...

But nevertheless I have been trapped into joining both the Liberal and the Labour Club... I did put myself down for the Boat Club, but later backed out when I realised some of the implications: six afternoons a week of practice when the races are on, and guaranteed blisters on hands and in the other place! So besides forsaking my studies I would have to forsake both my favourite pastimes of cycling and playing the piano. So I have decided to play a hectic and popular game called squash.

Yesterday the freshmen were 'matriculated' – for which ceremony we had to turn up in dark suits, cap and gown. I borrowed a cap (= mortar board) and white bow tie. The Vice Chancellor said something to us in Latin and we just bowed at the right places...

This was only the first term out of nine; later I produced regular essays at last, somehow passed the intermediate exams and stayed the course to the end. In my second year I got a college room, shared with Keith Potten who was older than me but I suspect he had been chosen as my room-mate because he was young for his age. We became close friends, gave parties together, talked endlessly about girls and luckily for our domestic harmony we had different tastes. I joined the French Club, unusual for someone not reading French, and served two terms as its secretary. As a result much of my love life in Oxford involved French girls.

Girls were famously rare in Oxford in those days and any that were pretty and charming quickly became *femmes fatales*. Miche was an au-pair girl with one foot in the university: she was pretty, witty, stylish and French. I never had more than one portion of her heart.

Colette came from a different milieu – a chateau in the Auvergne. This never became more than a friendship with romantic undertones, and I was not the only one invited to the autumn grape-picking down at the chateau. Her real love was England in general and Oxford in particular in all its glamour and eccentricity.

There was something wistful about Colette de Pomyers, as if she had been let out into a wonderland but remained on an invisible leash. We were friends for two years. After leaving Oxford I got a letter from her that could have come straight out of Balzac.

My dear Walter,
This is going to be a very short note because I am more than usual short of time. The reason of it? Well, I can hardly believe it myself,

27

but I am actually going to be married in two weeks time. It is very sudden; you are, I am sure, going to be very surprised. My fiancé is an officer in the cavalry. He is a captain, much older than me, very nice. His name is the Count Abrial. He is just back from Indo-China... He is attaché to the Sixth Division and we will live in Compiègne near Paris. I do hope my English friends will learn very quickly the way to my new home...

I know you will find it difficult to believe these news. Why did I take such a decision? Well, you know that my intentions were to go back to England at any cost. I found it almost impossible because of the difficulties in finding a job. My family who were very upset with me did their best to make things as difficult as possible for me too. And by the end, though with the best intentions in the world, made me promise to marry this officer. So, you see, this is what I am going to do. I am decided to face my new duties and difficulties as well as I can from now on. But of course, I am rather distressed for so many reasons. Jacques' kindness will help me, I hope. Dear Walter, do come and see me whenever you have an opportunity to come near Paris...

yours,

Colette.

PS I shall be married on the 15th of April.

I never came to see you, Colette, because I went into the army and then I was a self-centred young journalist, a married man to whom you had ceased to be relevant. Could you have still been in Compiègne 20 years later when I was Paris correspondent of the *Guardian* and we lived in... Compiègne? I see on the Internet that you have buried Jacques. *Et vous?* Should I accept your 60-year-old invitation and find my way to your house?

My heart in those last balmy Oxford months belonged elsewhere – to Valerie who was back in Didsbury, Manchester. Val was a model in a dress shop and later a trainee nurse. I wrote to her every day and she to me. She was 17. I have in my hand 46 of her loving, funny, inconsequential letters which tell of her day, her work, her friends (all male), their weekend hikes in the Peak District, her dog Chummy, her enjoyment of the classical music records I had left her, her tempestuous relationships with her mother and elder sister

Jacqui. I can find nothing worth quoting now: Val never tried to be quotable.

When my father first saw Val he found her attractive (I could see it in his eyes), sporty and funny, and he said to me afterwards that she was a 'rough diamond'. Eight years later, when I brought home Dorothy, aged 18, he gave her the same look and made the same remark. He was right both times.

But I must quote something from Val after all.

> Please, dear boy, drop the subject of the Commemoration Ball. It's quite upsetting to me when you write about it and yet I know damn well I cannot manage to go... If I can't like you in your ordinary suits I'm sure you in a dress suit would make no difference. I'd like me in little shorts!
>
> Ahem! Tuesday's letter! It was very amusing, but it sounds as if you are really annoyed with me! What are you meant to be, amusing or annoyed? Dear Walter, I wish everyone wrote letters like you, each one is different from the other. Could you really imagine me weeping and wailing for your company? Just who do you think you are that I should be honoured in the fact that you take an interest in me. See!

At last I grew into Oxford which in that last summer term was a blur of parties, romantic intrigues and gossip. All of us, students and academics, played the game that Oxford, and only Oxford, was real. Finals loomed but they, too, were as unreal to me as John of Gaunt and all that 'modern' history I had tried so hard to study in an adult manner. The big week arrived. I put on my gown and went into the Schools, more or less with my eyes closed.

After the exams, when I had gone down and was away on holiday, John Prestwich wrote to me in longhand:

> 20 August 1951
>
> Dear Walter. I am sorry about the Third. However you had a good deal out of reading History in the three years here, and I don't think you need have any regrets. I don't see that on the marks the examiners could have done anything else. Your best mark was

βα/1 in the general paper and your lowest γ+ in English II, though a more charitable examiner gave it βγ 3+.

I gather that Keith is with you in Austria and I hope that you are enjoying it. Let me know what happens to you and what you do on leaving the Army; and if you want testimonials and references when the time comes, ask for them.

I never asked John Prestwich for a reference. Long ago I had decided that if I got a First I would stay on at Oxford and become an academic; if not, I would be a journalist. And that was what I had really wanted all along. I never, ever, minded getting a Third. And now, goodbye to the Middle Ages and into the army – a new world I was determined to enter not so much as a soldier but as a reporter. No news desk was waiting for my copy but there was always Mother and Father, Vicky and Marlene, and Valerie, to write to.

Chapter two:
Willing warrior, would-be reporter

In Oxford I had been too young. In the Army, two years older than the other recruits, I was just right for my third and greatest adventure. I liked the Army, from the first barrack-room days with boys who were loud, bad, funny, sweet, unintelligible. The day I put on my brand new officer's uniform and drove Father's car through the gates of the Manchester Regiment... Discovering the Orient on a troopship to Singapore while in charge of a draft of unruly Black Watch soldiers... Riding with loaded pistol on the night train from Singapore to Tapah... Days and nights alone in the jungle with my very own platoon of Manchesters who are of course the best soldiers in the world, and later with my platoon of wild Ibans from Borneo whom I grew to love... My first article in the *Manchester Guardian* written without permission under the pseudonym Blake Walter... Christmas in A Company camp when the officers served the men turkey and mince pies and, late in the night, my platoon invited me to their tent and were drunk enough to say I was the best second lieutenant in the Company (there were only three)...

> 22592157 Pte Schwarz, Coy A Squad 7 Intake 83. no 1 Trg Bn (sel)
> ROAC, Parsons Barracks, Aldershot, Hants
> 3 September 1951
> Dear Folks, Having a very nice time in the Army! Hell is promised us for next week – but up to now all is cleaning, sewing buttons, vaccinations, parades... I like my new uniform – esp. the magnificent boots. I like marching about the place (although marching away from your meals is much worse than marching towards them) and I like the people here.
>
> There are 21 of us in Squad 7 – all nice blokes, the really unpleasant faces having found their way to other squads. The corporal in charge of us treats us well – a cockney soldier as one sees them in films. The CO is positively gentle... in his opening address he told us not to take life too tragically, to write often to

our parents and to come to him in case of any trouble. I haven't got into much trouble yet, though having my hands in my pockets has several times been ascribed to the circumstances of my birth.

Bad times followed – black, downhearted weeks of waiting at a place called Blackdown while the Army decided what to do with me. Weeks of bullying corporals, sadistic sergeants and dreary fatigues. It was a black day when I was RTU'd (Returned to Unit, which means rejected) from the Intelligence Corps in only my third week of training, with no reason given. Years later I learnt I had been put in the I Corps by mistake because I still had a foreigner's security classification. I opted for the next best thing – officer training – which turned out vastly better. Lucky boy.

I was a man now, getting sweet letters from my sweetheart Valerie who told me what films she saw, when she went hiking in the Peak District with 'friends' (*What friends...?*) But still I kept writing at length to my family. Mother and Father wrote back and sent food parcels with black bread and salami; Vicky and Marlene wrote often.

> 28 September 1951
>
> I'm sitting on my bed as I write this. People are busy cleaning kit for tomorrow... someone is crooning a sentimental song, a high-spirited Scotsman is arguing with a sweet little Welsh boy about the respective merits of their homelands. Oaths and curses fill the air incessantly but always in good humour. Outside someone is barking 'left-right - left-right' as some other squad returns from breakfast... The food is dreadful but it doesn't worry me... We rise at 10 to six every morning – inc. Sunday. Lights Out is at 10:15 pm but in this merry company life goes on till 11.

Why did so many people dread their national service, try all they could to avoid foreign postings and aim for a quiet life as near home as possible? I opted for active jungle service in Malaya which I could have avoided; the risks seemed small because death and injury were not yet real to me. The army gave me further confirmation of my good luck in having become British, because most conscripts were good-humoured, tolerant and brave, with a deprecating, anti-heroic, sense of humour. And most career officers were gentlemen, even when they were pompous and boring. I think I did a good job in Malaya but twice I blundered badly, and dangerously, and both times the bigwigs were understanding and forgiving. But the deepest reason why I liked the army was the same reason I wanted to be a foreign correspondent: I loved new places and new people.

After my false start in the Intelligence Corps I was in limbo, hanging around in an Ordnance Corps training camp, bored and prone to getting into trouble.

B Coy RAOC, Dettingen Barrracks, Blackdown, Hants

18 October 1951

Dear Folks, I have been working a solid 16 hours a day... It all started with my losing a knife back at Aldershot. Having two forks I swapped with someone who had two knives. Not until I had left Aldershot did I discover that my new knife bore the letters NAAFI (the forces' canteen service) on the blade. Well, last Thursday we were suddenly ordered to stand by our beds for a surprise inspection. In the panic that is customary on such occasions I hastily stuffed those things that were lying about under my pillow – a few dusters, a handkerchief – and my knife... And the first thing the sergeant-major did was look under the pillows.

Things happened very quickly after that. Within an hour I was marching in the company of several other petty criminals (people with dirty lockers, untidy blankets, etc) dressed in best BD (battledress) best boots etc, towards the Company Commander's office. There was no arguing with Captain Johnston. Pinched or swapped, innocent or guilty, it was a chargeable offence to be in unlawful possession. Three days CB (confined to barracks) for the lot of us. About turn. Quick march. Left wheel. Right wheel. Mark time. Halt. And there we were in the guardroom waiting to be instructed in the routine of defaulters. You report to the guardroom at 7am, 6pm, 8pm and 9.45pm. Between 6am and 8pm you do 'fatigues' (= charring). At 9.45 pm you have to be dressed to the hilt, spotless and shining, for an inspection by an officer. If the slightest detail is amiss your 'time' is doubled.

33

I will never forget those evening parades. I was always behind time with my preparations and I had to mobilise the entire squad to help me. One was pressing my greatcoat, another polishing my boots, a third cleaning my brasses. At 9.43 they were all dressing me. Standing in the heavy great-coat while one person was fixing my gaiters and the other adjusting my belt, I felt like a medieval warrior being dressed for battle.

The 9.45 parade is terrifying. It is a 'staff parade' for the guard, fire-pickets and defaulters. After the roll call the three groups stand in perfect silence waiting for the officer. After about 20 minutes he arrives and inspects the guards and the fire-pickets. Dismiss! He then goes inside the guardroom and the defaulters, 20 of us, march in one at a time to be inspected. Thanks to squad 128 I passed all three nights, but it was touch and go… The first night was so nerve-wracking that when he said 'about turn,' (to inspect my back) I turned to the left instead of the right (a horrible crime in the army) and nearly got another seven days for it.

On one of those evening fatigues I was sent to scrub floors in the kitchen of the officers' mess. One of the cooks asked me why I was on CB. He said: 'I suppose you'll be out of a knife now.' I admitted that I was, and he kindly produced an old knife covered in rust. 'Clean that up and it's yours,' he said. Grateful, I worked for half an hour at it with sandpaper and Brasso. When at last it was gleaming I fingered it proudly. On the blade, in shining letters, I saw: *British Red Cross and St John.*

At last I got my chance to become an officer. At our USBI (selection board interview) we were asked about current affairs to make sure we weren't communists. And then the dreaded four-day WOSBI (War Office selection board). We candidates were obsessed with sinister rumours – they were bugging our conversations, delving into our remotest past, photographing the way we ate, slept, defecated. But no, we had to write down what we would do in various tricky situations and we commanded real soldiers across baffling obstacles like deep rivers and high walls. It was, I thought, efficiently done and very sensibly they accepted me for officer training at Eaton Hall. My problems were over.

Eaton Hall, near Chester, home of the Grosvenor family since the 15th century, was a hospital in both world wars, then an Officer

Cadet Training School until the end of national service in 1960. Chester is only 40 miles from Manchester, so I was practically at home.

> O/C Schwarz W. 16 Pln 'C' Coy, Eaton Hall OCS, Chester
> 20 May 1952
> Dear Folks, Fantastic is the only word to describe it – a jumble of aristocracy and army. Splendid drives leading to magnificent, secluded monuments, lined by Nissen huts! The Hall itself is not beautiful – but the gardens! These are at the back of the Hall, the only part that seems untouched by the Army. Inside the Hall is the same nightmarish mix-up. Marble busts and billiard tables, harmoniums and NAAFI chairs...
>
> I live in one of the stone huts which line 'Belgrave Avenue' – the straight drive from the Hall to the Obelisk which perhaps you saw. The beds are in twos, and my neighbour is as nice a fellow as I could hope to have met. He is a stage manager for the Glyndbourne Opera. His father is the leader of the Royal Phil. Orchestra.

The handsome boy in the next bed, David McCallum, told me he planned for a career in the theatre (he was to be the celebrity TV star in *the Man From Uncle* series). David was a good room-mate and we spent the last exhausted hour of each day on our backs discussing all that had happened.

We both enjoyed Eaton Hall, with never an idle moment between tactical training – flanking attacks, defence in depth, patrolling techniques, endlessly practised in breathless outdoor war games. We learnt how to fire or throw every weapon from sten gun to bren gun, from grenade to mortar, that our future platoons might possibly use. Like schoolboys we hero-worshipped Captain Fenner, a handsome red-beret parachutist who enthralled us with war stories.

But this was still the army and there was drill on the concrete parade ground. The NCOs called us 'sir' but that didn't stop the terrifying sergeant-major telling me on parade that I was 'a useless idle nincompoop, sir!' and handing me the punishment known as

35

'obelisk' – running with rifle and full kit half a mile down the avenue, round the obelisk and back.

While at Eaton Hall I suffered the classic soldier's misfortune: I lost my sweetheart to a rival back home. Val's letters stopped. Back in Manchester for the weekend, I couldn't get her to answer the phone. I loitered desolately near her home until I saw her come out with her new man. He looked like a hiker. I accepted defeat, was desolate for at least a week until the outdoor rigours of Eaton Hall helped me recover.

The eight-week course was over. McCallum and I and our fellow cadets lined up in a grand parade with our parents and siblings looking on, and we were officers. I opted for the Manchesters because they were my local regiment and they were serving in Malaya which sounded like an exotic and glamorous destination, something to write home about. The Regiment sent me its silver fleur-de-lys badge to sew onto my officer's hat. But first I had to go to London to buy the hat, and my swagger-stick, at Bates in Jermyn Street, which has sold the same hats and sticks since the First World War and still does.

Practising for my future career I started a diary.

Ladysmith Barracks, Ashton-under-Lyme, Lancs. 30 August 1952
Today I put on my officer's uniform for the first time and joined for duty at the Depot, Manchester Regiment. A regimental policeman and a guard were at the gates as I drove through, resplendent in the family Humber, so that the first salutes I have received were of the smartest. In spite of repeated resolutions, I smiled sheepishly. Mother, who with sister Marlene was present to take the car back, told me not to smile.

A handsome subaltern received me at the mess and helped with my luggage to my room – thus shattering Mother's hopes that menial soldiers would appear to carry it. I am to live with two others in a miniature barrack room containing six army beds and layers of dust. The view from both un-curtained windows is entirely coke, colossal piles of it. The regimental home appears to be in the middle of a coal mine.

The handsome subaltern was Martin Blackburn who was, three years later, to be usher at my wedding.

I reported to the Adjutant who told me the rules of the Mess. Ladies' names will not be mentioned, on dinner nights the sherry will be passed from right to left, smoking will begin only after the Queen's health has been drunk, and the first cigars will be taken from the box on the table.

To the Orient with a cargo of soldiers
17 September 1952
Sailed from Liverpool in the Empire Pride... Feeling very much an officer, I drove out of Ladysmith Barracks in a 3-tonner, with two soldiers to act as porters.

The family, who saw me off at Prince's Landing Stage, was one of many hundreds in a moving scene reminiscent of a war film. As we waited for the gangway to be hauled up the soldiers crowded on the port deck, exchanged last cheerful shouts with the families and sweethearts on the quay. A few mothers and little sisters were in tears and hidden away below decks I saw a soldier sitting with his face buried in his hands. The men began singing songs, and the inevitable 'Why are we waiting,' voiced a universal desire that this protracted farewell should be over and the long adventure begun. It is difficult to take these boys seriously as potential warriors, but their youthfulness certainly heightens the pathos of the parting, and also the sense of adventure. When the gangway finally rattled aboard, delicacy prevented the cheer that would certainly have arisen if the quayside had been unpeopled.

The Pride is indeed a proud ship. Her fresh white paint seems to portend fairer climes and romantic places and her shape is simple, clean. The troops are overcrowded, and seem miserable now, or at least subdued.

I felt suddenly happy as we edged past the long suburbs of Liverpool, on through a highway of clanging buoys towards the open sea. In that moment the Army ceased to be a bore and a nuisance and, as the Pride dropped her pilot, opened her duty-free bar and changed course for the South, to become a fantastic adventure.

The contrast between officers' and troops' living conditions is almost feudal. The Pride is a freighter with 100 first-class passengers and a cargo of soldiers. They live in an underworld called a troop-deck, full of long tables in closely packed rows where they eat and above which they sleep. When the hammocks are up it is impossible to walk about unless bent double. But more pathetic is to see them up on deck. There is one long bench, set back from the rails, which is always full with its quota of a hundred or so. The place along the rail on which a hundred more can lean idly and watch the sea is also full. Between is a sorry no-man's land of displaced persons.

We officers, if also somewhat cramped in our accommodation, live in luxury. First-class cabins, first-class food, and service of oriental standards (the crew are Indians). We dress for dinner, and in the evenings the sight of the troops milling around on the deck, peeping in at the immaculate officers in gorgeous uniforms, emerging from the spacious dining room into the spacious lounge to sip whiskies and gins, is like something from Dickens at his angriest...

18 September 1952

In the evening I went to visit the troop decks – not on duty but pretending to be. Morale seemed surprisingly high in those sultry storehouses of personnel. The hammocks were already slung and half of them occupied by seemingly comfortable bodies. I could feel adventure and comradeship in the air; the strangeness of this new life seemed to have won over the discomfort of it. I asked one or two men how they slept, and all replies were cheerful. A sergeant who, inevitably, had appeared to walk round with me, added that it was a job to get 'em out in the mornings, sir.

I was i/c of No3 Station, composed mainly of a large Black Watch draft bound for war in Korea. Tough, ill-disciplined young Scotsmen, hard to deal with but very likeable – I supposed because they were just a shade too young to be frightening. A certain number always appeared without belts, gaiters or beret. 'I couldn'a find it, Sir,' 'I lost It, Sir,' came out with such a cheerful, couldn't-care-less and yet not disrespectful promptness, that I could never bring myself to say anything more harsh than 'Don't do it again.' The notorious razor-slashing Glasgow ruffians, or high-spirited potential war heroes? I couldn't decide which way to look at them.

21 September 1952
This morning it seemed impossible to believe that I was in the army. The Mediterranean was too blue, the weather too perfect, the gentle breeze of the ship's motion too delightful. A swarm of dolphins, eager for company, were keeping level with the ship. Every now and again, for sheer joy of living, they jumped a foot high out of the water and, with an expert flick of the fin which protruded grotesquely from their shiny bodies, nose-dived back again at an exactly premeditated spot. This blue lake is like a glorious theme and the dolphins' little leaps are a graceful figure of accompaniment, repeated and repeated in the left hand.

Writing all this I thought I was practising to be a journalist. Or was I a baby travel writer?

26 September 1952
At 5.30am the engines stopped after nine days of uninterrupted throbbing. Port Said, a mass of yellow lights a few hundred yards away, seemed at once like the Promised Land and the end of the world. The lights were warm and welcoming, and as we headed straight for them it was impossible to believe that there was any ocean left in the world but that which lay behind us. A pilot ship, black, sinister guardian of the port, began winking instructions

through the gloom. As the pilot, a fat complacent Egyptian, climbed the ladder the sun rose. We could almost touch it for we had arrived in the East where the sun is at home.

Bumboats. Abrupt, unceremonious introduction to the East, they came up on all sides as soon as we had anchored. Sunburnt Arabs in gaudy shirts on a blue water, selling melons, wallets, glittering rings, watches, sweets. It is forbidden to trade with bumboats – a safeguard against infection and being swindled. As a result, the first personal contact between the lads, who were crowded in wonder on the decks, and Levantine commerce was amusing. Imitating the hawkers' accents and entering into the spirit of their trade, the men began to barter and haggle without the slightest intention of buying. '10 shillings? We can get 'em twice that size in Liverpool market for ninepence.'

A gangway lowered to the water for official comings and goings. First, in a very fast and luxurious launch, came General Naguib's customs officials. Then the British Army. In smart khaki-drill shorts, looking as if they owned Egypt. A military policeman, miraculously smartened up, was on duty at the top of the gangway, barring the way to illegal entrants with the tolerant firmness of a London bobby.

The Canal. Military road and railway along one side – all traffic British. Native settlements, sun-baked and sleepy, at intervals on both sides. Old men in flowing gowns, women carrying tall baskets on their heads, camels.

Night. I could see nothing on the bank but black, unidentified shapes. A soldier on the lower deck jeered: 'where d'ya get that home posting?' The dark canalside came to life. 'Gertcha! Suckers!! Fuck you Jack, we're all right here!' I think the soldiers of the Empire Pride got the impression that the wide world is peopled by little brown scoundrels and British soldiers.

27 September 1952

In the Red Sea the sweat flows in rivers down my trunk and arms. I charged 13 of the Black Watch for having dirty or no PT vests after repeated warnings. They will do extra fatigues and/or be confined to the troop-deck for a day. The sight of the soldiers on their decks at night is weird. The boards are a solid mass of naked, sunburnt flesh. Only about a third of them can sleep on the open decks. What it must be like for the rest, down in the troop decks, is beyond imagination.

I assembled the Manchester draft for occasional chats. To these mild, nondescript boys I could be paternal and cheerful. I had talked myself into a considerable regimental pride and lost no opportunity of telling them what they had to live up to – not letting on, of course, that I was even newer to the Regiment than they were.

I tried explaining why we were going to Malaya, our colony threatened by Chinese Communist insurgents. I told them about the Emergency, now in its third year, our struggle against the 'bandits' who hid in the jungle, the world-wide threat of communism, the difference between Chinese and Malays in Malaya.

The Manchesters were unmoved. Apart from two whose fathers were obviously communists I could coax no questions or comment out of them. When at the end I asked what they would say if they met someone in a pub who said they were mugs to be in Malaya and that the British had no right to be there, I heard only a murmur from the back: 'Tell him to fuck off!'

I had no political qualms about taking these boys into a colonial war. The British army had saved me from the Nazis; now I was thrilled and honoured to be helping it save us from the communists. I could never have been a pacifist. You have to defend yourself.

28 September 1952

At the request of the sergeant I told the Manchesters I would inspect them at 15.00 hours before disembarking on shore leave at Aden. It goes without saying, I said, that the Manchester draft would be the smartest on the ship. When I did inspect them they were very well turned out in their new jungle-green uniforms and I felt that the Manchesters were indeed a fine lot.

In those days before television, before mass tourism, stepping ashore at Aden, my first footfall in the orient, was momentous.

41

2 October 1952

I lingered behind and lost my three cabin mates who were bound for the Officers' Club – the last place in all Arabia that I wanted to visit. The next two hours were a delicious nightmare. Black-sleek-skinned, black-glossy-eyed, black-curly-haired Arabs. They stood outside their open shops, and I ran the gauntlet of them as each bade me enter… I sidestepped the shopkeepers, to be waylaid by small black boys with bare feet and enchanting white smiles, wanting sixpences. A procession of taxi-drivers offering to take me to the Officers Club. (My civilian clothes were my badge of rank.)

A narrow street led off the main road where shops were for the natives, hovels without doors or simply tables in the street, selling brown rice, melons and a host of things I could never name. I began feeling surrounded. I held tightly onto my camera, and with my right hand I made my cigarette case bulge from my pocket, a ridiculous precaution for they were undoubtedly peaceful and well-disposed.

On the floor, propped against the wall, was a black, shrouded shape, in roughly human form. The black cloth seemed to have a head, shoulders and a limp mass of a body. After 13 days at sea in a shipload of soldiers, I had seen my first woman. I stood rooted in horror. Coming closer, I saw two slits in the hood, and surmised that there were eyes beneath. .

Hungry taxi-drivers again. 'You come and see sights,' said one, when he had understood that I did not want to go to the Officers' Club… Darkness fell as we drove along a wide, hilly road. Here there were Super Snipes and Jaguars, containing fat, determined-looking Europeans in shirtsleeves, tired with Anglo-Iranian oil worries at the end of the day. A boy appeared from nowhere to take me round. First we came to a kind of illuminated parade ground, with a score of people standing in irregular pattern, but all facing the same way, doing a strange kind of gymnastic… it was shamefully long before it dawned on me that these people were praying.

When we found the taxi again, I paid off the boy and wanted to know where we were going now. 'I take you where you want to go,' said the taxi-driver mysteriously, and we set off once more down the hill. My three cabin mates gave me a little cheer as I arrived at the Officers' Club, just in time for a moonlight swim in the pool and an iced lager.

My friends were charitable enough not to believe a word of my story, for they took me to be an officer and a gentleman, not a common tourist. They were about to take a taxi back to the jetty, an hour before we needed to be there. I took my leave of them and went up the narrow street again.

The Arabs were bringing their beds out of the dark, airless houses, setting them up on the pavement or in the middle of the road, and settling down to sleep. The sleepers wore the same clothes as the wakeful, and they had no covers. Some were still sitting around in dingy cafes, and from one of them came a stream of piercing, monotonous Arab music that filled the village. I went into the bazaar, but it had become a dormitory. Dozens of beds were installed and all was still except for the goats who wandered silently about, nosing for food. These Arabs were very poor and very dirty, but they seemed to live as one enormous family. I saw many things in that native quarter, but one thing I never saw anywhere was a closed door.

I returned to the ship at 9.30 pm after four and a half hours ashore. Nothing of moment had occurred in my absence, except that a drunken soldier had declared he wanted a drink and hurled himself into the sea.

Four days later, another shore leave.

6 October 1952

After the bumboy in Aden came the rickshaw man in Colombo. We must have been a rare sight as we walked through the monsoon rain all the way from Kollupitiya to the Fort; he with his cab unoccupied, and I walking in the road, so that I could speak to him.

'Rickshaw, master?' His bare feet and his oiled wagon made no sound, and only my own steps were audible as I strode on in sullen silence.

'Three miles to town, master.'

'No! Go away! Leave me alone!'

It began to rain and as I turned up the collar of my raincoat he raised the hood of his rickshaw.

'It rain, master.'

A silence.

'Only two rupees, master. You go to town, I go to town, so I take you for only two rupees, yes?'

'Master wants to walk,' I bellowed, all the louder as I felt that my anger was no longer genuine. 'Master two weeks in big ship! Master likes walking! Master climb big mountains. Master hates rickshaws!'

'I find no work, master. I plenty children, no work. Only two rupees – special price, Master.'

'What are you – beggar or rickshaw man?' I demanded of the horrid man, still at the top of my voice because I felt elated. I was speaking my mind at last to the Asia that one sees in the streets of big cities; spineless, without dignity, degraded – by white rule or their own inherent character (the question nags at your nerves and makes you shout at them).

My taunt seemed to have found its mark; at once I liked the detestable little man. I began to probe, with suitable contempt, into his circumstances.

'Not beggar, Master. I rickshaw man. Ten rickshaws, all mine. But no work, I Ceylon man, not Indian man. Indian men very bad. I make journey for ten rupees, Indians for five. Very bad. Indian men steal and do funny business.'

I had gone ashore soon after nightfall (only officers had shore leave that night, and most of these had decided to stay on board)... had supper in a Chinese restaurant. Some sailors started a dispute about the bill and within minutes fists were flying and startled Chinamen were sprawling on the floor. I was the superior officer of these sailors and I conscientiously obeyed the Eaton Hall teaching I had received for such contingencies: I went on eating my chop suey. The first duty of an officer is to avoid getting hit by his own men.

The Pride was anchored in the middle of the vast harbour and dwarfed every other ship. The monsoon was blowing and immediately outside the harbour the sea was livid. As we slipped past the anchored ships towards the narrow entrance to the harbour, waiting for the waves to chastise us, I understood the lure of the sea. It is not the salt spray, the immense horizons, the promise of adventure. It is an affair of the bowels. The roll of a ship, once your system has mastered it, becomes an opium. It fills you with an all-pervading sense of well-being and when it has

44

ceased there is no rest for you. As soon as we had crossed the line of the breakwater and the decks began to heave I groped my way forward, feeling like a dipsomaniac at opening time, to the bows. For two hours I clung to the nose of the vessel, where I could forget the ship behind me and be alone with a foot of white steel and the terrific sea. I hurtled down 50 feet to the water and soared up into space. For two hours I clung to the white steel, spitting the salt water back into the sea, nearly screaming with ecstasy.

11 October 1952

We reached Singapore in the evening – an infinitude of bright lights. The Pride, nosing along the dark coastal waters with engines at half, seemed like a furtive intruder whom no-one had noticed. We stopped engines, drifted discreetly into a dark cove, dropped anchor and waited until morning for somebody to notice us.

Night mail to Kuala Lumpur

12 October 1952

The cruise is over. Our harassed sergeant is anxious that I take over the administration of the Manchesters draft. Currency exchange, baggage problems and bewildered Mancunians wanting their officer to confirm wild rumours that we were going to Penang, not going to Penang, going to Perak, staying in Singapore till noon, till midnight, till next week. I scarcely noticed the Chinese girls clad in pyjamas who waited on the quay to unload baggage. 'No we're not going to Penang, we're going to Tapah.' 'No I haven't the faintest idea where Tapah is, or how we're going to get there. Fall in on the deck and shut up!' There were Malays also, just as I expected them, looking as if butter wouldn't melt in their slightly silly, prominent mouths. 'Sir, the corporal has lost his belt.'

It was obvious to all ranks that Singapore was a much better place than Aden or Colombo. 'They don't seem, to press you so much,' said a Mancunian. And then of course the place was Chinese 'and the Chinks are a much better lot' than the Arabs or the Sinhalese. They looked busy, prosperous, intelligent and clean. 'The only trouble is there is such a bloody lot of them,' so that you could hardly walk along the pavement. Old Chinks with wrinkled skins and pathetic little umbrellas against the sun and rain, middle-aged Chinks selling lots and lots of rice or eating it or both, pretty young Chink women all dressed in bright wide-legged pyjamas, chattering incessantly but never catching the eye of a lecherous stranger, and millions of embryonic Chinks looking awfully intelligent for their age.

The washing hangs like festive banners on poles from the upper windows; in narrow streets the banners meet in the middle, so that you walk under a roof of pyjamas. The houses stand end-to-end, their bright colours merely form a base to the even brighter Chinese signs splashed all over them; they are all supported by pillars so that the very pavement is an arcade. On ground level the shops are filled to overflowing with any desirable article from anywhere in the world; upstairs you just see the gaudy wall with a wooden window, each with a yellow face at leisure in it.

Every street is identical; they cross each other at right-angles in a hundred identical crossroads and each long street looks like the main thoroughfare because it is so teeming with life. For this reason it is said that Singapore lacks character. You get the frustrating feeling that everything is Chinese and yet you are by no means in China. There is a restless, makeshift air here: a pioneer air, a refugee air.

The night mail to Kuala Lumpur. The Manchesters queued with their mess tins for their tea on the platform and then they queued for their ammunition. The officers (half a dozen of us) were given pistols with 12 rounds. The men paraded on the platform, charged their magazines and were given instructions about when to shoot, when not to shoot and about the posting of sentries. When we had crossed the causeway onto the mainland I went to visit the draft in their carriages – made sure they understood their instructions and that sentries were properly briefed, returned to my second class berth, put my loaded pistol under my pillow, pulled down my mosquito net and slept solidly for nine hours.

When I awoke, twenty miles from Kuala Lumpur, everything was as I had read about it. Waterlogged rice fields worked by bent Chinese with wide saturnine hats to act as shields against the sun and drains for the rain. There was the rubber, which theoretically grows in neat rows and in practice is an untidy forest. And the kampongs – villages with huts raised on stilts against the floods. And the jungle, the immediate background to everything. The

46

only thing my books seemed to have overlooked was the beauty of it all.

13 October 1952

We arrived at Tapah Road station. I rang the battalion adjutant to ask for transport and told the men to fall out for a smoke. A typical enough army situation, sitting by a station waiting for the army trucks, loveable in their ugliness, to come lumbering up and take you all away. When they are late, as they usually are, the soldiers are wont to give a cheer. This time we waited half an hour but there was no cheer. A convoy of closed, armour-plated trucks appeared, each with a Bren gunner at the ready perched atop the cab, and an escort car with a Lewis gun and a wireless. 'So that's how it is', I thought, and gave an order to charge magazines again.

The barracks of the Manchesters at Tapah, which house Battalion HQ and C and D companies, are the prettiest I had ever seen. Its buildings are of atap, a bamboo plant. The whole place looks like an aboriginal village, a garden city and a fortress all in one.

In the officers' mess, a long wooden bungalow, the chairs and settees, spaciously placed, are tastefully marked with the green fleur-de-lys of the Manchesters and the dining room was rich in regimental silver. A Malay waiter and a Chinese waiter bypass each other at the doorway, and the mess sergeant rules over a little squad of Mancunian batmen who take turns at serving drinks and meals.

Mess talk is unashamedly 'shop'. C Coy commander made a 'contact' this afternoon, wounded a bandit with his carbine, but the fellow got away somehow. It is a sporting anecdote - good-humoured annoyance at the bandit's escape and the same scientific interest in his self-preserving skill as if he had been grouse in Derbyshire.

Quite different are the brave young subalterns returning from patrol in sweat-sodden jungle clothes, weighed down round their middles with grenades, carbine magazines, map case and compass. Although they are frightfully British and tight-lipped and reticent and grown-up about it all, their Malaya is an adventure and an enthralling responsibility.

I have an 'atap' room with latticed windows and a space between the walls and the steep roof, so that a multitude of strange little creatures, mostly lizards, have free access. The officers' quarters are at the edge of the camp and the jungle is only fifty yards away, so there is a perpetual whir and screech of jungle voices, particularly at night. One strange bird keeps making a noise exactly like the tzt! tzt! of a disapproving tongue and it disconcerts me that whenever an unworthy thought enters my head the bird says 'tut tut tut.' With its high, framed mosquito net, white and transparent, my bed looks princely.

The CO, to put me in the picture, took me in his staff car to 'morning prayers,' the daily conference held jointly by the police and military on the operations of the day. I had the impression of a multitude of traps and cunning plots, each maturing independently to a carefully co-ordinated fruition.

Next day I went in the daily ration truck to Ipoh, the nearest big town 40 miles away and capital of Perak. In no time you get used to travelling in this country: the slight tensing every time you come to a corner or an obstacle or high jungly ground at the roadside, the semi-conscious mental 'appreciation' ('...if we are ambushed from the right we can debus to the left and do a left-flanking attack behind those trees...'), the relief when the road is straight and you can feel safe at 50 mph.

In ambush

7 October 1952

A staff-sergeant knocked at my door, saluted with special smartness. 'The compliments of the Adjutant, sir – you are being posted to us.'

'To you?'

'To A Company, sir. We are ready to leave when you are.'

So I packed my black tin trunk, placed the same six little cartridges in my pistol, and was taken away over 20 twisting miles to Sungkai. Jungle alternated along the road with rubber plantations, but when they told me we had entered the Company operational area I could see nothing but rubber on both sides. At intervals there were paths through the trees, with trim plaques displaying the estate names – 'Chengai', 'Narborough', 'Kruit', etc.

We turned into one of these estate tracks, but instead of the planter's residence or estate office or coolie lines we came to A Company's cosy little camp. A homely, sprawling bungalow which used to be the planters' bedroom contains the officers' quarters, the mess, dining room, cookhouse and the sergeants' mess. The rest is canvas. The men walk about without shirts and the camp is quite unimposing, very quiet, almost apologetic. In our Mess there's only a dear little major of a company commander, the Administration Officer and we three platoon commanders. The Company's job is to protect all the rubber estates in the area directly, and indirectly by chasing the bandits in the jungle.

There was something touching about this sad, quiet colony of fifty Mancunians among the alien, jungle-covered hills. You can ask any of the men when they come back to England - they will tell you it was all right in camp but they will be at a loss to describe it. It is just A Company.

2/Lieut Tony Davis, in an aertex shirt and a pair of embarrassingly wide-legged shorts, strode out of the Mess, smiled warmly over his jungle-pimply face and shook my hand with the restless energy that characterises everything he does. He gave orders for the disposal of my luggage and brought me inside. There I found a very civilised looking middle-aged gentleman clad exclusively in shorts and sandals; as he put down his coffee cup and rose to welcome me I understood that he was the Company Commander and that it was a lucky thing for me to have been posted to A Company.

22 October 1952

Dear Folks... You can't set foot outside this camp unless you are in an armed party. If you were alone, you would probably see the bandits quickly enough! And yet, just now, I wouldn't want to be anywhere else in the world but where I am. The whole thing grips you, somehow, and it never occurs to you to feel sorry for yourself... I feel very fit indeed, and am waiting impatiently for December to come, when my platoon will really be mine, and my apprenticeship over...

Tony took me in hand. We walked round the camp together and he talked. There are eleven operational men in each platoon. Each has to protect three rubber estates. But that doesn't mean there's no jungle-bashing: the bandits live in the jungle and if you can't catch them in the rubber you have to go and find them. I was to take over 1 Platoon. Mike Rhodes had 2 and Tony's was 3.

Next day the Major assembled all the operational men of the three platoons in their dining room for a Company briefing in which he showed his sterner side. 'The operation tomorrow is one with which you are all familiar. No information has come in for nearly a fortnight now – but the road ambush last week on the police vehicle was a reminder that the bandits are still in the area. Our only course is to put out as wide a net as we can. I want each platoon to split up into three patrols of six, so that we shall have nine ambushes in all.'

The men sat on benches or on the floor, shirtless as usual, listening in absolute silence to their respected commander. A company briefing was rare and it was appreciated. Our sweet, civilised major showed his sterner side when he went on: 'Each of you has sufficient experience now to be able to open fire when you judge fit. Don't be too cautious. We're at the stage now when we want a bandit at all costs. When you're certain of killing one, shoot – and don't worry about the rubber tappers. I don't want anyone coming back to camp saying: I couldn't shoot because a tapper was in the way. If a tapper is in your line of fire it's just too bad. Remember he's probably a food supplier or something anyway. They're not innocent, not a single one.

The Major's briefing was for a routine 'blanket ambush' at various points on the boundary between rubber and jungle on all nine estates of the Company area – an operation that saw me out on my first patrol. I was to go as an ordinary rifleman under Tony's command.

I did not question the Major's bland assumption that all tappers sympathised with the Communist insurgents even though, when we saw them at work from our ambush positions, they looked as peaceful as can be. Our enemy was the Malayan National Liberation Army whom we called bandits in order to denigrate them, and because we only met them in small, furtive groups. The MNLA was the military arm of the Malayan Communist Party and was supplied by the Min Yuen or Mass Organisation. Who supplied the Min Yuen we had no idea.

For me this was a war in defence of free Britain: I had no other ideology. My sixth-form master had summed me up as a liberal of the old school; at 15 I was thrilled when the United Nations was born; in that same year, 1945, I felt bereaved when Churchill lost the post-war election, unaware of the national yearning for progress and justice that had swept my Tory hero away. Since then I have been against the Tories, unenthusiastic about Labour except in 1997 when Tony Blair's New Labour won us all over. The only political cause I embraced, at age 50, was that of the Greens – and even that I took on board as a good story first, an ideology later. In old age, I dream that the world economy will be reshaped to abolish economic 'growth' as the measure of national wellbeing and replace it with something more intelligent and sustainable.

I began patrolling under the command of my own respectful sergeant and our little band of quiet, unimaginative, good-humoured, brave Mancunians. I liked them all and I thought they liked me. It was hell struggling through the *belukar* (bushes so thick that you would call them impenetrable) under a diabolic sun, getting bitten to pieces. I liked dashing around in a jeep as if I owned the place; I even hopped into an aeroplane for a reconnaissance flight of my area, telling the pilot to go wherever I wanted. It was hell lying for hours in an ambush position before dawn, struggling against sleep and mosquitoes and wondering what sort of a bloody mess you would make of it if some bandits really did appear.

In our cosy little officers' mess the Major was like a father to us, like a widowed 19th Century gentleman with four sons who called him Sir and whom he called Michael, John, Tony and Walter. He loved France and also Austria, so relations between him and me were good from the start.

Trying to kill my own chaps

Number One Platoon was soon to be my own and I considered it important that they should respect me from the beginning. Luck was not altogether with me in this, for the very first thing I did to my new platoon was try to shoot them dead.

We had received intelligence that two bandits had been seen on field 9A of Chengai estate, so we went out on a three-day operation of early-morning ambushes on the jungle fringe. We would make a jungle base by night and creep unseen back into the rubber at first light, find a good hiding place and set up an ambush.

6 November 1952

We came to a clearing and made our base. There were 17 of us – two corporals, two Iban trackers, a CLO (civilian liaison officer) and ten men. When we got to field 9A we sat down by a stream and waited for first light to get into ambush positions.

The more spread out you are the better your chance, so I suggested to the sergeant that we split into two groups – he takes his party off to the left and I take mine to the right. Now I would have a little command of my own. We would ambush until 11.30 am and nobody was allowed to move before then. We would then RV on the higher ground above us. So, at 5.30 am we parted – they to the left and we to the right. I had with me Sultan the CLO and two private soldiers. The sergeant had an Iban and three men. Before he left we synchronised our watches.

Day dawned almost immediately and I found an excellent piece of cover for an ambush position. It was on low ground, hard by the stream, bush-covered and the ground sloped gently up on both sides presenting a good view uphill. I placed one soldier facing back (west) toward the RV, another facing south, Sultan facing east and I faced north. We were in a thick clump of belukar.

The hours of waiting slipped by. Jungly noises increased as the sun rose higher, and the startling rustle of monkeys in the treetops. At every disturbance I gripped my rifle tighter. The tappers came, singing and shouting at their work, but our hideout was perfect and I was sure they could not see us. Hour after hour I stood there, straining my eyes for bandits. I had little idea what they would look like – I had been told they might wear anything from rags to jungle-green uniforms just like ours. But they would be armed, and no armed party could be moving about the rubber other than bandits.

With the sun beating down I began to lose some of my enthusiasm. They never seemed to come, these bandits. I began to look more frequently at my watch and pray for 11.30 to come when we would stretch our legs. 11 o'clock at last – only half an hour more. I decided to pull myself together – this last half hour I would be really watchful.

And then I saw them. Unmistakably. One, two, three armed figures, right on the hilltop that I was watching. Creeping along with about five yards between them. I felt no fear but beads of sweat were forming on my brow.

In fact I was so excited that I acted like a machine, without volition or awareness. I pushed my safety-catch forward, cleared away some of the foliage that was getting in the way, took a quick aim and fired.

They were still there. They stopped and crouched, as if they were waiting for another shot in order to locate it before returning fire. I fired again, and a third time.

The sweat was running down my face now. There was a wild relief and a pleasure in savagely shattering the long hours of stillness and inactivity. I reloaded to fire again but the round jammed in the breach and there was a pause while I extracted it. Suddenly came the voice of Wheeldon, the soldier in the bush behind me.

'They're our own chaps, sir.'

For a moment the words did not sink in.

'How could they be our own chaps?' I shouted back, 'It's only 5 past. And the sergeant went the opposite way.'

But Wheeldon's voice had broken the spell and I couldn't fire again. I looked out and could see no-one. I knew suddenly and certainly that they had been our own chaps and that I had probably killed three of my platoon. Bandits would have fled at the first shot and not just stayed there waiting for another.

Everything was silent. I mustered my last reserves of strength and shouted with a voice that echoed through the estate: 'Is anybody hurt?'

From the top of the hill the answer came that, had I been religious, would have made me fall on my knees. 'No!'

I clambered out of my hideout and stood up. On the top of the slope the sergeant and his men were standing, looking down at me. I clumsily crossed the stream and slowly climbed the slope. The sergeant had his hands on his hips, looking at me with a strange smile. His three men and the Iban stood there, still spaced out with five yards between them, looking at me, without a word.

'What the hell's the time?' I said. The sergeant held up his watch. It showed 11.32. 'Who else has got a watch?' One after the other the soldiers shook their heads. I asked the Iban: 'have you got a watch?' He pointed to his pocket. 'Get it out, for God's sake.' He got out his watch while we waited. It showed 11.10, the same as mine. I called back for Sultan, who came panting up the hill. 'What time do you make it?' 'Ten past 11, sir.'

The smile died on the sergeant's face. 'It's those bloody sentries – they borrow my watch and they put it forward during the night to shorten their watch – it's not the first time it's happened.'

'What the hell were you doing up there anyway? You were supposed to be down here on the left. I was expecting you over here.'

'We couldn't find any cover down here, so we had to go up the hill to find a position.' The sergeant and his men had been in the wrong place, right in my line of fire, and come out at the wrong time.

We returned to our jungle base. The question of consequences arose immediately. The sergeant was strongly in favour of hushing it up. For my part I had no desire to come back from my first op. and tell the Major that I had shot at my own men. But as an officer I was paid to tell the truth. How could I lie in front of my platoon? And besides, how could it be kept secret? Three shots were fired on Chengai Estate, a few hundred yards from the coolie lines and the special constables' post. The shots would have been heard and reported, the Major would want an explanation. And how could I trust the whole platoon not to talk?

I decided that if there was a fuss in Sungkhai about three shots and the Major was bursting for an explanation, we would talk. If the shots had not been reported or had failed to arouse interest, we would not.

I got the platoon together. I said it was a scandal that sentries should have tampered with the sergeant's watch (no-one owned up to doing it) and that if it happened again, charges would be brought. However I proposed to let the matter drop, and if possible prevent it from going any further. I told Sultan, the CLO, that if anyone asked him about the shots, to say I had fired by mistake at a wild pig.

The shots had caused little stir in Sungkai. The constables on Chengai said they thought it was bandits killing a pig. The Major mentioned casually that he had heard a report of three shots and said with a smile that he had 'hoped it would be you killing bandits.'

In command

I took over command of my platoon and became absorbed in our routines of patrolling and ambushing, navigating precariously with inadequate maps and no landmarks in a jungle that all looks the same. We sometimes took 'guides' who themselves got lost. We got used to leeches creeping into our clothes, settling on their favourite place, the penis, and sucking blood until they became so firmly attached they had to be burnt off with a cigarette.

In the early days I felt like an impostor with men saluting me who had been at the job for 18 months. But soon I enjoyed the power, like when you first drive a car only this machine is human. To be in command means that you are never tired, never depressed, never bored. The men were happy in our jungle evenings when they had built their 'bashas' (huts), heated their rations and rested, secure in the knowledge that I had picked a safe place, set up a roster of night guards and planned ahead for the next day. I never felt sorry that my own basha was the last to go up, my own food the last to get cooked, because I was doing the more attractive things first.

I was sent on a three-week course to the army's jungle warfare training base in a remote spot near Johore Bahru. The army has a genius for courses – action-packed, fast-moving. But coming from our busy little theatre of war I thought the tactics they taught were too cautious, with too much emphasis on self-defence.

> 2 December 1952
>
> It's really no longer a matter of defending oneself; the bandits are already too much on the run: more stress should have been laid on the tremendous problem of locating them. Elementary tracking is not enough, for the bandits are much cleverer at it than we are. They should have taught more about rational methods of location i.e. calculation of likely places. A second criticism is that they taught us too large and unwieldy patrols. Bandits are best caught with patrols of six or less.

General Templar was in command in Malaya – the man who gave the world the wise observation that guerrilla warfare is won 'not in pouring in more troops but in the hearts and minds of the people.'

The Americans later mouthed the slogan in Vietnam, Iraq and Afghanistan, with less success than we had.

December 27 1952

Christmas at Sungkai was very hot. I unfortunately missed the tea party for the local children. Fifteen bandits were reported on Narborough Estate. The terrified tappers had been sent scurrying back to their lines in the middle of the morning. It was too late to do anything useful but we had to do something, so we called for an air strike in the surrounding jungle, and the afternoon of the tea party saw me sitting in the midst of a grumbling platoon on Narborough, watching the planes dive one after another over the jungle. When it was over we went in to do a 24-hour search of the area. It would have required 24 weeks. We did not even find a bomb crater.

We returned in time for Christmas Eve. I found myself in the men's canteen being filled to capacity with beer by my platoon. Admittedly the men were all tight but the fact remains that a toast was proposed and solemnly drunk to 'the best platoon commander in the company' and I was proclaimed in song to be a jolly good fellow.

On Xmas morning the sergeant-major brought tea round to the bleary-eyed men in their beds. Christmas dinner was served to the men by their officers! There was so much to eat that at least a third was left over. I saw the wide-eyed wonder of the little Tamil scullery boy at the sight of all the turkey and potatoes and pudding being shovelled into dustbins.

We officers escaped into our Mess for some hurried turkey sandwiches. There were only four of us but in the evening we put on our mess kit and ate a formal Christmas dinner complete with sherry, champagne (the present of our thoughtful Chinese contractor), port, toasts to the Queen and all the turkey that still remained in the men's kitchen.

By 10pm discipline had reached rock bottom. A soldier, literally on his knees with drink, came crawling into the Mess, muttering thickly that it was about time the men had the pleasure of our company. For this unheard of lapse the man was given a drink and sent back with the promise that we were coming. They were having a drunken concert; one personality after another was named and forced to sing...

The Battalion CO had paid us a short visit earlier. At midnight the signallers reported that his escort car, which maintains regular wireless contact with base throughout the 20-mile journey to Bn HQ, had suddenly gone off the air. So John, being the soberest of us, set out with a medical orderly in another scout car to see what had happened.

Then a major rang from Bn HQ at Tapah. Between loud hiccups, he said he understood that the CO had been ambushed, and what were we going to do about it? John reported by telephone that the scout car was upside down in a ditch; the CO, however, was safe in Bidor, a half-way village. So John extracted the driver, spitting beer and blood, from the scout car, escorted the CO back to Tapah, and returned to the festivities.

The Company's lights were out, I had discarded my spirit-stained mess kit and was about to turn in. There was a knock on the Mess door, and a member of my platoon asked to see me. He announced that the platoon was holding a private celebration in one of their tents, and would I come? So I went. In their candlelit tent the men were naughtily cooking some of their jungle rations for a midnight feast. They told me their private opinions on the various ways of their platoon commander. It was 3am before I could tear myself away.

Coming back from the jungle warfare course I was fresh and happy to get back to my platoon. Alas! Almost the first operation was another fiasco in which I blundered badly and this time I did not get off so lightly.

It happened like this. Relations between the army and the police had become strained in our area after a police patrol walked into one of our ambushes and two policemen had been killed. Under a new arrangement the police were to operate only in the rubber, the military only in the jungle. The planters, hard-drinking and hospitable as ever, were our good friends but they hated the new strategy and tried to sabotage it. They wanted British soldiers on their estates. But they were overruled and returned with many oaths to their bottles.

Before the next operation we officers were briefed by the Major. 'Now that we are out of the rubber estates, the old arrangements whereby the police must keep 200 yards away from the jungle fringe of course no longer applies,' the Major was saying. But I listened with only half an ear: that didn't concern me for I would be well in the jungle all the time.

Our three-day operation was in the jungle at the back of Narborough estate. We were to go parallel with the rubber, southeast to an area with a stream running through it. But the estate track was not marked on my map, so I had to plot a jungle course without knowing where I was starting from, and in the jungle there are no landmarks. All I could do was go southeast until we hit the stream.

The going was hellish. Apart from the *belukar* there was *llalang*, stifling-hot grasses 6-8ft high. After three hours we should have reached the stream but we did not. My new sergeant, a weak and flabby individual of about 40, was beginning to feel the strain. He thought we had gone too far East and past the source of the stream, so we should go southwest, back to the rubber edge to establish our position. I said no because we were not allowed to enter the rubber, and continued on my course.

After another hour there was still no stream and the sergeant's advice was becoming more persistent and more breathless. By this time I reckoned we must have gone well south of Narborough estate; if we went west now we should strike a paddy area that was marked on the map. So we went west.

After half an hour we reached – not paddy but rubber. I thought it must be one of the many locally owned, un-named estates we called 'Kampong Rubber' that were not marked on our British maps. The sergeant now suggested that we proceed inside the rubber along the jungle fringe until we came to the stream or some other landmark. I still objected that we were not allowed to enter rubber at all. The corporal said that surely the police had to keep 200 yards inside the rubber. The phrase sounded familiar. I didn't remember, didn't want to remember, that this rule no longer applied. So I gave way, inexcusably, against my better judgment.

With perhaps an obscure presentiment of disaster I made sure that we were properly spaced out. I walked in front, the column stretched a long way behind me. When the rear elements stopped unaccountably, I could see nothing amiss from where I was. Bit by bit news began to reach me. They had seen a 'man in white' in the distance. On the top of a hill in the rubber, about 100 yards from the fringe, stood the planter Ronnie Boxhaul, in white shirt and shorts, and the area's police chief, Jock Ness, in jungle green, with a police patrol. We were on Narborough after all, and fate had decided that on that huge estate we and they should meet.

Their patrol had been resting on the hill before going home when they had spotted armed figures walking along the jungle fringe. Jock had rapidly sited his men, placing his bren gun in a commanding position and given the order to open fire. But the bren gunner said: 'they've got white arms like Europeans.' 'Don't be an idiot,' Jock had replied fiercely, 'there are definitely no military in the rubber. Open fire.' But the bren-gunner said: 'they are spaced out, like soldiers. And they have military weapons.' And thus it was that my platoon, exposed by a combination of bad counsel, weak leadership and bad luck to mortal danger, escaped with their lives thanks to the level-headedness of a young Malay policeman.

Having got my exact bearings from my two unsmiling friends, I headed again into the jungle where I belonged. We soon found our stream, made a base for the night, and set up our aerial. The major's voice came through, with the unmistakable incisiveness of wrath. He ordered me to abort the operation and return to base.

We found the whole Sungkai area in a state of uproar. The police had gone on strike, refusing to go out on patrol. The planters were exuberant at the spectacular failure of the plan that they had opposed and were holding drunken counsels of war. There was talk of A Coy moving out of Sungkai in disgrace. I pulled off my sweaty garments with a sense of impending doom.

The major, sweet and fatherly no longer, received me formally in his office. I made no attempt at defence, apologised profusely for the embarrassing situation I had placed him in. He said he had no alternative but to relieve me of my command and to ask me to consider myself under open arrest, pending the arrival of the Battalion's 2/ic to take a summary of evidence.

Major W T Thompson, OBE, DSO, 6ft 2in tall and with corresponding bulk, 2nd in command of the battalion, ex-Cambridge, a proud, formidable potentate who amused himself by inspiring terror in soldier and subaltern alike, came down the next day to take a summary of evidence. His only other pastime was the manufacture of spontaneous puns. He was not easily discomposed and the present incident presented a challenge only in the opportunities for punning.

He did not ask to see me. He took notes from the major (who afterwards related the scene) sitting in mock-pompous state behind his notebook, in masterly imitation of a provincial magistrate, enjoying himself hugely. 'Am I to gather,' he boomed, 'that Schwarz came out of the jungle and encountered the Jock Ness monster in a rubber field?'

Colonel Walsey who as a shy, gentle CO was a contradiction in terms, came down himself the following day with Tony, my old friend who was now the adjutant. The Colonel sat down at the Major's desk and called for Schwarz. Tony, whose frank, youthful and familiar face wore such a mask of seriousness that I almost burst out laughing, sat at the other desk.

'I – er – suppose you know, Schwarz –' began the CO with his customary fatuousness for which I was now wildly grateful – 'what this is all about?'

'Yes, Sir,' I said.

That seemed to discompose him a little, but he recovered and said this was a serious business. However, the company commander had spoken in my favour and he did not propose to let it go any further. He appreciated the navigational difficulties I was up against – 'in fact I really don't know how some of you young chaps find your way about the jungle at all – I'm sure I couldn't. But orders are orders, Schwarz. If people didn't obey orders what sort of an army would we have? It would be like the – er – Portuguese army.'

And so I was forgiven, Major Gill was my surrogate father once more and normal operations continued.

My own Ibans

I was just back from a three-day jungle patrol. Although as usual there was no 'contact' it was a successful operation and when I returned, hot and tired and happy with my gallant little band, I should scarcely have turned a hair if someone had told me I was to command 1 Platoon for the rest of my life. Then came this bombshell.

> 6 January 1953.
> Signal to: O.C. 'A' Company
> from: Adjutant. 1 Manch Tapah 3 Jan 53
>   Subject: Language courses.
>   1. 1 Manch have been allotted an Iban Platoon which will arrive on 17 Feb 53
>   2. 424052 2/Lt W.Schwarz is appointed Platoon Commander.
>   1440197 Sgt Swetman G. is appointed Platoon Sergeant.
>   3. a/m officer and NCOs will attend Malay language course commencing 12 Jan 1953...
>   6. They will report to RSM Foster at Kuala Lumpur airfield (RAF P&F section) at 0830 hrs 10 Jan 53 and will fly to Kota Bahru...

Here I was being given exactly the sort of job I wanted before I came here – and cursing my fate!

> 7 January 1953
> I am to work with lovable British soldiers no more, but to command 60 tiny, yellow, grinning, longhaired, superstitious Bornese savages. Ibans are tattooed from head to foot with weird designs, and in spite of having operational kit they burden themselves with all kinds of weighty lucky charms. They are passionate in love and hate; if they like me they will wait on me hand and foot; if they dislike me I shall live in nightly fear of their little curved knives.

Ibans are Dayaks from Sarawak, Borneo, who are famous headhunters, scalping their victims and keeping the cured scalps as trophies. In Malaya we had used them individually as trackers for their uncanny skills. On patrol I would always put my Iban in front because only he could see bandit tracks. He would suddenly stop,

61

peer at the ground and say here was a track. I could see nothing. How old? An hour, a day, a week or a month, the Iban would say. How many bandits? One or two, a dozen, a hundred. They could tell from upturned leaves, a crushed blade of grass, a tiny trace in the earth.

More Ibans wanted to join us than we could use as trackers. But why, when the British army chose to have its first ever operational platoon of Ibans, did they choose me to command it? Did they think, after my two early blunders on the rubber estates, that I could be entrusted only with natives? I prefer to think they found me cosmopolitan enough to cope with a foreign language and foreign savages.

13 January 1953

Malay language course c/o Malay Regiment at Kota Bharu.

Their language is the gentlest of lullabies; any word that is loudly spoken is ipso facto incorrectly pronounced. Perak was over-run with Chinese; Malays were the underdogs and their fragile character was suppressed. Here in Kelantan I am in the real Malaya, where Malays hold their handsome heads high. What a lovely people they are! I have never seen such peace and beauty as here, although I live in a military camp. There is a tranquillity and a tenderness and a vast, unobtrusive 'savoir vivre' about Malays. The first thing a British officer of the Malay Regiment has to learn is that he must never raise his voice to the men; a raised voice has no effect except incredulous bewilderment and an abrupt loss of respect.

The place is alive with children – little brown naked creatures, so healthy and so beautiful that I would willingly adopt half a dozen and bring them home as presents for the family, but in cold, confined England they would probably die. My lessons finish at lunch-time so that I can spend the afternoons stalking these creatures, hunter-like, with my camera. At first they ran away but soon they began calling me *tuan gambar* (picture mister) and I now enjoy many a *s'lamat pagi* (good morning) or a mock military salute from the tops of trees, from ditches or from underneath the raised houses. Malay women, with their long shiny black hair, large kind eyes and hanging breasts which they cover up on the approach of a stranger, must be the shyest civilised creatures in the world.

The men are never more than five feet tall, their frank, brown faces so boyish that the thought of their being soldiers makes one want to laugh or to cry. And yet, in their neat brown shorts, spotless shirts and Malay 'songkok' hats they are as smart as any soldier I have seen, and if they are more afraid of bandits than British soldiers are, they have doubtless had more reason to be. A broad smile is always just below the surface of their faces, and a natural politeness (far removed from the calculating fawns of the Chinese) is their most outstanding characteristic. My picture-hunts invariably finish with coffee and pidgin Malay on the steps of one of the huts.

I looked forward to my Ibans and I was the envy of many officers with duller jobs. I was to collect them at Port Dickson (near Kuala Lumpur), take them for two weeks of weapon training at battalion HQ in Tapah, followed by two weeks of jungle training in Kroh (North Perak, on the Siamese border). Meanwhile I prepared training programmes, accommodation and suitable food for my strange charges.

17 March 1953 Tapah

I'm a company commander, platoon commander, weapons training instructor, drill instructor, minor tactics instructor, sergeant-major all in one! The Ibans are very keen, which helps a lot. Much more energetic than Malays, if not quite as charming. To help me with the training, administration, discipline and welfare of 60 Ibans I have only one moody sergeant and one pretty useless corporal.

We shall do three to four weeks' training. Then two sections (24) will go off as trackers attached to companies and three sections (36) will remain as my operational platoon. About two thirds of them speak Malay, an easy language which I now speak quite fluently…

The battalion has high hopes that my Ibans, because of their innate tracking ability, can overcome our chief problem which is finding the bandits. The job which now occupies all my waking

63

(and sleeping) thoughts is to see that they will know how to deal with bandits when they find them…

I need never again fear getting lost in the jungle or being uncomfortable in it, for besides being born trackers they are skilful in constructing shelters, and are eager to please, help and protect their officer. I am also fortunate that my two British NCOs, in spite of their faults when training in camp, are both good on operations.

21 March 1953

On a jungle mountain expedition. It was hard to keep up with my 21 Ibans who were in their element, with three Sakai, an aboriginal race who know the jungle even better. Apart from my corporal, who spent every spare moment reading penny-dreadfuls, there wasn't another white man for miles. We dashed cheerfully up and down the 3,000-foot mountain, following bandit tracks only a few hours old, and found bandit camps only just evacuated: they kept one step ahead of us all the time. In the middle of the night I was woken by terrified Ibans who said that the camp was surrounded by bandits. 'There are lights! Lights!' they croaked. It was the lights of a village at the foot of the mountain showing through the dense trees.

An Iban got bitten by a scorpion. The Sakai produced a black stone and placed it on the wound. Not to be outdone, I administered 4 'sulfa-meg' tablets and some antiseptic, taking care, in deference to an older culture, to replace the black stone afterwards. The man recovered almost immediately, both cultures thus retaining their prestige.

The Ibans' appearance in the jungle was fearsome. Most of them went barefoot and almost naked, some only in jungle boots and underpants – a grotesque combination. They carried bones and goats' horns and bits of animals (or human beings, I could never tell) strapped around their torsos.

We had a visit from General Sir Hugh Stockwell, who had commanded British troops in Burma and was soon, in 1956, to command the Suez invasion. He told me I was to let my Ibans go into the jungle dressed exactly how they like. 'If they want to go out with only a feather up their arse then you mustn't stand in their way,' were his words.

They kept asking me most earnestly if they could cut off the bandits' heads, and I feared that I should not be able to prevent them. The walls of their houses back in Sarawak are lined with human heads, the insides having been skilfully removed and the skin cured to prevent decay.

The Iban corporal went round the camp twice every morning, once with the antimalarial Paludrine which they tolerantly swallowed to please their eccentric officer, and once with a glutinous black substance in a tin, into which each Iban dipped his finger and dabbed a bit onto his throat.

> 28 April 1952
> They have excellent manners and a first-rate sense of humour. They constantly offer to carry my pack and when we strike a base they build me the most comfortable shelter. I've now got an Iban batman. He estimates his age at 27 but cannot be more than 17 and looks about 15. He is a sweet-looking boy – perhaps that's why I picked him as it isn't nice to be woken up in the morning by the more formidable type of Iban with one grotesque, droopy ear. Of course he cannot write so laundry is a bit of a problem, and the art of blanco-ing belts eludes him. But he has a passion for brasses, and my pips twinkle like twin stars.

The Battalion commander appeared to have regained confidence in me as he planned to recall the other two sections of Ibans who were with the sergeant, so that I could take the whole lot (48) into the jungle as part of a Brigade operation.

> 19 May 1953
> Dear Folks... The Brigade operation was good fun. A change to have others on the spot to take orders from... The Manchesters had only one contact and, of course, it was made by my Ibans, who have an uncanny nose for bandits. This time I was with the patrol myself. It seemed nasty and horrible, to suddenly shatter the stillness of the jungle, previously broken only by the hilarious hoots of monkeys, with gunfire. We didn't kill any bandits as they were too quick for us, but everyone is very pleased with the Ibans, who also found two food stores, while the rest of the Battalion found nothing at all.

My Ibans made their first kill in another Brigade operation which was the subject of my first article in the *Manchester Guardian*, a back-pager called *The Clearing*, submitted without authorisation under the pseudonym Blake Walter.

Manchester Guardian 10 September 1953

...The Ibans were on form. Rifles thrust purposefully forward, almost as if they were in the habit of discharging them with accuracy, fiercely tattooed bodies and bare feet poised for action, they seemed to coax the undergrowth into silence... They found a camp in the clearing, shot a bandit and were crowded round him when our captain came upon the scene and shouted to me: 'Call them off – they're bashing his brains out.' The bandit wasn't dead. We radioed for a helicopter to evacuate him.

The machine circled once and then hovered over the clearing, a delicious orgy of noise and science in that hushed and primitive theatre of war. It landed precariously on the uneven ground. To complete the wonder of the moment a brigadier jumped lightly down from the plane. It was the first time we had seen anyone in olive-green shorts and shoes in the jungle. Instantly we took stock of our shortcomings. I had not shaved for three days... We saluted.

'Jolly good show,' said the brigadier. "Have you got him ready?'

Now tied to a pole like a boar, the bandit was laid at the feet of the brigadier. At that moment the engine of the helicopter spluttered, coughed and was silent. 'She's stalled,' announced the pilot from the cockpit... He kept pressing the starter, causing violent shudders through the machine... To add to the consternation the bandit at the brigadier's feet suddenly decided he was not dead after all, and started heaving and groaning horribly.

'He isn't dead,' observed the brigadier. 'No,' admitted the company commander apologetically. The pilot got out of the machine and announced that owing to the sloping ground the petrol had all run out of the front tank to the rear tank and could not be induced to return. The brigadier said: 'Get it levelled,' The Ibans exuberantly set to work with their parangs... When the nose had fallen forward the pilot pressed the button again, but there was only a whirr and a shudder... 'Couldn't we rock it?' suggested the brigadier. At which the whole company, British and

Iban, officers and men, lent their weight to the helicopter. The bandit now began to snort. The Captain gave him some morphine and he was quiet again.

'We'll have to get on the blower,' said the brigadier, seizing the mike. 'This is Sunray Brigade speaking,' he boomed, and with a dark patch of perspiration slowly forming on the back of his jacket, transmitted his troubles to headquarters.

It was after six o'clock when the drone of aircraft was heard again over the jungle. Two more helicopters appeared above our clearing. One circled defensively while the other hovered... Acclaimed by a great shout from the audience on the ground, a petrol can appeared through a hatch and was lowered on a rope.

The clearing vibrated once more with the noise of the engine and the trees trembled with the wind of the rotors. The brigadier beamed and shook hands all round while the bandit, now immobile, was hauled aboard. In another minute brigadier and bandit were whirled up beyond the treetops, and an indescribable peace descended on our base.

The bandit died, the first and only kill in the seven months of my Malayan service.

25 May 1953

Dear Folks... I have contracted a disease that all soldiers out here get sooner or later. It has no medical name that I know of, but among soldiers it is known as 'boat-happy.' Its chief symptom is an unnatural serenity in the face of discomfort, a perverse cheerfulness in carrying out unpleasant orders. A subsidiary symptom is an obsessive preoccupation with the names and movements of troopships, and with the sailing dates of various release groups. More alarming is a certain loss of touch with the immediate environment. When vital matters of anti-terrorist strategy are being discussed the patient tends to assume a dreamy, introspective expression, and offer some strangely irrelevant remark like 'the Empire Trooper docks at Southampton on April 30th, so she should be on her way back in May. That means she'll be sailing from Singapore in July...'

I sailed for home in the Empire Windrush, the captured German cruise ship that had carried the first wave of Jamaican immigrants to Britain in 1948. Ten months after my voyage she sank in the Mediterranean after fire broke out in her engine room. I took in the sights and sounds of Asia and Africa with more equanimity than on the voyage out. My family had moved to London and I was in a hurry to become a journalist.

4 August 1953 (letter)
The future being uncertain is a slight blemish on my good spirits. How I envy those who are coming home to a pre-arranged job, or to a waiting place at Oxford! After the rigours of the jungle I don't despair unduly at the prospect of a year or so's good, honest reporting for the *West Salford Advertiser*. If there was plenty of fun in the jungle, why should there be less so in West Salford?

Chapter three:
How to be a journalist

'Schwarz, know anything about football?' the chief reporter asked out of the blue.

'Not a thing.'

'You will. You're covering Oxford City on Saturday.'

Two months into my first job, on the *Oxford Mail*, I was quite used to sitting in the press gallery of the magistrates' court writing down who was fined £5 for riding a bicycle without lights. I was covering rambling debates in the city council about whether new street lights should go on the left or the right of the road – and stayed alert much of the time although I was still a dreamer. Every other week I was a film critic, enjoying free tickets and the imagined prestige of passing judgment elegantly in the four paragraphs that I was allowed.

But football! I knew the rules but not the right words to record the ebb and flow. It was all right in the end because we journalists are kind and co-operative (except when we have an exclusive story when we become mean and devious) and my colleagues helped me translate my notes into football language.

I had come home from Malaya to London, not Manchester, because the family had moved. I think Father might have stayed in the textiles capital but there had been pressure from our fun-loving mother who found Manchester a backwater, and Vicky and Marlene were of course delighted. Our big house had a garden backing onto Golders Hill Park which has a duck pond and a deer garden and is big enough to take a proper walk in. Technically we were in Golders Green (NW11) but in spirit, we insisted, this was Hampstead (NW3). Wasn't the Heath just up the road? Our street was called The Park, and we residents had a key to a private gate.

I wanted to be a journalist – now. What should I do? How is it done? Schools of journalism were not yet in fashion. There were only two routes: write to every editor in town and out of town and hope for an interview – or use your contacts. I did both. Having no previous experience, I got only polite rejections, except from the *Evening Standard* whose editor, Charles Wintour, gave me an interview. Wintour was famous for his wintry manner but he liked me, told me to find a job in the provinces (he didn't have one in mind or offer any contacts) and come back to him in six months.

My only contact was our family friend, Derrick Sington, a *Manchester Guardian* correspondent who had got my Malaya backpager, *The Clearing*, into the paper. Sington had been one of the four officers who were the first British soldiers to walk into the horror of Bergen-Belsen concentration camp at its liberation on August 15, 1945. The commandant, Josef Kramer, greeted them at the gate. Of the four, three were Jews, including Chaim Herzog, who later became President of Israel. Among the emaciated inmates of the camp Derrick met Traute, who was to become his wife. When we children came over to their house for tea, Traute showed us the number tattooed on her arm but she never spoke to us about Belsen.

Derrick knew Harford Thomas, editor of the *Oxford Mail*, wrote to him about me and told me to write also to Thomas. I got the job. Harford was a gentle and humane boss who a few years later was deputy editor of the *Guardian* when I was the foreign leader writer.

The *Oxford Mail* is an evening paper and I was too busy on assignments to see much of the editor. I had to learn how to write for a real newspaper, not for my parents or my diary. The people who taught me were people I never met – the sub editors. I learnt the trade by opening the paper and seeing, often to my chagrin, what the subs had made of my story. Especially what they had left out. My finest prose was not edited at all, it was deleted. This is the moment in a journalist's career, the moment of truth, when you decide whether you are in the right profession. Which is more important – the fine prose or the facts?

But I had also to learn to respect the facts and tell the truth. As a baby journalist I wrote my stories for the chief reporter who had sent me out and who was the first to see them, and when they appeared in print that was the end of the matter. I did not really believe, deep down, that my stories were read by real people. Until the day I covered a popular Christmas lecture for children in one of the colleges. It was over-subscribed and some children were turned away. I wrote that children were in tears, which they were not. Next morning in my digs the landlord was telling this story at the breakfast table. 'It's a real shame, you know, the poor little kids were crying their eyes out... It's all in the paper.' The penny dropped. A news story is read and believed and ought to be true.

I did get my chance for the finer sort of writing when Harford Thomas sent me out on the occasional feature. If I went out early in the morning and promised to be back by 3 pm at the latest, I could borrow the Mail's red delivery van, in which I felt grand and important. I was still young for my age.

I hated an assignment the chief reporter gave us on quiet afternoons: 'nip round the colleges, have a squint at the notice boards and see what stories you can pick up.' This practice was illegal but that wasn't why I hated it: snooping on the students felt like an intrusion on their charmed life. Worse, I felt forced to revisit an adolescence in which I had been out of my depth. I had little nostalgia for The Queen's College. Just the occasional ghostly moment as I passed, say, the little wood at the top of Park Town where on dark nights I had kissed Miche.

The *Oxford Mail* sent me on a Pitman's shorthand course. I didn't stay long enough to become proficient but to this day I write a few common words in shorthand and save time. (Time is, indeed, one of the words). In this electronic age, shorthand should not be despised. Nervous interviewees are less intimidated by a notebook than by a tape-recorder, and journalists still benefit from shorthand to capture that vital quote that would be tedious and time-wasting to retrieve from a tape.

I join the rat race and find Dorothy

Six months were up. I had promised to write to Charles Wintour but I didn't because I was happy and had forgotten about the *Evening Standard*. But now Charles Wintour writes to me! Asking how I was getting on and would I like to send him some cuttings? I sent the Brize Norton piece and a few news stories, went to see Wintour and was offered a job.

My friends on the *Oxford Mail* were unanimous: 'Don't take it! Don't go to Fleet Street. It's a rat race – you're far better off here.' I joined the rat race.

Now I lived in the family home again, commuting to the *Standard* in Fetter Lane, just behind Fleet Street. The office seemed to me grand and imposing and so did the journalists: Milton Shulman the film critic, Quentin Crewe the acerbic travel and food writer, Nicholas Tomalin, Angus McGill, Larry Marks and others.

I joined the *Londoner's Diary* team under Tudor Jenkins, the veteran 'Londoner' who knew the secrets and scandals behind every star, toff, millionaire and scoundrel in town. We sat at desks arranged in an oblong, where Jenkins could see us and call us when he had an assignment for us. Quentin Crewe in his wheelchair – he had muscular dystrophy – was my neighbour and we spent happy hours in cynical wisecracks while we waited for the Jenkins call. We each had our telephone which we used for our interviews and Quentin was always on his phone to his posh friends and relations, some of whom he wrote Diary pieces about.

We did not go in for much ruthless revelation. Tudor was not vicious or even unkind: scandals were only hinted at and there were plenty of warm, kind stories as well. *The Londoners Diary* was well accepted by most of the people we wrote about and even its victims were often pleased to be publicised. For every memory of someone slamming down the phone on me, I have ten of people going on and on.

As if there was not already enough excitement in my life, I now met Dorothy. This happened because my big brother Vic, handsome as ever with plenty of girls, had been invited to an elegant party in Wimpole Street. The house was large so Kay Seymour allowed her young sister Kathryn, still a sixth-former, to invite a friend or two – and Vic brought me along. There was dancing. I was shy and alone among those smart, older people, and when I saw a beautiful dark-haired girl with intelligent eyes and a mischievous expression, also alone, I asked her to dance. She was

72

one of Kathryn's schoolgirl extras. I felt suddenly liberated from this stiff and forbidding party and I could see Dorothy felt the same: we needed air. We went out for a walk.

I had my little Fiat 500 parked outside. I felt in my pocket for the key. She said: 'If you think I'm going in your car to neck you'd better think again.' Dorothy was quick with her thinking and with her tongue and has remained so. She told me she lived in Hampstead and I said I did too but we were both lying because we both lived in Golders Green, where we were eventually married.

We saw each other every evening after our first meeting, at parties, the cinema and friends' houses; it was four months before we met in daylight. Dorothy continued to be beautiful and sharp-tongued. She could often tell what I was going to say or even think.

In daylight at last, on Hampstead Heath, she took me down the sloping grounds of Kenwood to a private place she had loved all her life – a hidden tree beside the pond with a low branch you could swing on. Dorothy had been wandering alone on the Heath since she was nine, which of course would not be allowed today. She was escaping from a stifling Jewish upbringing with frilly dresses and pink wallpaper in her bedroom. She had made friends out on the Heath, including the odd dirty-old-man, but she never came to any harm. In the fifties children had freedom to roam.

To love Dorothy I needed to love Tio, her fierce little Papillon who challenged dogs twice his size – the precursor of many dogs, cats, horses and parrots that were to enrich and plague the rest of my life. When he was not fighting, Tio was deliberately charming, but only to important people because he was a snob. He would bark at poor people. To the right people he would sit up prettily to beg, but would sometimes topple over because he had broken his pelvis in one of his many battles. He was disobedient and often went missing. Yes, I did love Tio, who was to come with us in the adventures ahead.

Mother called Dorothy the Princess of Golders Green – a double dig, at her family's evident prosperity in the textile business, and then, of course, we looked down on Golders Green because we lived a little way up the hill.

Dorothy

Father found her attractive but too sharp and irreverent to be the English rose he would have considered ideal. Max and Cissie Morgan found me too dreamy and poetic to be a substantial prospect for their daughter but they made me welcome, inviting me to Friday night suppers with chicken soup, chopped liver, *gefillte fish* and *challah* bread, and Pop Morgan reciting the blessing in Hebrew. I enjoyed the warmth of those Friday rituals, absent in my own family.

We have had a volatile romance these last 55 years. Crockery hurled, blows struck, partings for ever, love letters, laughter, infidelities. Best of all: adventure. I am, as I have said, a dreamer. I dream alone. Dorothy lives in the real world with more passion and intelligent insight than is good for her. She is constantly knocking at my door. I like travelling alone, hiking alone, listening alone to music. Dorothy, less self-centred, was more spoilt. When we went out together I was frugal in my habits, she was five-star, which lead to our earliest bickerings.

She was more romantic, as a girl should be. We used to come late at night to my family home in The Park, stop in the kitchen for a drink and tiptoe all the way upstairs, past my parents' room, to my attic bedroom. One night as we arrived I was hungry and ate some bread and cheese. She was appalled. One does not feel hungry before sex, let alone eat Emmenthal.

I bought her a diamond wedding ring. Quentin Crewe and I, as we waited for our next assignment on the *Londoner's Diary*, discussed the appropriate inscription. We came up with *noctes cenaeque deorum* (nights and suppers of the Gods) which is still on her finger.

The *Londoner's Diary* sent me to celebrity parties, with or without an invitation, and here I was not shy, as I had been in Wimpole Street, because I was a reporter.

We had to meet visiting celebrities in their hotels, and when Jean Cocteau arrived in town Tudor Jenkins naturally called on Schwarz, a French speaker, to go. Cocteau was in bed where he immediately invited me to join him. I declined but I still got a good interview and before I left he wrote me a sweet letter in praise of London. I described him as 'a small, lean, wizened man of 65 with a virile growth of white hair' and quoted him as saying: 'I haven't a *centime* to my name' but pointed out that he had a flat in Paris and a house in Cap Ferrat.

On Saturday afternoons we reporters could earn extra money by helping out at our sister paper, the *Sunday Express*, in the hectic hours before it went to press. Each time I was impressed by the shiny black glass of that palace in Fleet Street, pleased to be allowed through the heavy revolving doors. Mostly we just checked and updated stories already written by staff reporters.

But one Saturday I was sent to Cowdray Park in Sussex where Prince Philip was playing polo. Not to cover the game, just to be there in case he fell off or committed one of his gaffes. Dorothy came along with Tio. Prince Philip did not fall off or make any gaffes so I had no story. As he sat drinking at the bar Tio, the show-off, the snob, went up to HRH, sat up and begged precariously on his bad pelvis and was rewarded with peanuts. Even this did not

75

qualify as a story and I felt inadequate. Disconsolately I drove my little Fiat back home. I felt that any claim for expenses should be minimal: I put down a gallon of petrol and a drink with a sandwich at the bar.

Three days later I was sitting at my desk at the *Standard* when the phone rang and an angry voice bellowed. 'Schwarz? This is the chief reporter, *Sunday Express*. Don't you ever eat? You were away at tea time, so claim for tea! You were away at dinner time, so claim for dinner! And your out-of-town daily allowance and your mileage allowance! And don't you ever buy drinks for people? I'm sending you back your form to be properly filled in!' The phone went dead.

I did my best with the expenses claim and as my career progressed I became a little less puritan, a little more imaginative with expenses. But alas! Those extravagant days began to be over long before I retired and I am told they are quite over now.

Have wife, will travel

In June 1956, on board SS *Angelica* between Athens and Crete, I recorded in my honeymoon diary that we had been married at Golders Green synagogue in a blaze of photographers (local press only) ponderous Jewish clerical wisdom and Viennese waltzes.

> I awoke as if to a day of execution. The hired morning coat hung, black and strange, like a mourning coat, over the bed. Mother, who looked in through the door, advised me gently to hurry so that I could have a peaceful instead of a hurried 'last hour'. And all morning the sense of waiting to be fetched by a man in a big black car…
>
> Outside Golders Green synagogue stood our usher, Martin Blackburn, dressed like a tailor's dummy, grinning in a diffident, Aryan, Anglo-Saxon manner as the guests arrived. Inside were sparse, predatory groups of aunts who had come too early. If they were Schwarz aunts they sat smiling sheepishly, throwing me desperate glances of encouragement. If they were Morgan aunts they rushed up and kissed me.
>
> Dorothy came down the aisle. The minister muttered under his breath to the cantor: 'what a beautiful girl.' The cantor moved not a muscle.

I had my back to her but I could see her reflected in the Gates of the Ark. She was magical. Child, wife, beauty and mischievous urchin – it all came through from under the veil in an instant. It came through to me, to the minister, to the cantor and the whole congregation…

Tio and Dymocke, each with a pink ribbon, were the first to greet us outside. In the Rolls Royce on the way to the reception at the Grosvenor House Hotel, Tio slept. We felt he had accepted our marriage.

We shook hands with all the guests in the foyer, the four parents, we and the dogs forming the receiving line. Some guests ran the gauntlet bravely, with what they considered tact and understanding for the harassed hosts. They looked straight ahead, proffered fingers apologetically and vanished. Other guests, less diffident, loquaciously held up the queue. Others (Morgans only) slipped large sums of money into my pocket…

We were very happy in the evening in our room in the Grosvenor House Hotel on Park Lane. We shed our finery and had a bath. Dorothy giggled a bit and became coy and virginal. Then we walked through Hyde Park at the end of the day, dressed like new pins, savouring London and our marriedness. We dined at the Caprice at the best corner table. Charles and Mrs Chaplin, Sir Bernard and Lady Docker were there. The man next to us said he guessed we were just married.

Then we walked to the Savoy. We were very much in love by this time. We called in briefly at the Morgan family dinner party, feeling it rather an anticlimax to re-appear after our disappearance, but worthwhile for the sake of Papa Morgan.

We went to bed at 11 pm. We got to sleep at 5 am. We did not stay awake because we were making love. We made love because we couldn't sleep.

Still in our matrimonial daze, we staggered onto an airplane and made for Athens.

Our first married home was the coachman's flat above the old stables of a Georgian-fronted mansion on the edge of Wimbledon Common. In this house Dorothy's school-friend Hildegrace Seligman had grown up with her parents, grandparents, three sisters and two brothers. Hildegrace was now married but the rest of the family still lived there in style with about a dozen Papillon dogs of whom two, Tio and Dymocke, had been given to us. The Seligmans, who were hospitable and generous, offered us the flat for £5 a week.

Peter Seligman was boss of the APV engineering group. A lot of entertaining went on, we were often invited and the lavish but always tasteful food remained a model for us in later years – whole roast hams, whole stilton cheeses, the freshest strawberries. The grandparents, Grace Wheatley and her late husband John, were both distinguished artists (Grace was an FRS) whose pictures lined the walls.

In our coachman's flat we behaved badly. We would come home late, bang the door and argue at the top of our voices. Our uncurtained windows overlooked the mansion's guest bedroom which was occupied by a clergyman, but this did not stop Dorothy walking naked from the bathroom to the bedroom. Trying to wash a floor for the first time in her life, Dorothy began by pouring a bucketful of water onto it; the water seeped down into the ceiling below. Grandma Grace cared lovingly for her Rhode Island Reds, but our inadequately supervised Dymocke, a fiendishly clever dog, learnt to climb like a cat up the wire fence into the poultry yard and killed one of the hens. Grandma Grace, too refined to expostulate in person, left the dead chicken on our doorstep, covered in a tea-towel. In summer we made love in what we thought was a secluded copse on Wimbledon Common but a troupe of boy scouts came by, in single file, each trying without success to avert his eyes – a scandal that reached the mansion. Our kind and beautiful landlady, Elisabeth Seligman, lent us a small Matisse lithograph to enhance our flat. We didn't like it all that much and hung it in the bathroom where it deteriorated. Elisabeth was mortified but never reproached us for this or for our other sins.

We loved the Seligmans and had no idea we were behaving badly (decades later they told us). We were spoiled and insouciant, convinced that the world owed us a living. The Seligmans forgave us and we have remained friends. They are still larger than life. Elisabeth died but Peter has remarried aged 93.

I had had enough of the *Londoner's Diary*, a life that was becoming routine. Ever since I wrote that school essay on the ideal occupation I had wanted to be a foreign correspondent. I could have tried to get on to a national newspaper as a reporter and wait for a foreign posting, but I was in a hurry. I decided to take myself abroad and make my name.

Dorothy was willing. She wanted to see Israel – 'the land of my fathers' – and perhaps live there. Her father had been born in Zikhron Ya'aqov near Haifa. I felt no such affiliation but Israel was fine by me – a better place for news than most, and I had relatives there. We would go on our own and I would be a freelance. Lucky boy: you cannot be a freelance foreign correspondent with a wife who is not game for adventure and likely penury.

But first, we were going on our honeymoon – so why not Israel, to reconnoitre? And so, subsidised by the cash stuffed into my pocket by Morgan wedding guests, we set off in our new clothes for Rome, Athens, Crete and Tel Aviv.

This was 1956. Tourists wandered alone, not yet in tidal waves, and were welcomed as individuals, especially if they were on their honeymoon. In Crete we spent days almost alone and quite unsupervised in the bronze age Palace of Minos.

18 July 1956

We have been trying to feel at home as guests of the Minoans. We brought our melon and apricots and Cretan cheese. We sat down in the Queen's cool, quiet chamber and had a light lunch sitting on a ledge of red stone leaning against red pillars, followed by a siesta. An urn decorated with an octopus design stands in one corner; above it is a fresco of blue dolphins over a blue and white floral design. The birds sing as they sang for the Queen…

We scrambled on rocky tracks among the villages and borrowed a donkey for which no payment was asked. We distributed the remains of a watermelon among the children. Then we were beckoned inside the cool house and a table was laid for lunch. The family had eaten already so we lunched with the young man alone, in the bare, cool, clean, whitewashed room. While we conversed in sign language and with the aid of a French-Greek dictionary he produced, a woman brought eggs cooked in olive oil, tomato salad and rice wrapped in vine leaves. The young man, we learnt, had a deep affection for the British from the war.

In Israel we were welcomed, even feted, by relatives, officials and journalists alike – all pleased that two young, good-looking, educated Londoners were thinking of coming to live here. This was the young Israel, only eight years old, 11 years before the Six-Day War, still needing to show the world it was real and here to stay.

My cousin Erica was married to Emil who in peacetime was a vet, in wartime the purveyor of provisions for the army, at all times a non-stop propagandist for his country. Emil drove us to Sdom, the Dead Sea and Beersheba. The drive out took four hours and Emil in his monotonous voice never once stopped lecturing. My other cousin Max was a prosperous orange planter, an extravert and another indefatigable propagandist. Max called for us at our hotel to drive us round Israel's agricultural area. Among sandy, weed-ridden wastes by the sea he said: 'A few years ago what is now Tel Aviv looked like this. In another few years all this will be Tel Aviv.' I noted in my diary that propaganda was obviously Israel's national sport:

> The game is subtle, relentless, has few rules and is enthusiastically played by everyone. Play begins with an unnatural eagerness to show visitors 'all the sights'. In nine places out of ten there are no sights but this makes no difference. Your Israeli friend or relative or chance acquaintance always expresses horror at the shortness of your stay and immediately takes you to see 'everything'. He will draw your attention to each factory, village, herd of cows, with words and gestures that invest these everyday phenomena with a miraculous quality.
>
> There is no downright bragging: that is against the rules. Only gentle exposition. Of the factory you are told that it produces so and so in such and such quantity every year and was built so many years ago. Of the cow you are solemnly informed of the breed, the size of the herd and the number of such herds in Israel. No inference is drawn: the silent implication is that no intelligent person should find it necessary to be told that all this is more than wonderful, more than spectacular, it is miraculous.

Where was Israel, behind all this propaganda? The Dursts, friends of Dorothy's family, gave us an answer. Dr Durst, a gynaecologist, quiet and gentle, invited us to his home for two nights. His 22-year-old son Arie, as polite and soft-spoken as his father, drove us there. The following evening Arie and Dorothy went to see *Gone With The Wind*.

As they walked away from the cinema something happened which she has fictionalised in a story she calls *Survivors*, in which Arie is called Poldi.

> Halfway to the bus stop, he grabbed her arm, dragged her into a dark passageway, and, with his palms flat on either side of her head, pinned her against the stone wall. The top of his head reached her collarbone; she could see his dandruff.
>
> 'Poldi?' She wasn't afraid; a raised knee in his balls would free her in a second. She waited. Nothing happened, no kiss, no fingers kneading her breast.
>
> Then a torrent of mixed-up Hebrew, Polish, German and English was poured into her reluctant ears. 'Listen. This is true. Not stupid film.'
>
> Poldi isn't an only child; he has a little brother called Victor. The family, together with another Jewish couple, six souls, escape from Poland in 1942. They reach Amsterdam where Dutch sympathisers hide them. Months drag into years; they are often hungry.
>
> The Nazis are losing; the war is almost over. Someone blabs. The Gestapo arrive at the disused warehouse. A canal runs alongside. They are captured. No, not all. Just the other couple, Masha and her husband, Lonick. Feather-brained Masha has gone to the ground floor and is rolling a ball – 'It has red and yellow stripes' – along the dusty factory floor to Poldi's baby brother. The Gestapo march the woman, man, and toddler outside. Lonick protests; they break his jaw with a rifle butt.
>
> One of the Nazis, 'not very old, maybe twenty,' holds Poldi's brother by the heels and swings him around and around. Baby Vic laughs. The young soldier whirls faster. The baby begins to wail. On the third circle, his head smashes against the iron gates. It takes six circles to split the skull in two. 'He has strong head.' Poldi taps his own skull. Poldi and his parents are watching through a gap in the attic eaves. Poldi's mother's hand is pressed over his mouth. 'Her rings cut my cheek. Our luck, our one luck, the Gestapo take Masha and Lonick but they don't come back.
>
> 'We stay upstairs. Victor's body floats down the canal. Past our window. Papa won't let Mama fetch it. War ends three weeks later. We arrive in Israel one year later.'

Poldi's story, Arie's story, helped us to begin to understand why Israelis are so fanatically convinced that they live in a unique land in a unique situation where different standards apply. Most Israelis bore Holocaust scars from horrors experienced at first, second or third hand, and many still lived in the traumatised world described in David Grossman's magnificent novel *See Under Love*. Mrs Durst, Arie's mother, had never fully recovered her wits: she was absent, switched off. Arie became a surgeon, a professor at the Hadassah Hospital.

Israeli doors were open for us, almost as if I were an important journalist. We met Foreign Ministry officials, sat in the press benches in the *Knesset*. Ted Lurie, editor of the *Jerusalem Post*, received us warmly and said I could make a good career in Israel once I learnt Hebrew. Jon Kimche, editor of the London *Jewish Observer and Middle East Review*, who was in town, invited us to dinner at the house of his brother David who was something in the Foreign Ministry but quietly known to really work for *Mossad*, the secret intelligence service.

Back in London I was still on the *Evening Standard* but our thoughts were in Israel. I went to see Jon Kimche whose review, a polemical weekly edited and mostly written by Kimche, needed an assistant editor. I got the job. The *Jewish Observer and Middle East Review* had no other staff except the indispensable Daphne who saw to the layout and printing. I would work in London for six months and then the *Review* would take my stuff from Israel, paying a small retainer.

Kimche was brilliant, opinionated and difficult to work for. He was often away on trips he didn't talk about, leaving Daphne and me to cope. One never felt he was writing or telling all he knew. Jon was left-wing, often critical of Israeli policy, which led to trouble with Jewish organisations in London who were financing the *Review*. Every Wednesday was crisis day when Jon's editorial had to be vetted by his paymasters: if they wanted changes he would go white with fury and rush out to argue his case.

We had to cover Jewish and Zionist meetings in London, and this was my undoing. Sitting through a discussion on the petty politics and internal squabbles of fundraising, my attention wandered. Back in the office Jon wanted to know who had said what – and there was no fooling Jon. He was furious, cancelled the arrangement for my retainer in Israel: he would only pay for any articles he might publish.

To Israel overland, with Tio

We did not fly to Israel because that would have been conventional, boring and expensive: we decided to go overland in a car we would sleep in, a car we would have in Israel. Tio would come along for our protection and for his good company. We would go through France, Switzerland, Austria, Yugoslavia and Turkey where, since we could not drive through Syria, we hoped to find a boat to take us to Israel.

We bought a Ford Squire which was not designed for sleeping in, so we improvised a makeshift conversion with two wooden frames to support a mattress. We could sleep in this car only after all supplies and luggage had been taken out, so Tio the watchdog was essential. If there were campsites in those days we had never heard of them: we would spend our nights in fields, on beaches, beside streams. Of course I wrote a diary.

> 4 May 1957
>
> Tio seemed strangely disquiet at first, which was apparent from the eerie way he did as he was told. Did he know he was abroad? What peculiar smells had France? He was not disposed to investigate at roadside halts, and he had a new way of moving around with tragic deliberateness and a reproachful look that had something of pity in it: 'I hope to God you people know what you're about.'
>
> Bedtime was a subject we kept off – each of us had our private nightmares on the subject. Would our bed space be too short? Would the French not laugh us into the nearest hotel?
>
> But it turned out miraculously easy... we turned off the road just short of Soissons on the way to Reims, drove up a cart track and came to a gigantic Dutch barn, with hay stacked on one side, a cart on the other and a big empty space in between. We drove into the space as confidently as if we had reserved it in advance through a

travel agent. Respectfully, the rats scuttled away as we entered – though each of them would have been large enough to have put up quite a decent showing against Tio.

We climbed onto the empty cart, where we reckoned the rats could not or would not interfere, cooked a meal of fried eggs and salami, and made our bed. The whole thing was done in no more than two and a half hours. What with the wind, the soup took nearly half an hour to get hot: it never boiled so the noodles were not quite their usual selves and the eggs made no sound as they were broken into the pan. While Dorothy tidied up, I made the bed. This involved unloading all the baggage and arranging it on a pile of hay, looking rather like a well-stocked government surplus store. Next I had to unscrew the bench of the rear seat – four screws and eight washers. Then I placed in position the two specially constructed wooden supports. All that remained was to collapse the passenger seat, tilt forward the driver's seat and strap it to the steering wheel, connect our special interior light system to the car battery, place into position the mattress, blankets, rug and pillows, make Tio's bed behind the collapsed passenger seat, and all was ready for the night. It really was night by then.

Dorothy slept like a log. I remember only the sound of rats' teeth crunching something, being incredibly hot and wondering what on earth we shall do in Turkey if there are no Dutch barns there.

We found no more Dutch barns but ventured confidently into Switzerland.

5 May 1957

We turned off the road onto an enchanted track through a valley, beside a river, across flowered fields. It started to climb. It passed quite a selection of places to spend the night – barns, a cave, a tunnel – all suitable. But there was no stopping on that enchanted path: we had to see what happened next. The track assumed a bottom-gear gradient which it kept up for three miles. At the top, finally, was a sloping field, wooded on one side, on a plateau. It was the ideal place and in no time the car was in position, the baggage unloaded, the bed made, supper cooking.

I had just taken my second spoonful of piping hot soup when Tio barked. Three men in shabby grey peasant suits descending purposefully on our ménage. It was a perfect spot for a robbery but the men had only come to tell us to get the hell out of their field. We packed up and moved back onto the track, where we had a good night – just behind the house of one of the peasants who turned out to be friendlier on his own and offered us wine at bedtime. Next day in the sunshine: cow bells and church bells.

In Austria: snow blizzards – the coldest May of the century. Innsbruck had been my last home in Austria, aged 7, but it was too cold for nostalgia. We did, however, call on my aunt Julia Brull who received us with measured warmth and a wealth of family anecdotes and talked enthusiastically about a camping site outside the town. But it was so cold that we got no further than the Hotel Roter Adler just round the corner from this inhospitable aunt.

In Salzburg we stumbled about in snowstorms looking for food and then we took the road to St Gilgen, lovely in the wintry sun: this was picture-postcard country. In Graz we followed the AA's recommendation – to the Hotel, a rambling, old-world place that for some complex and obscure economic reason let us have a double room the size of a small house, with service to match, for 53 schillings, or 13 of our shillings.

6 May 1957

…But the prices on the dinner menu bore a much closer resemblance to economic reality so we began surreptitiously to move our tins and cooking utensils upstairs to our palatial room. I tried to scurry past the reception desk with a battered suitcase creaking ominously. But authority apprehended me, made me put it down in front of the big desk, rang a tremendous bell that resounded through the foyer – and the suitcase was borne upstairs by a porter. The chambermaid lurked in fascination in the corridor as behind locked doors our dinner cooked on a velvet tablecloth, on which we had spread paper from the drawers of the dresser. Later, when all was out of sight and the chambermaid was allowed in, her sharp, Slav-like eyes darted about but found only circumstantial evidence.

Graz we liked – it had an easy-going grace that seemed peculiarly Austrian. The natives have a unique way of giving you street directions so that even if you understand every word you have no idea where to go. 'Well now if I were you I'd go there – no I wouldn't, I'd follow all those cars that keep on passing by here

86

till you get to the doings, then round by the back of the big red house you'd better ask someone.'

The sun came out as we headed for Yugoslavia. The contrast between Austria and Communist Croatia, which until 1918 had been part of the same country, was stark and immediate.

8 May 1957

A silent, drab, sad, dusty place. No traffic. Processions of sad, worried looking people in dark clothes walked silently along the roads. For the first two days in Yugoslavia we had the impression that some mass transmigration was afoot.

The sleeping question imposed itself quite soon. People stared open-mouthed at us just because we were driving along. Mouths opened wider whenever we stopped – and wider still when we actually got out. How wide would they get if we bedded down? Perhaps we should get away from all this, drive up some lonely by-road into a wood or abandoned heath. But would we be murdered in our sleep? We began rather abortively to bicker about it but Dorothy found a louse or two on Tio and this occupied her while I found a promising side street.

We turned off onto a track through flat land, all farmed in strips under an age-old open-field system. Peasants stopped their ploughing, children stopped in their tracks, as we lurched down the track. We came to rest on the bank of a river where half a dozen children were tending two cows. We unloaded our implements and paraphernalia and began brewing tea. The children cowered behind a hedge, giggling. Not even the sight of Tio's antics with his ball, though they enjoyed it, emboldened them. After our meal I brought over a plateful of Grandmother's kirchel cakes but it was not until I had distributed each individually that any attempt was made to eat them.

9 May 1957

There was no immediate need to explore Yugoslavia, for it came to explore us. Mostly children in charge of cattle grazing on the meagre grass on the edges of the fields. Their job was to shoo the cattle away from the crops. They were shy, good looking, dressed in smocks, shirts, torn jumpers, long woollen stockings. The boys wore caps. All were thin. I beckoned to two boys to take their picture. They just stood there. I showed my camera, grinned, beckoned, began to walk towards them. They fled.

In Zagreb I had a relative, Nikolia Krpan, whose family overwhelmed us with hospitality and complained non-stop about the Tito regime and its petty bureaucracy. They could not even get a passport to leave, let alone foreign currency.

Next day we were on the road again, looking for a place to sleep.

11 May 1957

We parked among ploughed fields. While I walked round a hedge to reconnoitre a position, a peasant who was ploughing with a prehistoric apparatus and two cows came over to the car, opened the door and sat down beside Dorothy who was sitting reading a book. Dorothy ignored the peasant entirely, went on reading, whereupon, according to her account, he got out of the car, closed the door and began to talk politely through the window, in which position I found the pair of them. Dorothy's comment: 'he's jolly handsome.' We had no common language, only a German-Serbo-Croat phrase book which specialised in air travel and bathing establishments. However he was a bright peasant, scanning the book for appropriate phrases with more agility than we had.

Driving south from Belgrade we came into a land of potholes, unsurfaced tracks, streams, ditches and boulders across roads marked in red on maps. Beyond Skopje the road was excellent with superb mountain views.

15 May 1957

We had stopped for lunch to celebrate Dorothy's 20th birthday in a clearing near the summit of a pass, when we heard Tio's scream. Two sheepdogs had caught him, one at each end, and were beginning to tear him apart. The shepherd beat them off. Tio was bleeding copiously, dragged himself under the car and wouldn't move for half an hour. Then he crawled out, I seized him by the scruff and put him on the passenger seat – the only one, so Dorothy squeezed into the rear by the tailboard. We headed back towards Skopje, speculating unenthusiastically about the probable veterinary resources of Macedonia. We pulled in by a village clinic where a medical student offered to show us the way to the vet. Somehow we made room to accommodate him too in the car. We had to cross a torrent on a flooded track. The student threw his hands in the air and said 'Ah, Macedonia!' and pointing at the enormous puddles he shuddered: 'malaria!'

We came to a fully equipped veterinary clinic, but the vet was out – indefinitely. So we rushed Tio to Skopje where we were directed to another vet clinic where a competent-seeming vet who spoke German expertly muzzled Tio with a bandage, swiftly exposed his wound, probed, penicillined and bandaged it – and we were on the road again.

Tio was lucky. In this country of poor peasants, thin children, appalling roads and shortages of almost everything, every village had its vet clinic, clean and competent. Tio's bandages were changed. He got better. He always did.

18 May 1957

In Greece people look happy. They smile at you. We stayed the whole day in our dream place by the lake. We walked along the shore to the village of Arrissa and bought provisions from the tiny shops without the need for a common language. An aged farmer appeared who had spent some of his youth in Canada; he joined us for wine and then we went into his spotless white house for more wine and to be introduced to the various generations and branches of his family.

20 May 1957

Salonika, an oasis of fruit, honey and yogurt, was a magnificent city with a row of 18th century villas in Venetian style along the sea. Doggedly un-touristy, we avoided the recommended churches.

We gave the car its 3,000-mile service at a Ford garage. When we asked why a youth was feverishly stripping the carburettor to its bare components, the manager beamed and said: 'They are sending us a mechanic in two months' time.'

21 May 1957
We found our baby tortoise outside Cavallo in a field where we picnicked. We called him (or her) Cavallo, emptied our heating utensils out of their box, put Cavallo in it with suitable furniture and, after a little discussion on the pros and cons of owning a tortoise, drove on with him.

Another dream camping site just short of Alexandropolis. Down a narrow track through a cornfield right to the sea. The track ended there so there seemed no possibility of being disturbed. Impetuously we rushed down to the water, threw all our clothes off and communed with nature under a caressing afternoon sun.

But then – oh horror – Tio barked. I looked up and saw two men with rifles standing on the higher ground beside our car, looking down at us. After a decent interval they approached and began to communicate in sign language and fragments of German. They tugged at my arm and bade me follow. Dorothy stayed with the car while I followed the men to the other side of the field, where they cocked their rifles. We came to a hole in the ground and stopped. It dawned on me that the men were hunting a wolf. This morning they had captured seven cubs from the lair. Now at dusk they were awaiting the wolf. They told us to keep very quiet around 8pm which was zero hour. In the night we heard wolves howling but no gunshot.

Istanbul was the most exotic town we had ever been in but as darkness fell we couldn't find a hotel.

22 May 1957
…We cruised about for an hour or two, then asked a policeman. He leapt into a passing taxi, signalled us to follow, and roared up a hill. The hotel was full. We tried half a dozen others, even the fabulous Hilton – all full. Dorothy thought they were not really full – the problem might be my filthy jeans and windjammer. She tried coming with me, taking Tio as a badge of luxury, but the result was the same.

At 1.30 am we decided to camp in what looked like a back street and began bedding down, but despite the late hour limousines and taxis roared through it, and a succession of very fierce dogs kept racing up and down, snarling at each other and taking very little notice of Tio who barked at them. Passers-by screwed their necks back to look at us but were too big-city to gather round and stare. Policemen strode up and down. When one blew a long blast on his whistle we thought the game was up and we were about to be arrested for attempting to burgle our car. We learnt later that the whistles are routine, like the nocturnal calls of Shakespearean constables.

Still room-less and stained with the dirt of many days and hundreds of miles, we went to the American Express to collect our mail and ask about travelling to Israel. There was plenty of mail but the other thing went badly. If you want to travel abroad from Turkey you have to pay in foreign currency, so the Turkish lire we thought we had been so clever to buy in Switzerland, at such a good rate, were quite the wrong thing to have. There was nothing for it but to hawk our cheap Turkish lire for expensive sterling or dollars for whatever we could get.

We found a cheap hotel at last but spent our daylight hours at the Hilton, the most elegant and sophisticated hotel we had ever seen. Tio, the snob, loved it there too and made acquaintances for us, which we needed badly because we now had to sell Turkish lire. An American serviceman told us a taxi driver had offered him double the official rate for a dollar – 10 instead of five – but that he had turned it down because he enjoyed a special US government rate of 12. However, because we were young, and British, he let us have 15 dollars at the rate of 8. 'It sure burns me up to see you kids in trouble.' Then Tio got us talking to some Belgians who changed a further ten dollars at the same rate. A week's operations yielded only $25, but a British oilman promised to have £45 sent over from the UK at the rate of 25, so we were more or less in the clear. All we needed was a boat.

The thing was impossible, against the regulations, not feasible in the time available. So we were assured by Michael Richard, the *Daily Telegraph* correspondent whom Tio had found for us in the hotel bar. Richards hated Turkey and the Turkish government and, one suspected, the Turks. He was appalled at the naivety of our arrangements.

'Draw out your foreign currency allowance in Iskenderun? The Turks won't allow it. My dear fellow you'll be in Asia. It takes four days by train from here to Iskenderun. As for telegrams, they never arrive.'

I was thrilled to meet Richards, my first real live foreign correspondent. He invited us to camp in the rose garden of his house on the Bosphorous, where it joins the Black Sea, and treated us to a barrage of pessimism. 'Camping out in Anatolia? You don't know what you're doing. They won't allow it. They'll rape you and murder you. My dear fellow you just don't know what this country's like.'

> 28 May 1957
> We called in at Adriatica Lines. They had a boat but it was full. Try Hellenic Lines, they said, it's just up the road. We couldn't find Hellenic Lines – people kept sending us back and forth. It was very hot and sticky. At last, hysterical with frustration, I wrenched open the nearest door and screamed at a dusty little man behind a counter to direct me to the Hellenica line. 'What d'you want?' asked the man with maddening inquisitiveness. 'I want a ship to Israel,' I yelled at him, adding as a hysterical joke: 'Have YOU got a ship?' He had. A small Israeli merchant ship called the Eyal, sailing in a few days' time from Izmir. It didn't normally carry either passengers or cars but it happened to be returning almost empty. Something might be arranged.

We drove onto the ferry that takes you from Europe to Asia and then 350 miles to Izmir. Ignoring Richard's warnings we camped off a high coast road overlooking the Bay of Izamit.

It was the loveliest view we had had yet. Quite a poor village when you drove through it but seen from above it was a miniature Venice, with a square and a row of venerable white mansions at the water's edge: the sun did wonderful things with it. We were not raped or murdered. The few peasants who passed avoided our eyes and said nothing.

31 May 1957

When we arrived the shipping agent at Izmir, Mr Arcas, had never heard of us. It was 5pm, the ship was to sail at midnight. It could not be done. He was a fat, heavy, jovial Turk who gesticulated, sweated and shouted. 'You cannot go. Customs are closed. Banks are closed.'

Arcas, beneath tremendous eyebrows, had sharp eyes. 'Have you any foreign money?' When I said I had he grabbed my arm and marched me down the street, changed his mind, marched me down to the customs shed where he had a long impassioned talk with many shrugs of his shoulders in apparent apology for the inconvenient stupidity of Britons who thought they could get off in a hurry. Then he rushed me to a travel agent who sent a boy with me to a bank, where I had to change £10 into lire at the official rate and get a receipt. I was brought back to the travel agent and asked to pay him 10 lire as commission. I paid up and turned to Arcas. 'But where is your ticket?' stormed Arcas. 'He should have given you a ticket – two tickets for five pounds each paid in Turkish Lire.' I returned to the travel agent, who said he couldn't give me a ticket because he wasn't the agent. Arcas was the agent. He made a phone call and discovered another man was the agent. So he grabbed me and took me in a car to another street, another office. But this other man was not the agent either. They telephoned Arcas and after some heated tri-cornered dialogue it was decided that the travel agent would give me a receipt for the Turkish lire and Arcas would issue the tickets.

Back at Arcas's there was pandemonium while a lightship was produced. This cost me a further 50 lire. Then I went to the customs, where groups of officials began reading aloud from books of regulations concerning the unprecedented case of our car. At last, after a great screed had been committed to paper, the customs formalities were effected in true Turkish style. They made me bring all the suitcases from the car into the office – the first time this had happened on our entire journey – while no attempt was made to glance inside the car, which was packed with a suspicious-looking miscellany of boxes and tins.

We drove the car up wooden planks placed at a precarious, slipshod angle onto a lightship. There was our car which we had come to love, bobbing up and down in the hands of Turks, totally uninsured. Finally pushing through a crowd of immaculate marines who had just landed, we boarded a tiny motorboat that took us out to the Eyal.

1 - 5 June 1957

We had unlimited access to the Eyal's bridge where we learnt about navigation. We had our meals in a small space with the crew, few of whom washed, and spent a lot of time wondering how typical of the Israeli merchant fleet the incredible idleness of the crew of 15 could have been. The ship was so dirty that if you walked from the cabin to the bridge you looked as if you had been down in the hold. The cargo was salt, and tannin stains were everywhere. The crew appeared to be taking a pleasure cruise but the first mate explained that this was Sabbath: tomorrow work would begin. A little desultory painting and hosing of decks – rather more as sport for they hosed each other – was all that happened during the long working day. The only serious work was on the repair and beautification of a little model sailing ship the crew had acquired somewhere. It lay keel upwards on the deck while the captain meticulously painted it blue, was dissatisfied, scraped the paint off and painted it again.

Tio was enjoying the voyage in spite of its proletarian ambiance. He had made the ship his own, crossing from side to side, forwards and backwards, jumping up onto the hatch cover as a short cut. This habit of his was a very bad idea indeed.

Haifa at last, in its splendid bay in the evening. The engines stopped, the ship docked. We were to disembark in the morning. Preparing to unload, the crew opened the hatch cover. Tio, unaware that they had done this, jumped up as usual – and disappeared from view into the darkness far below. Peering down, we could see him at last, immobile and surely dead. They lowered a ladder for me. He was alive but scarcely moving. The captain agreed that Tio must go ashore and arranged for us to be rushed through immigration and customs on shore leave. We took a taxi to a vet but the vet was out. We went to another vet, who was also out. At a third vet's house we were told that all the vets in Haifa had gone to the annual vets' party. We went to the party. A very merry vet came out, felt Tio all over and said that he would live: he had a greenstick fracture that would soon heal.

Chapter four:
Living on our wits between Israelis and Arabs

In Israel we lived for a year and a half on our wits. We ate well when the money for an article came in, the rest of the time we enjoyed the *leben* (cheese made from yogurt), *labane* (goats cheese balls), *pitta* (flatbread), *falafel* (chickpea balls) – all of which were delicious, good for us and cheap, thanks to generous food subsidies in force at the time. After a while Dorothy's father, who owned an apartment in Israel from which his rents could not be sent abroad, instructed his agent to pass us £5 a week – almost a living wage.

We depended on our youth and enthusiasm and the hospitality and kindness of Israeli friends and relatives. We thought of ourselves as free spirits without the new-age ideology that hippies were later to have. We would kiss and cuddle in the back of a car while an earnest and patient Israeli was trying to show us the wonders outside. When Dorothy stole bunches of tomatoes, handfuls of figs or sweet peppers from a field, I chided her and refused to help, but shared in the spoils.

From Haifa we drove to Jerusalem and stayed in an immigrant hostel that offered us a room with balcony at a subsidised rent. Young people from all over the world stayed in this vibrant place but we were fussy and spoiled and found it too noisy. We rented two rooms of a house in Bet Hakerem, the old, affluent suburb that looks down on the city from its houses of mellowed stone. Tio now had a garden as a base for snarling at passing dogs. Ma Raban, as we called our long-suffering old landlady, kept complaining we were stealing tasty mouthfuls from her part of the fridge, which we denied absolutely and to this day I insist that sometimes we were innocent.

I sat in the government press office reading press releases, envying real correspondents of real newspapers.

I had a cable credit card for the *Daily Herald* which printed my news stories but alas, nobody I knew read the *Herald* and every important newspaper in the world already had a correspondent in Israel. Trying to creep under the barrier, I sent the *Observer* a feature about life on the surreal barbed-wire border between East and West Jerusalem, which cut streets in half. They liked it and sold it worldwide in the *Observer* Foreign News Service but they had made a mistake: the paper had its Israel correspondent who was furious and insisted that Schwarz be kept out of the OFNS as well as the Sunday paper.

I decided to concentrate on features about economic development in the Negev where Israelis wanted to be pioneers in making the desert bloom. The Negev seemed to me romantic and a good story. It was of interest to Jon Kimche, so the *Jewish Observer* published my stuff every week. Now we could buy a bottle of Carmel wine – strong, a bit rough in those days – with our *leben* and *pitta*.

The expert on desert agriculture was the botanist Professor Michael Evenari. Michael and I got on well, not least, perhaps, because his name before he came to Israel had been Walter Schwarz. He and his wife Liesl and our respective dogs became friends. They had no children and went a little way towards adopting us, inviting us to Passover evening in their home in Jerusalem, and on treks to their desert base at Avdat, the ancient Nabatean settlement 30 miles south of Beersheba.

What excited Michael about the Nabateans was the clever engineering which allowed them to grow food in dry soil using dams, canals and reservoirs. They would contour an area of land into a shallow funnel, plant a single fruit tree in the middle and wait for the minuscule rainy season – only a shower or two but just enough to break up the soil. Then the water in the funnel would flow down to the tree and sink in; the ground would seal up and retain the water. Michael dreamed that modern Israel could adapt these methods.

The brown sand-swept ruins of Avdat were a mystery for all of us, even the professor – a place of peace and romance. Soon after we left Israel the ruins were excavated, partly restored and turned into a national park. Now you can see Nabatean wine vats, Roman baths and Byzantine churches.

Michael Evenari was a humanist with a sophisticated European manner in contrast to the febrile chauvinism of many Israelis. But underneath this exterior he was as uncompromising a nationalist as any. We were talking one day about Israel's then nascent nuclear weapons capability, little known, little talked about and kept off limits for journalists by the censor's red pencil. Michael paused, his eyes narrowed and his mouth tensed – a face I had not seen before. 'If the day should come, Walter... if they should ever come to get us here... Boom!'

The first tarred motor road through the Negev desert – 250 kilometres from Beersheba to Eilat – was finished at last. Two days before its official opening, the first civilian car to drive down the road, by special permission, was ours. On board: the two of us, an Israeli freelance photographer and Tio. It took two days, with a night stop at kibbutz Mitzpe Ramon. The desert road skirted the enemy on both sides – Jordan to the West, Egypt to the East, and finished at the Red Sea at Eilat, beside the Jordanian port of Aquaba. Was it dangerous? It did not occur to us to ask. The border with Jordan was marked only with an occasional flag.

We stopped for a picnic at a place where the road almost touches the Jordanian border. Tio, left to his own devices, dashed away in pursuit of a gazelle – westward into Jordan where we could not follow. For a nail-biting hour we waited (not the first such hour in Tio's life) until he nonchalantly reappeared.

Eilat, today a mega-resort, was a sleepy village of pioneers and eccentrics. Living coral reefs lay under the water. Dorothy went snorkelling. A few feet from the shore she came to a living reef sheltering a myriad rainbow of fishes. When we returned to Eilat 15 years later the reef had gone, all living corals broken off by souvenir hunters.

On our honeymoon we had met the editor of the English-language *Jerusalem Post,* Ted Lurie. Now, a year later and short of cash, I asked him for a job. He was a kindly man and he gave me a part-time position for two months, replacing an absent features subeditor. Without Hebrew this was the best I could hope for. Still a junior hack, I enjoyed manhandling other people's copy.

The Arabs in Israel

The Israeli government press office invited foreign correspondents to Nazareth for a ceremony celebrating the advancement and well-being of Israel's grateful Arab citizens. Only three of us bothered to go. I chatted to the Arab dignitaries who were present – and found them less happy and less grateful than we had been led to expect. I had entered a new world.

Two hundred thousand Arabs – Moslem, Christian and Druze – had stayed behind in Israel in the 1948 war, refusing to become refugees. This was one tenth of Israel's population. With Israeli help Arab farmers had become wealthier than rural Arabs in surrounding countries. But many were devastated when their land was confiscated for new Jewish settlement. And all the Arab towns and villages in Israel were placed under military government, which meant that Arabs needed passes to travel and made them feel like second-class citizens. (By 2009 the Israeli Arabs had multiplied sixfold to 1.3 million, nearly 20 percent of the population.)

I wanted to learn more and soon returned to Nazareth which had remained an Arab town, and still is. I enjoyed the slower pace and quieter tone of Arab life after the brash hyper-activity of Jewish Israelis, and I was welcomed by Arab officials and dignitaries because not many foreign reporters came their way. The Arabs' attitude to Israeli life seemed to me reasonable and moderate. Christian Arabs, especially, did not talk like militants and did not identify with the Muslim majority outside, let alone with terrorists. Muslim Arabs sounded more militant but they, too, became our friends, which displeased Israeli officials and also some of my own relatives who thought we were naïve, a sucker for 'terrorist' propaganda.

Here was disagreement, controversy, maltreatment of the underdog – a better story than the Negev desert and the foreign press was not covering it! There was so much misunderstanding between Israelis and 'their' Arabs; could my articles help explain them to each other? Soon I was writing on this subject for the prestigious American Jewish journal *Commentary* which was often critical of Israel. The fee they paid seemed to me fabulous. I sent a proposal for a book to Faber and Faber; they accepted. *The Arabs in Israel* was published soon after we left Israel in 1959.

For Dorothy's 21st birthday treat, and to research my book, we decided to hire two donkeys and tour Arab villages in Galilee. We would sleep in fields and orchards while the donkeys grazed and Tio stood guard. It seemed a good idea for a holiday away from the dusty sameness of roads, taking along our bedding (we did not think we would need a tent) and cooking things without having to lug them on our backs in the sun. Now we could get to know Israeli Arabs in their remote villages.

The idea met more raised eyebrows in Israel, where donkeys are common, than it would have done in England, where they are not. Israelis had not yet a tradition of eccentricity. Used from childhood to doing things collectively, they could be as conventional, even prudish, as, say, frontier Americans in the pioneer days.

'Why don't you take your car,' we were asked with dull uniformity. And then, when it dawned that we were decadent, 'Why not camels, then?'

The Arabs, though hidebound by tradition, were more understanding or at least more diplomatic. Perhaps they had sharper memories of the mad British. Or perhaps, living at a slower speed, they had time in their lives for whimsy. For advice about donkeys and other matters we approached our friend in Nazareth, Sami Geraisi, a local government official who had educated me in the complex predicament of his people. Sami said he would like to come with us – but it would have to be horses; he would never live it down in the villages if he were seen on a donkey.

We started in the village of Cana, where women still drew water from the well, as they did when it was turned into wine at the Marriage Feast. They still carried it off on their heads but they used jerry cans and it remained obstinately water. The Nazareth-Tiberias road, carrying on its errands the faster, more purposeful world of

99

the Jews, wound narrowly through Cana, overhung with dusty pomegranate trees,

No-one ever thought of stopping for a drink of orange juice or an ice-cream at the village shop. Was it a shop or a kiosk? Its back was of stone, its front of wobbly corrugated iron. It sold everything edible and potable from eggplant to homemade soda water. The wistful Sami in Nazareth had given us a note for the owner of this shop, Gamal Hanna Elias Abu Taisir, enlisting his help in the matter of the donkeys.

Abu Taisir, a big, badly shaved, handsome man in sweaty shirt-sleeves and braces, middle-aged, with unkempt hair (no *keffieh*) and lazily satirical eyes, read the note in silence, re-read it, looked us both up and down in a sleepy way, scrutinised our ridiculous miniature dog with a tolerant expression and said at last (in an upper-class English drawl): 'Have some whisky.'

The 'whisky' turned out to be arak, the local spirit tasting of aniseed. It had been an honest attempt at translation. Besides, it was soon apparent that 'have some whisky' was a line of poetry to Abu Taisir. It evoked the good times and gentlemanly comradeship of the days when he was an officer with the British.

His dog-eared pay book, volunteered from under a pile of receipts, showed he had been a warder at Acre prison, where Jewish and Arab extremists alike were held, sometimes tortured and occasionally hanged. For Mr Elias (Abu Taisir), as for thousands of Palestinians of his generation, the years with the British were the best in their lives. At least the British had been gentlemen imperialists.

Mr Elias did not regret the end of empire although it had reduced him to the ranks of shopkeepers, from which despised living he had now to provide for his wife and three unmarried daughters in a single, stone-floored room. He did not own a donkey. Only the Moslems in Cana had donkeys, he explained with a tinge of contempt. He was prepared to hire some for us. 'You can start tomorrow. Tonight you sleep here.'

The living room in the Elias' house was as spacious and unfussy as the man himself. It had beds of various sizes for various sizes of daughters, a sturdy table, an ailing dog and the traditional roomy alcove near the high ceiling for storing grain, olives, perambulators and pickled eggs.

As this was a Christian house there was no fuss about feminine elusiveness. Mrs Elias and the daughters shook hands and beamed hospitably; the girls were soon busy fetching goats-milk cheese (served in balls drenched in olive oil), hard-boiled eggs, olives, omelettes, flat bread, jam and tea, while their mother chatted in what French she could remember from her convent days. The warmth and simplicity of the Elias's hospitality remain as a model with both of us, fifty years later.

There was a convenient bedroom for us – the room that had been prepared for Elias' son Taisir, who was due to marry the girl next door, Jeanette. To get to it we groped our way through a courtyard full of hens and pigeons and climbed an uncertain staircase – to be dazzled by a splendid bridal chamber. The bed took up most of it. What remained was filled mainly by the triple wardrobe, yet there was just room for a couple of deep armchairs and a lot of space on the walls for sentimental landscapes in technicolour and lush paintings of southern European beauties with rosy cheeks and long eye-lashes, reclining on sofas. Bed and wardrobe were of mahogany carved in decadent patterns reminiscent of Habsburg emperors (perhaps because it had been made by a Jewish carpenter from Prague, now living in Acre); curtains were chintz, pillows and cushions were velvet. The bedspread had been expertly embroidered by Jeanette herself. Everything glowed with newness and expensiveness and style – or rather styles: the room respired with the intermingled ghosts of eighteenth-century Vienna, Bedouin tents and Tel Aviv.

Taisir himself, a schoolteacher, was one of those positive, forward-looking materialists who did not mind living in Israel one bit. He told us it cost his in-laws three thousand Israeli pounds to furnish the room and buy the trousseau. There was only the one magnificent room, though. The kitchenette was wholly in the spirit of the courtyard below and there was nothing that could be called a bathroom. Taisir, meanwhile, ventured into the dark world of Muslims to see about our donkeys.

We settled for the equivalent of ten shillings a day per donkey. If the Christians had donkeys, explained Mr Elias, we should have had them for nothing. They turned out to be small and unsteady-looking. One was dirty grey – not quite so small; the other was brown – not quite so dirty. They had saddles of canvas stuffed with straw and moth-eaten saddlebags made of sacking.

The whole village turned out to see us off. They gave us sticks to beat the donkeys with, taught us to say 'Ha! Ha!' to make them go, and 'Shhhh!' to make them stop – which was how we came to call them Hawan (Ha-one) and Hatu. Until we were clear of the village we had to take Tio on donkey-back with us because some of the small boys had started beating him as well as the threadbare behinds of the donkeys.

We could see the next village quite plainly from the main road – a matter of ten minutes' walk on a track across fields. It took us an hour. Hawan and Hatu had started at a nice jog-trot, like all the other Arab donkeys one sees. Then they seemed to realise this was no everyday work trip. They continued to respond magnificently to the command 'Shhhh.' But to 'Ha-Ha' they merely nodded their heads in token agreement. Even the sore spots on their behinds were only relatively sensitive. We grazed them in a field for a while, but the owner appeared on the scene unexpectedly. What they needed was a proper meal, of the kind that comes in bags, Dorothy decided. But she wasn't sure exactly what.

Our general idea was to buy food for us and the beasts in the villages and sleep out. But this thoroughly European idea did not come up to the standards of Arab villagers.

At two o'clock in the afternoon we found Tur'an village virtually asleep. The world of tarmac roads, cars, electric light, running water and the ubiquitous Israeli greeting 'Shalom!' seemed far away. Cana had been a mixture, a half-Christian village with Israeli traffic keeping it awake. Tur'an was Arabia. A boy was leaning against a wall. We asked him where we might buy some food in the village for us and the donkeys.

'*Ahlan-wasahlan!* (welcome),' he replied, beckoning us towards his house. Here we sat on chairs arranged formally in a line round the walls. We were offered sweets, then cigarettes – quietly and with dignity by the schoolboy himself. Other people arrived slowly: the boy's uncles, cousins and second cousins who, by Arab custom, had put in an appearance for a guest. No women. Then we had bitter coffee – a single gulp in the bottom of a daintily-flowered little cup – merely as an appetiser for the real coffee to follow: strong and sweet. It came on a tray with an embroidered cloth.

They must have found us difficult to place, but they showed no sign of it. Conversation flowed in desultory fashion – it is not an essential part of Arab hospitality – and we were assured that the donkeys, meanwhile, were being similarly, or equivalently, feted.

Back in the street, another boy got hold of us. Arabs were always doing this – getting hold of us. This boy wanted to show us the village, though he admitted there was nothing special to see. But he would show us the new school, even though it was closed just then.

On the way to the school he mentioned en passant that our donkeys had not really been fed at all while we were having coffee. He had been standing there watching all the time and they had not had a bite. However, if we cared to visit his house they would certainly be fed, and so would we, and we could spend the night. There is an element of fierce rivalry in Arab hospitality.

Not knowing whom to believe, we declined the invitation, visited the school and coaxed and bullied the poor donkeys, whose stomachs were now unknown quantities, up the steep hillside until we were just out of sight of Tur'an. We made a base at the edge of an olive grove which had a few oats (wild, we assumed) growing between the trees. We went to sleep to the sound of Hawan and Hatu munching, and awoke seven hours later to the same sound.

Heading north towards Lebanon on a steep mountain track, our donkeys put on an early-morning spurt lasting half an hour or so, before resuming their grudging amble. After a while we got off and walked: it was less tiring. We began by leading them, like horses, but this way they had to be dragged; it was better to drive them from behind like cattle. When beating grew ineffective we took to prodding them with sharp sticks.

Splendid views over fields of hollyhocks, anemones, irises and small, flame-coloured gladioli, with a surprise view down to the Sea of Galillee. Not even the sight of the Arab farmers we met – or were overtaken by – whose donkeys trotted underneath them willingly and effortlessly, could depress us. They did not greet us but looked away, as if in embarrassment; we had no means of telling what they made of us.

More remote even than Tur'an was Be'eina, down the next valley. It stood on a track that was not motorable even in summer. Our brash greeting was met with only shy, embarrassed smiles; the people seemed too polite, or too scared, even to stare. Women squatted on floors in large rooms with only gaps for doors, amid goats and chickens and children. Even the children, who formed an inquisitive procession behind us, were wary of coming too close. Brazenly and self-consciously, we dared to wash ourselves at the village well. It was as if we had stood on our hands.

By now we had learnt the rules: never try to buy anything, for in an Arab village every stranger is a guest, and never admit we intend sleeping out; always pretend we were urgently on the way to the next village. Arabs disapprove of sleeping out. It is an insult to the village. It exposes one to 'wild beasts' – ill-defined creatures who are said to be especially fond of donkeys. But it was rarely possible to evade Arab hospitality. Certainly not at Arraba, where they had an answer to everything.

The Arrabans got hold of us when we were still some distance from the village. A boy helped us prod the donkeys across a cornfield, through which they were refusing to pass except on their own terms – one mouthful to every two paces.

'You going to Arraba?' he asked.

'Yes – and then on to Rama.'

'Not this day.'

'Why not?'

'This night you will sleep at Arraba. In the house of my father. He is the *mukhtar. Ahlan-wasahlan.*'

We passed through splendid olive groves and were taken to the *mukhtar's* house. The room was square and bare except for a dozen chairs round the walls facing inwards. Some of the chairs were already occupied by other visitors of a miscellaneous and listless character. Feeling like wallflowers at a desultory dance, we waited, watched, hoped, but nothing happened. We sat there for hours. There was a policeman from Acre who was waiting to see the *mukhtar*, a tax collector from Eilabun who was merely sitting, and two or three others. Nothing happened. Now and then someone said something. Or someone left, or arrived. A barefoot old man came and squatted on the floor and played with beads for an hour or so. Someone brought coffee. It was two and half hours before someone said quite casually that the *mukhtar* was away and not expected back that day.

We wanted to leave but there was no-one to say goodbye to. The boy, having done his bit for the honour of the family, had gone. Another boy unrolled a straw mat on the floor and deftly covered it with plates of olives, goats milk cheese, yogurt, sour milk, hard-boiled eggs, flat bread and a pot of tea. Knives and forks were added as an afterthought. The two of us were invited to squat on the floor and eat. Everyone else sat watching. It is an acquired skill to enjoy food while others watch, but the freshness and pure flavour of this home-produced food overcame our self-consciousness. Eventually Abdullah, the *mukhtar's* eldest son, arrived. As he was now our host, we made our adieux.

'Good-bye? You are not leaving?'

'Yes, we must be in Rama tonight, we absolutely must. They are expecting us.'

'But you can stay here. Go to Rama tomorrow.'

'Thank you. Thank you. But really...'

'My young brother goes to school in Rama. He walks every day over the mountain. He will guide you in the morning, early, any time you like, six o'clock, five o'clock...'

Now we got impatient. Why should we be dragooned by the obscure laws of fanatical hospitality into spending a whole day merely existing? – 'No definitely not. Thank you so much, but we have to be in Rama tonight.'

'You cannot go.'

'Cannot?'

'There are army manoeuvres up on the mountain. It is forbidden to pass.' He had played his trump card.

'But will there not be manoeuvres tomorrow just the same?'

A discussion broke out. Some of the Waiting Ones thought the manoeuvres were already over. Others were sure they would go on tomorrow. Yet others thought they were not on the route to Rama at all. In any case, we realised we were beaten.

In the evening Abdullah arranged our entertainment. He had a blind old man play the *mujewes* for us, a twin-reeded pipe that looks like a cross between an oboe and a flute and sounds like humanised bagpipes. Someone accompanied him on the coffee-pounder, the ornate pole sticking out from a jar that can be made to give out an erotically pulsating rhythm.

'You will sleep here, yes?' said Abdullah, indicating the floor. We agreed gratefully. One of the Waiting Ones, the tax collector, said: 'I see we are to be bedfellows. I, too, am sleeping here. Welcome.'

Just then a pale and earnest-looking youth came up and asked us to spend the night in the house of his uncle. 'It is not good, a lady sleeping in the room with strangers. In my uncle's house there is a room just for you.'

It seemed sensible, but what would Abdullah say? The youth assured us that it would be all right, yet when Abdullah heard about it he sounded angry and we felt guilty as we went to bed in the uncle's house.

Our new host, Mahmoud, knocked on our door in the morning to ask if we were ready for breakfast. He rummaged under our bed and took out a chipped and dusty china bowl full of sour milk and carried it off to the kitchen. He came back and poured water over our hands and brought me jasmine-scented hair-oil. After an excellent breakfast we tried to say goodbye, but we knew in our hearts that it was no use. Mahmoud said he would walk with us over the mountain. We did not argue. For the twenty miles to Rama he told us about Arab nationalism.

We by-passed Rama village and made for a likely base in an olive grove. Camping was difficult among the olives because between the trees the ground is ploughed. But our stony bed felt comfortable after the bewildering rituals of village hospitality. We had just gone to sleep when a villager who had lost his donkey came out looking for it with a torch, gently calling its name. He almost stumbled over us. With great presence of mind, he hurried back to the village to fetch – not the local constable to have us arrested but the local schoolmaster to invite us to spend the night in the village. We pretended to speak nothing but French, not even dumb show. Around midnight we could hear the lost donkey stamping and galloping and braying hysterically among the olive trees.

We had Israeli friends to visit at Bar'am, a kibbutz on the Lebanese border. Hawan and Hatu now came into their own, giving rides to a queue of kibbutz children (how sunburnt they seemed after the pale Arabs), and afterwards they could eat their fill in a lush field.

After the daunting hospitality of the Arabs, a brusque welcome from the Israelis came as a relief. 'I suppose' said our kibbutz friend, 'you would like to have a shower now and rest alone for a little.'

Dorothy goes home

We had been in Israel for a year and a half, the adventure had paled into routine and we were homesick. With my book to write I had less time for freelancing, so I could hardly support the two of us. We had started to bicker. I am introspective: she says I am cold. She is demanding: I say she's too intense.

Dorothy went back to London to enrol in history at Birkbeck, London University's evening college for mature students. Not that she was that mature, in my opinion.

I saw her off at Haifa and drove back to Jerusalem, calling on Arab and Jewish friends, relaxed and happy on my own. Not for long. We wrote to each other every day.

107

Shikun Rassco, Jerusalem
26 September 1958

Loveliness. There is no-one to talk to here. So I'll talk to you:

Wal: What on earth was the matter with us?

Dot: Don't know

Wal: From the time we said goodbye to the time I reached Jerusalem I did nothing but love you... And at the same time I felt relieved. I enjoyed those days, I was alert, relaxed, optimistic, purposeful, conversational.

Dot: What was the secret?

Wal: Simple. Nobody was there *demanding* it the whole time... What do two wilful people do to live together? They recognise that they're two wilful people - have spheres of influence, divide up the empire.

Dot: Could that have worked in the life we were leading in Israel?

Wal: It couldn't. It didn't. But just suppose we'd had a proper home, you had some work or were a student, lots of friends, a garden and maybe a few children... If you'd had all that in Israel everything would have been different. I could have done many of my trips alone, without you fretting. Gosh, how I'd have sped home bringing flowers and chocolates!

1 October
Nazareth: Café Galilee on the terrace 2pm
Darling,

Here's a nice lull between interviews to sit in this delicious sun-cum-gentle-breeze, sort out my notes, listen to Mozart's 39th from Abu Nasser's loudspeaker, watch life on the little street that leads to the souk. Here comes a Greek orthodox priest in the big black hat, a girl leading a donkey, a boy with a barrow of tourist goods (they leave me alone now, I'm an habitué) a pomegranate stall, a flock of schoolgirls in blue tunics who *smiled* at me (making a nice point for the book about how *normally* Arabs grow up as distinct from neurotic Israelis), a couple of Druze sheikhs, a fat woman balancing a sack of potatoes on her head, a big man on a small donkey. And here comes the mad fortune teller.

Dorothy's letters were anguished. In London, living among our two affluent and busy families, she was lonely, in limbo. Married but without her husband, she faced unspoken reproaches and questions about her absent husband's prospects.

Jerusalem
8 October 1957
My poor darling you're having a tough time. I suppose it's the environment of other peoples' security, prosperity and hard work, in the midst of which we two seem so insubstantial. Here we lived in our own world – partly a dream perhaps yet secure in our own freedom and private ideals and romances...

Darling, it's really out of the question that I come home before the New Year. People are usually experts when they write books; I'm very far from being an expert on the Arabs in Israel, except in the shallowest journalistic sense. I have constantly to check facts while I am writing. Dozens of facts which don't seem important when I'm interviewing loom large when I'm writing, so I have to dash back to the source again. Don't worry, I'm doing my best to be a 'success' and I'm all set for a sensible job in London, getting 'settled' etc.

I've been thinking seriously about the question of money and parents and so on. I think I can see what has happened. When we got married I was quite unused to any parental help and managed my life without. Then your dad very kindly pressed various forms of grants and aid on us - not in cash but in services that tend to go unnoticed e.g. fruit every week, tankfuls at Pop's filling station, etc. Then the bad thing happened – I began to get used to it and take it for granted...

Now, semi-consciously or unconsciously, they reproach us both for being irresponsible and you're the one who has to face the music for the moment.

You can tell your mum and dad and brother that I have not been too proud to accept freely offered help from them because I didn't use it for a holiday. I used it doing my best to make a success of my career, i.e. going to Israel instead of plodding on in the *Evening Standard*, where I was earning excellent money. Unfortunately I haven't walked into a good job at the end of it, which was the main purpose.

In London Dorothy stood up for me and wrote to me in a spirit of conciliation.

London 13 October 1957

I want you so. To talk to me and encourage me. I'm a little scared about your hair cos I am sensitive to appearance. But even if there's hardly any left I suppose I'll get used to it. Please Wuff don't come home fat and bald and spotty. When I dream of you physically I dream of your soft skin and flat belly and long twiny legs – and I hear your voice which is so warm. I see you most of all reading in bed with your arm around me (not Tio!) and I can feel that gorgeous soft spot between your neck and shoulder.

I realise how lucky I was in Israel and how foolish not to enjoy my luck more. I also puzzle about why we grated on each other and I try to think when he comes home it just won't arise any more. Maybe we'll have grown out of it.

I rented a room in Jerusalem's German quarter, and cut down on my freelancing to work full-time on the book. I only ate full meals when invited out: in my shared kitchen I ate those delicious subsidised cheeses and vegetables with pitta bread.

23 October 1957

Darling,

Speaking as a man who has had a piece in *The Spectator* a couple of weeks ago, even though it was cut a little and appeared down the page – but very early in the paper, as one of the more important articles – all about the Israeli angle on the crisis, even though it was sent off with so little hope that I had forgotten all about it till I received the compliments of the British Embassy staff on its excellence – cheque for 8 guineas arrived simultaneously...

My book *The Arabs in Israel* concluded that by ordinary human standards the Israelis had not mistreated their Arabs: they had admitted them to their parliament, extended to them their own social services, watched them grow more prosperous and been gratified by the result. But there are other standards. 'The messianic vision that has lighted up our path for thousands of years... has imposed on us the duty of becoming a model people and building a model state,' Prime Minister Ben Gurion said in a speech reprinted in the government handbook.

110

By those high standards the Israelis had failed. They had failed to educate their own public to rise above bigotry (not too strong a word to describe the attitude of many Israelis to all Arabs, right up to the present day). They had dispossessed and oppressed Arab citizens by devious and disingenuous means through its military government, the abolition of which I recommended: it was to happen eight years later in 1966.

In those pre-digital times I took my own pictures (today a wise foreign correspondent leaves photography to the professionals). The shot I'm proud of was in Kfar Baram village which had been demolished by the Israeli army in August 1953 'on security grounds'. My camera looks out through the forlorn doorway of a ruined Arab house to the new Israeli settlement on the skyline.

When it came out my book – the first objective account of its subject – was attacked by both sides, which I took as a tribute to its fairness. Pro-Israelis, including Jon Kimche in the *Jewish Observer*, said I was naïve in believing what Arabs told me. Pro-Arabs said I gave Israel too much credit for good intentions. In the middle was James Morris who gave it a rave review in the *Times Literary Supplement*. He particularly liked the chapter on the donkey trip.

Twelve years later, on holiday at our beloved rented cottage in North Wales, we were flirting with the impractical idea of moving permanently to the Welsh hills. James Morris was advertising his house for sale near Criccieth so, on a whim, we went to see it. The famous writer received us warmly and showed us round his magnificent house and gardens. We said we would think about it and were preparing to leave, when James asked for a word with me in private, in the library.

'Walter, this is going to shock you…'

I interrupted with an off-hand gesture: 'Nothing shocks me, James, I'm a journalist.'

'Next month I am going to Morocco for an operation to change my sex.'

'Oh? I hear quite a lot of people are doing that now.'

His face fell. I had said the wrong thing – a faux pas of which I am ashamed to this day. I should have realised that James's sex change was to be an epic – the subject of his/her next book, and I should have expressed wonder and amazement.

As if this were not bad enough, some twenty years later I made another faux pas, when Jan Morris, still a friend because she is kind and forgiving, came to see us in Paris. She had been commissioned by a travel magazine to write a review of the Ritz Hotel and she invited me to join her for dinner there, so that she would not be dining alone. My problem was that having known Jan as James – a fellow hack when all is said and done, even though she is a better writer and more famous than me – I never thought of her as a woman. This was my problem, not Jan's, because of course she really is a woman. The head waiter ushered us to our seats with a flourish and handed me the menu. I sat down without pulling out Jan's chair for her. Me, I was just having dinner with a colleague. I carelessly tossed the menu before her to discuss what we should eat. The head waiter looked shocked at my bad manners but Jan was too polite to complain. The perfect lady.

Chapter five:
Africa

We are back in London in good time for the Sixties, which suits us because we think of ourselves as liberated. Dorothy buys a Vespa scooter which I consider silly until I try it, love it and adopt it for my own. Her generous father has bought us a house in Hampstead Garden Suburb. For our country residence I buy a thatched, semi-detached worker's cottage at Steppingley, Bedfordshire, a mile from Britain's first motorway which is being built. The Duke of Bedford's estate sells it to me for £300. The motorway is about to quadruple its value.

The Middle East behind us, we now live in the spirit and ambiance of Africa. I am assistant editor of *West Africa* magazine, a job I found by chance through a friend who had calculated that my book on the Arabs in Israel might carry enough prestige.

When *King Kong* comes to town I call at the Princes Theatre to welcome the cast and report their arrival. The exuberant jazz opera about life in the shantytowns around Johannesburg, sung, acted and danced by black South Africans, opens on 23 February 1961. Two years before the Beatles' first television appearance, King Kong raises the curtain on the swinging sixties. *Time* magazine brilliantly reports the impact.

> With raw flair, swivel-hipped sex, lurid color and fundamental rhythms, *King Kong* has clapped a rough hand on English shoulders to lead its new audience through the shebeens (speakeasies) and back alleys around black Johannesburg. Great gum-booted miners dance with precision, township spivs glitter with menace as they re-enact a primeval war dance; shebeen Delilahs strut their stuff in the sinuous dance of the patha patha (touch, touch). Racy, swinging rhythms interweave tribal chants, European liturgical music and 1925 Dixieland stomps. Such certified-hit solos as *The Earth Turns Over* alternate with pennywhistle blues and a road gang's traditional chant.

113

I go to the stage door thinking that the cast, straight out of apartheid South Africa, will be shy and bewildered. They are indeed bewildered – riding buses and tubes with whites and never stopped for their papers. But not shy.

We throw a party for them at home. Twenty come. At 1am neighbours call the police to complain about the noise. The officers come through the front door into an eerie silence – a house almost empty. Our guests have vanished, using long-practised Johannesburg magic. The police are good humoured, relaxed. Slowly the guests emerge from under the kitchen table, creep out from wardrobes, arise from behind the sofa. They greet the officers, touch them to see if they are real, offer them drinks, sing and dance for them.

West Africa magazine was part of Cecil King's Mirror Group. We wrote mainly for business people but as the only journal covering the whole region we were read by its politicians and civil servants. The new African countries were popular in Europe – a hope for the future in a decade when we believed in progress. At *West Africa* we supported the radical Kwame Nkrumah in Ghana, the statesmanlike Tafawa Balewa in Nigeria, even the ranting leftist Sekou Touré in Guinea, with only mild admonishing when things went badly wrong. I started writing some of the editorials, a useful skill later at the *Guardian*.

David Williams, diplomat and humorist as much as editor, had friends in every West African capital and was on first-name terms with many potentates. He was as kind and gentle a boss as my first one, Harford Thomas at the *Oxford Mail*. There were only three of us on the staff; we could always wander into David's office for a gossip.

West African politics had a lighter touch than Middle Eastern. There may be crises, coups and wars but people never forgot to laugh. Perhaps some of their brand new states, economies and ministries still lacked mystique, so the funny side of pomposity could shine through. On tour, a politician, businessman or lawyer would often sit down to eat with his driver and other servants, who were likely to be members of his family.

Working with West Africans lifts the spirit and works wonders for social life. Their diplomats, rarely diplomatic at party time, and their businessmen, never letting money dampen exuberance, dance and drink and seduce, and love to welcome English friends to their circle. At their parties we danced wildly and badly and felt we were part of a new age.

At the same time, being with Africans and their London friends dragged us out of our self-centredness and made us aware of the nightmare of *apartheid* and the struggle against it. At those same hilarious parties we would meet Bloke Modisane, Sylvester Stein, Colin Legum and other writers and activists committed to the freedom struggle. Our Garden Suburb house became a meeting place. Colin and Margaret Legum became family friends and remained so until their deaths in 2003 and 2007. I have never had anything like the commitment and dedication that Colin and Margaret had.

Nicola

While all this is going on Dorothy is quietly pregnant. Taking this like everything else in our swinging stride, we decorate baby's room, buy clothes and toys, hire an au pair and Dorothy goes to a class in natural childbirth. Her class-conscious mother insists on booking a private room for her in the London Clinic.

Here I am, a sixties man, present at the birth of our child. Dorothy with pillows behind her back practices the breathing she's learnt, while I wave my arm to the correct rhythm, conducting Beethoven's Pastoral Symphony. Dorothy is brave, ecstatic. Nicola is beautiful with a perfect tiny face and masses of dark hair.

She cries. Her back has a raw, unfinished look with a blob of purple. I am awed, out of my depth. She is wrapped in a cloth and I hold her. The doctor comes in to check. He takes me out of the room, mutters something I don't understand. He is calling in a specialist. He tells me to go home. I think this is all routine. I know nothing about babies.

They tell me the next morning that Nicola has spina bifida which means her spine hasn't come together. Her legs don't kick. She will never walk, she may soon die. We have only heard of spina bifida as something that happens to other people, like car crashes and cancer.

We live on two levels: the wonderful world of new parenthood, and a nightmare world of doctors conferring with paediatricians. In Nicola's first operation, at nine days old, they push the spinal cord back into position, leaving only a scar no deeper than a cat's scratch.

After a month the build-up of fluid in her spinal column gives her hydrocephalus – water on the brain which, untreated, leads to blindness and mental impairment. The only treatment is experimental – bypassing the obstruction to drain off excess fluid with a plastic valve recently invented by a plumber for use on his daughter. The surgeon does not advise it. He tells us to take the baby home. Babies like that don't generally live more than a couple of years.

We find another surgeon who inserts the valve at the Maudsley Hospital. Dorothy and Nicola move into a cubicle in a ward where patients lie in rows, their heads swathed in bandages. The pressure has eased. We can take Nicola home. We play at normality as we wheel her about in her new clothes. At six weeks old Nicola has large, grey, long-lashed eyes.

Now David Williams wants me to go to West Africa for six weeks, because I must get to know my area and because I need cheering up. Dorothy's mother offers to pay for her to come with me and to hire a nanny for Nicola. We are told it is not a good idea for Dorothy to get too attached to her doomed child. Should she go? Should I go? Five decades later we still have no answer.

Margaret, the nanny, loves Nicola and when we come back from Africa we ask her to stay on. Nicola smiles and laughs and eases herself on her forearms as other babies do; her favourite game is pulling at my tie and laughing when it swings forward. When hot milk is spilled on her foot and leaves a burn, she does not feel it. Her curly hair hides from view the bulge at the back of her head. Left in the sun she gets a tan.

Nicola is eight months old. She begins to scream and does not stop for hours. The family doctor says the valve has blocked and

116

fluid is pressing on her head. We take her to Great Ormond Street Hospital for Sick Children for a new valve to be put in. Dorothy stays with her; I visit every day after work.

The Spina Bifida Ward is friendly, a community of small patients, parents and nurses. In the next cot to Nicola's lies a three-year-old boy, quite blind, quite paralysed. Both parents are Greek doctors who did not allow themselves to acknowledge that their son had hydrocephalus until it was too late to save his sight. With neither sight nor movement, when he hears his parents' footsteps his face breaks into an angelic smile.

Nicola snaps back from her operation within days. Dorothy wheels her out into the square, listens to the compliments of passers-by on how sweet and healthy she looks with her tan.

We begin to think of taking her home but the valve blocks again. A new one is placed in her skull. After the operation we find her dying, being resuscitated in an oxygen tent. Dorothy tells them to stop and let her die. They bring her a form to sign. She cannot sign and resuscitation resumes.

On her birthday the hospital makes a cake. She is weaker and her head is shaved. She enjoys the birthday meal, propped up on pillows. Margaret comes to the party. Nobody from outside has sent presents.

We go to a Mali Embassy party in Paris, while Margaret and Dorothy's parents visit Nicola. It is a joyful Independence Day celebration and we spend the night in a hotel on the Isle St Louis. For weeks we have not made love. That night Habie is conceived.

Nicola is weak but cheerful, like a little animal with limited awareness. She can no longer raise her arm high enough to play the game with my tie, so she makes the symbolic gesture, a few inches from her bed, and smiles.

Her brain is infected. She tries to pull the tubes out of her head, her hands are strapped to her sides. She vomits everything she eats so she is fed by a tube through her nostril. She cries to be picked up but we are only allowed to stroke her face in the spaces between the tubes. If anyone with a white coat approaches she screams. They move her to a side ward.

She has meningitis. She screams so much that her vocal chords snap and there is no more sound. She goes blind. They tell us she no longer feels any pain. Why, then, does her mouth open and shut in that soundless scream?

We are at home, at supper, when the nurse phones. It is over. Nicola was in a coma when she died. She is lovely in a white nightdress with a camellia in her hands.

A gravelled path bisects the lines of graves. The baby's grandparents lie on one side. The children's graves have miniature headstones; it could almost be a pet cemetery.

[In telling Nicola's story I have borrowed from Dorothy's unpublished *Letter to My Daughters – Habie, Tanya and Zoë.*]

Into Africa

We flew into Bamako, the capital of Mali, and from the moment we first touched down in Africa we felt more alive. In this dusty, gaudy town Africa glides past on bicycles and bare feet surrounded by roaming goats, chickens and donkeys. And always, in the foreground and background, music and drumming and dancing and laughter.

In Mali we visited some of David Williams' repertoire of contacts and quickly made friends. The best was Bokar N'diyae who was to be ambassador in London and Paris, and godfather to our new daughter Habie.

In Ghana we were not invited to the exclusive diplomatic party in Kwame Nkrumah's palace but we went all the same, running through a rainstorm and arriving drenched. In this new Africa white faces still got through doors. In Nigeria, in the steamy pandemonium of Lagos, we learnt to dance high-life and we came home with an address book full of new friends.

Habie was born on 14 June 1962. Her legs kicked! I could not stop watching her legs kick. She was beautiful. Bokar N'Diaye had named her Habibatu, his first wife's name which we had shortened. We wheeled her round Hampstead Garden Suburb watching her legs kick.

Now – here we go again – I wanted to be abroad. I still wanted to be a foreign correspondent, even if, once again, I had to take myself abroad and be a stringer for whoever took my copy. Lucky boy, I had a wife game, once again, for adventure. Habie, too, thrived on travel and adventure and still does.

And here comes Andre Deutsch, a brilliant, charming, vindictive, peevish Hungarian-born publisher. Andre had founded *African Universities Press* to publish school books which he hopes will become set books throughout English-speaking Africa. He had installed a manager in Nigeria, quarrelled bitterly with him and was looking for another. He chose me. I was impressed with Andre and I served as best I could until he quarrelled bitterly with me.

We started well, with working lunches at *L'Escargot Bienvenu* in Soho, which was said to rear its own snails in the basement. Over snails we planned our future meetings. I was writing down the dates in my diary when Andre asked: 'Why use a diary? If your mind's on the job you don't need one. I keep everything in my head.'

With more optimism than sense I decided I would be a journalist in my spare time. Before leaving for Lagos I looked round for strings to my bow and started at the top – at the *Guardian*. It had just dropped Manchester from its title and moved to London, but the foreign desk was still in Manchester. I walked with awe down the musty leader-writers' corridor to find Geoffrey Taylor, the foreign editor. He and other others I met, or overheard in that corridor, sounded more like Oxford dons than journalists.

I had come at a good moment. Serious, left-leaning newspapers wanted to cover the promise of the new West Africa but didn't have resident staff correspondents. Geoffrey gave me a cable card for sending copy without prepayment. 'Send me something whenever you feel like it and we'll see how it works out,' he said. I got the same deal from the *Observer*.

But first I wanted to do my best for Andre Deutsch. I aimed to succeed as a publisher without knowing anything about publishing. I flew to Lagos alone, with instructions to rent a house to serve as the AUP office and our home. The best I could find was something grand – a three-year lease on both halves of a new 'duplex' – two little semi-detached houses that I joined together by having a doorway pierced through the wall between the two living rooms. I got the agreement and signatures of our two Nigerian directors (a prominent lawyer and a prosperous printer, both too busy to care), clinched the deal, started buying furniture and moved in.

8 March 1963

Darling,

I haven't been absorbed in anything, and enjoyed myself as much, work-wise, since the days of the Ibans... For you, too, darling, the secret here will be to keep busy – if we work together – a thing we'll have to learn. I haven't tried any journalism yet: simply no time.

If I could have gone to Ibadan today to see the opening of the Western House, it would have made first-rate *Guardian* and *Observer* copy. *Tant pis.*

Dorothy and Habie joined me by boat, Tio came by air. We hired houseboys and a nanny. Together, the two modest houses made quite a fine residence and Andre, who was renowned for his meanness, objected to the extravagance. Why two houses when I was told to get one? In fact the new AUP House, on still undeveloped land between the airport and the city, proved an excellent acquisition. Chief Rotimi Williams, Nigeria's best-known lawyer, chairman of our board, came down from Ibadan in the Western Region to hold a press conference, putting AUP on the map. I presided and enjoyed talking to the hacks as if I was not one myself.

I hired a young secretary who knew no more about publishing than I did and almost nothing about being a secretary. But Godwin turned out to be a rock, a friend through good times and bad. He took over the scooter that Dorothy had brought out from London and became despatch rider and trouble-shooter for the firm and the family.

In the bustle, improvisation and amateurishness of AUP House we were happy, with new friends in publishing and teaching as well as politics and journalism, a cook to feed us all, a houseboy to serve us and a nanny for Habie.

At 15 months Habie lived largely out of doors with the children of servants and neighbours. She talked early and volubly and soon acquired a homely Nigerian accent. Decades later she is still a great talker. She walked late, but the strength of her personality made up for that: she would crawl very fast around the lawn while her Nigerian friends, who could walk, chose instead to crawl after her. Since she was out of doors all day with her nanny, Dorothy decided that Habie needed no nappies.

Tropical life can be dangerous for small children, so as a precaution Dorothy had taught Habie to fear the word 'hot'. One afternoon the gardener killed a cobra in the shrubbery. The female snake had a nest: the little cobras swarmed across the patio. Habie began to crawl towards them. Dorothy yelled 'hot, hot' and stopped Habie in her tracks.

Before breakfast Dorothy was coming down the winding stone staircase from our bedroom to my office when I stopped her with the news. 'Kennedy has been assassinated.'

I threw myself into four tasks: sign up text-book authors, publish and print their books, promote their sale and sell shares to wealthy Nigerians. I hoped my enthusiasm would make up for my ignorance. In twelve months I got five books out and I sold some thousands of pounds worth of shares. When sluggish distributors failed to sell the books I loaded boxes of them into the back of the car and went on tour, visiting schools and book shops with my sales talk. This was unorthodox. Our competitors, the mighty Longmans, never dreamed of doing it. Andre thought me eccentric but was impressed by my energy.

I loved those tours, driving far into the jungly Western and Eastern Regions and up to the far deserts of the North, sharing the road with lurching mammy wagons branded with brash philosophy: *By their Fruits Ye Shall Know Them; Sea Never Dry; Venture is Success; After this – Mercedes; Baboon dey work, Monkey dey*

Chop – or sensible advice like *Horn Before Overtaking*. On the road people sleep, sell, hunt, demonstrate, dance. Women wash themselves and the family's clothes in ponds and streams. Painted signs compete for every space: CHAIRS FOR RENT, CITY GIRL POOLS, SHOW CUTS – LONDON-TRAINED DRESSMAKER. Hawkers offer yams, peppers, paw-paw, pet birds, transistor radios. Monkeys swing from trees. Children dance, even when they are all alone and there is no music.

I stayed in small hotels and rest houses, ate *egusi* soup, peppery fish with okra, yam, cassava and palm nuts. I drank big-size Star beer over lunch which kept me awake though it sends most people to sleep.

I loved talking to booksellers and teachers – the most open-minded and agreeable Nigerians. They liked me back, pleased to be visited, and I suspect some of the books were bought to please me. I sold enough to justify my tours and I called on the occasional rich businessman to sell shares.

I made mistakes. The first AUP textbook – a collection of Nigerian stories – appeared with no copyright notice on the flypage. Nobody told me we needed that. One of the larger investors wanted his thousands back because he had changed his mind. I told him he couldn't have his money back because that's not the way shares work. I didn't know how shares worked either.

And now politics happened and I itched to send stories. A general election was coming and there were all-too-credible accusations that powerful politicians were preparing, yet again, to rig the vote. The future of democracy in black Africa's biggest, richest and most populous country was in doubt. Nigeria had a free press and competent radio, so I could report the crisis in my spare time, with no more first-hand coverage than a few phone calls to official spokesmen and aggrieved politicians.

I started modestly, with trepidation, sending news stories with political analysis to Geoffrey Taylor in Manchester. He liked them! He asked for more! When I didn't file for a week Geoffrey sent me reminders! I had started writing for the *Guardian*, the paper my father used to read every day, and I didn't stop even when I retired from the staff 35 years later.

But here was a problem: the *Guardian* was read by, among others, Andre, who was not amused that his manager, ensconced in that extravagant house, should be wasting his time like this. Andre wrote to complain. I replied that I was a journalist in my spare time, that I had been a diligent manager, as he had often gratefully acknowledged, and that I refused to give up the *Guardian* and the *Observer*. There was nothing poor Andre could do – for the moment. Until Clyde Sanger came along to spoil everything.

Clyde was the *Guardian's* roving Africa correspondent. He cabled that he was coming to Lagos. I replied that we would both be away but he was welcome to stay in our house: Godwin and two of the servants would be there. Clyde had a lovely time. A week later he was at a London cocktail party where he met Andre Deutsch. Clyde to Andre: 'Lagos was great. I stayed in the *Guardian's* house there – a grand place called AUP House.' Andre choked on his drink.

We knew nothing of this London cocktail party when we were invited for the weekend to Chief Rotimi Williams' opulent home in Ibadan. We looked up to Rotimi who was a huge teddy bear of a man with a soft, cultured voice. The weekend started badly when Dorothy, noticing that Mrs Williams had become even more portly, asked her when the baby was due. Mrs Williams was neither pregnant nor amused. After dinner I was invited, alone, into the great lawyer's study for a business talk. He wasted no time. The AUP board had met. It had decided, as he put it, not to renew my contract. For the only time in my life I was sacked.

This was a shock, not a tragedy. I was never going to be a businessman. I decided instantly that we would stay in Nigeria where I stood every chance as a freelance. The country was in a state of chronic political crisis because the Christian south and east were restive under the domination of the Muslim north, an anomaly of particular interest to Britain because we had given Nigeria its independence in that lopsided way. Oil had been found in the eastern region – a source of gathering crisis with the threat of secession and civil war. And just along the coast, Kwame

Nkrumah's Ghana was in bed with the Soviets but its leaders were still delighted to talk in English to a visiting British correspondent.

Unlike Rotimi's wife, Dorothy really was pregnant. We decided to go back to London briefly so that she could have the baby and I could scour the market. I would take a quick trip to America where there was surely no limit: think *Newsweek,* think *Time* magazine. We bade our friends a temporary goodbye. We left Tio, and also a donkey we had acquired, in the care of friends, and African Universities Press in the hands of Godwin.

In Manchester Geoffrey Taylor was pleased at this twist of fortune and agreed to pay me a retainer. In London within a week I had a retainer from the *Observer* and *Economist.* The BBC world service signed me up as its Lagos stringer. No retainer, of course, from the stingy Beeb. Next, the august *Neue Zürcher Zeitung* hired me as its West Africa correspondent, promising to translate my copy into German and pay my money into a Swiss bank account, which ranked me with the wily rich. Pall Mall Press commissioned a book on Nigeria. And – the final spiteful triumph of a sacked publisher – I signed a contract with Hutchinsons to start an educational publishing venture for them in Lagos, in competition with Deutsch. They didn't mind my being a journalist most of the time. All this before I even got to the States.

New York, 16 September 1964

Darling, I've had my first interview this morning and recouped the fare! $300 a year (£110) retainer from McGraw Hill News Service. They supply news and features to business and technical magazines. Should earn an additional £2-300 in linage from them in a year because of oil news. Half a dozen more interviews to go. Everybody I rang was interested. Hope to leave for Washington on Sunday

Washington 22 September 1964

My only darling, just a bonjour before I rush off to a reception at the Mali embassy. Somewhat exhausted – I walk everywhere to save taxi fares and cover miles and miles a day. Everyone continues to be most helpful and interested, courteous, hospitable.

Among other things I've arranged to be broadcasting in French for *Voice of America*. They have a man in Lagos who can't speak it. It's become clear that we'll be more busy, not less, than in the AUP days and we'll almost certainly be able to live at the same standard. I'll need your help more than before. This Lagos venture will be immense fun if we can manage to keep our heads above water.

Powkeepsie NY 25 September 1964

Left NYC in a hired VW this afternoon ($44 a week, no mileage to pay) after seeing: *Newsweek* (now definitely on, with retainer after short trial period), *Saturday Evening Post* (they want a piece on Nigeria soon and will pay upwards of £550), *Reader's Digest* (very charming, interested, and they pay £600 for a piece); lunch with Hella Pick at the UN (in the delegates' dining room of course!). Will be seeing *Christian Science Monitor* in Boston. Did I mention, by the way, that Praeger is definitely going to publish the Nigeria book in the US? Babe, we're sure going to be busy in the next few months.

Benjamin Peter was born at the London Clinic – Ben because we didn't expect to have another son after him (we were wrong about that), and Peter was my best school friend. Ben kicked his legs. He was breast-fed, like our first two babies, unlike me who was reared by bottle, to which Dorothy attributes what she calls my loneliness of spirit. By the time Ben was circumcised – unlike me who never was, because in 1930 my parents thought it might be a liability – I had flown back to Lagos.

19 October 1964

Darl,

Thanks for the cable. Glad Ben is OK – presumably the butchery went off OK. I'm going to be a bit difficult about Ben I think – already he's started by getting something I didn't, not to speak of the milk etc. If he starts to grow up as free as Habie is, I shall get somewhat cross and jealous – but maybe I'll identify.

I have not yet been replaced at African Universities Press – the empty house and office are being looked after by the faithful Godwin.

With Rotimi William's reluctant permission I moved back temporarily into our old home until I could find us a new one (I don't know what Andre in London thought about it).

22 October 1964

In this great empty barn of a place I feel like a ghost. It's quite eerie – Godwin comes in, in the mornings and runs AUP by himself... I've found an ideal house for us nearer to Lagos at Yaba – fully furnished at £1,000 a year with phone; an old house, separate dining room, lots of enormous balconies, two large bedrooms and study-cum-guest-room, nice garden, garage, 2 boys' quarters... matured garden needs a lawn planted. Suitable for chickens but probably not donkey. Will return donk to polo club pending your arrival. He makes a truly fearful din but looks well. Tio still fine. So am I. Have started working for *Voice of America*.

Dorothy arrived with the two children. We engaged a nanny, cook, gardener and houseboy. Our new life added friends to the old ones and soon we were caught up again in the laughter and dancing and flirting of a city even more swinging than London. Politicians, diplomats, businessmen, artists and journalists went to each others' parties or met at the Kakadu nightclub, where the brilliant Fela Ransome-Kuti and his band played and sang in Afrobeat, a subversive fusion of American jazz and funk with West African highlife.

On Sundays we would drive out to the beach at Badagry, where palms grow on sandy beaches and the Atlantic breakers roll. We would take two-year-old Habie, baby Ben, and Tio – the snob who snarled at poor fishermen so they wouldn't come near us.

We put the baby to sleep on a coconut mat under a shady palm and took Habie into the warm waves. Tio, too fastidious to get his coat wet, stayed under the palm tree with Ben.

Tio barked. 'Dam that dog, he'll wake the baby.' I wiped seawater from my eyes and Dorothy yelled: 'Shut up, Tio' but he went on in a high, irritating, hysterical yapping. I went back to the beach to shut him up.

Under the tree the baby slept, his limbs flung out like a starfish. At his feet the little dog swayed back and forth on his delicate white paws and never stopped his high-pitched yapping. At the baby's head something else was swaying – a spitting cobra. Twelve foot long. Back and forth, back and forth. The dog made little darts at the swaying snake. Then the cobra spat – full into Tio's face.

Tio screamed, breaking the spell. I snatched a dried palm frond and thumped it on the ground. The snake lowered itself onto the sand and slithered away, the smooth, brown body humping as it gained speed. Ben had not woken up.

Tio was rubbing the side of his head along the ground and screaming. A young fisherman who had been mending nets ran up and shouted in Pidgin: 'Takem quick-quick into sea and washem eyes out.' I dunked the little dog under the waves over and over.

Back home, the vet gave Tio an antibiotic, saying the fisherman's advice had saved his life. But Tio was the hero who had saved Ben's life. His eyeball swelled like a ping-pong ball as he staggered around, accepting the praise and admiration which were his due and eating minced chicken and thin slices of ham. In a week the swelling subsided and his eyesight returned to normal. Tio had survived too many catastrophes to be beaten by a spitting cobra.

From crisis to worse

The federal election was due on December 30, 1964. With three weeks to go, the country was in crisis, with talk of fraud and harassment, even secession. The president, Nnamdi Azikiwe, was an Ibo from the Christian eastern region. The prime minister, Abubakar Tafawa Balewa, was a Muslim from the feudal northern region. The Ibos of the East were restive, muttering about secession if the election is rigged, yet again, to perpetuate the North's domination.

In the *Observer* I quoted President Azikiwe as saying, unpresidentially, that 'the atmosphere reeks of mutual antagonisms, bitter recriminations, and tribal discrimination. Indeed the whole federal edifice, with its delicate balance between tribes, religions and ideologies, will face its severest test yet.'

Observer: 27 December 1964

Acid-proof ballot boxes and thugs.

By Walter Schwarz

The trouble besetting the Nigerian election isn't just the citizens' well-known genius for compromise, which insists on all the Westminster trappings – from nominations and returning officers and even acid-proof ballot boxes – while more or less philosophically accepting mass beatings-up by political thugs and the illegal imprisonment of opponents by the authorities. This time it goes altogether deeper.

The precariousness of the balance between tribes, religions and philosophies which the British bequeathed the Nigerians four years ago has been progressively laid bare since then. It has been an arranged political marriage and has resulted in very little love and a great deal of disillusionment. The strains have now almost reached breaking point.

Did I sound old for my age? I was more explainer than reporter, a useful skill because Nigerian politics was so complex. I talked to politicians, officials, academics, businessmen and market mammies. I travelled to the regions where the story was but I was not a describer; my pieces were analytical, restrained, wise, with few scoops. Typically, in that long *Observer* piece, I left an exclusive interview with Nigeria's most powerful man – the Sardauna of Sokoto who ruled the dominant north – to the very last paragraph and reduced it to a single sentence:

> Cross the Rubicon (Niger) by the bridge at Jebba and you are out of the forest in the dry, windy North. This Hausaland is seen by the Yorubas and Ibos as feudalistic (the women don't vote) autocratic and, above all, not half so populous as it pretends. In the modern capital at Kaduna, the Sardauna told me with obvious conviction that he counts on winning all the northern seats 'except a very few that go astray'.

A friend, Father Raymond Kennedy who was the local boss of the new Catholic charity, Cafod, and who, unlike me, saw my stuff appearing in the newspapers, said he thought of me as an *haut vulgarisateur*. Vulgar as it sounds, I took it as a compliment because of the *haut*. Two years later, when I joined the *Guardian* staff as leader writer, the man who read all incoming cables, known as the copy-taster, asked: 'Are you really Walter Schwarz? I'd imagined someone much older.'

The simmering crisis of the 1964 election did not go away until the coup of 1966 and the civil war of 1968. The thwarted, reform-minded opposition had formed a grand southern alliance – the United Progressive Party – against the Muslim north. Every trick of election fraud was used against it, and the alliance failed to win power.

In the election in the Western Region, rigging by the ruling party was further refined and perfected and the Chief Minister, Chief Akintola, duly claimed victory against an opposition alliance widely deemed to have really won. Still the high-minded explainer, but not neglecting the funny side of it, I reported how the election was 'won'.

> *Guardian:* 18 October 1965
>
> ...The game is played in four stages. The starting point is that as many electoral officers as possible should either support or fear the government sufficiently to receive the papers of the government candidates and then make themselves scarce until nominations close. This time the Western Region Opposition organised several extensive manhunts for runaway officers...
>
> The next stage is the polling. The aim now is to exclude the Opposition's polling agents while admitting the Government party's. Presiding officers insisted – claiming it was laid down by the regulations – that agents' identity discs had to be countersigned by an electoral officer. Discs of the opposition agents were not signed. The next stage is the counting. Now the idea is to exclude opposition candidates and agents or make them sit so far away that they can't quite see what happens. Stage 4 is only the last resort: if your opponent still wins you can declare yourself elected all the same. Several Opposition candidates said on Tuesday morning that they had heard one result announced in their constituencies and another one on the Government station.
>
> What made this election different was the open and utterly uninhibited way it was done. Nigerians, who believe in

democracy and practice it daily in village councils, in their courts, through their relatively free newspapers and almost embarrassingly free speech, have now experienced an election which most of them believe returned the less popular party to power.

My best informant on the unsavoury politics of the Western Region was Wole Soyinka, the charismatic playwright and drama teacher who was to win the Nobel Prize for Literature in 1986. Wole venerates his Yoruba traditions and culture but his fierce nationalism is Nigerian. He was furious at the way the elections had been rigged. We loved him for his deep, laughing voice and the cynicism with which he masked his passionate involvement.

Wole was gregarious, a *bon viveur*. But at crisis time he liked to move freely, unobserved – a lone activist, an adventurer. He came often to our house in Yaba, always unannounced, using the house as a refuge. Sometimes we came down for breakfast and found Wole asleep on a sofa.

I was looking for one of Habie's toys. Hidden at the bottom of a chaotic pile in a cubby-hole I found a pistol. A real one, loaded. I covered it up again and left it there: the cubby-hole was above the stairs, well out of Habie's reach.

Next day Tio barked, I looked down our long drive and saw eight police officers advancing on the house.

'Is Wole Soyinka here?'

'No.'

'Where is he?'

'I don't know. I haven't seen him for a week.'

The officers were too polite to search the house of a foreigner and even if they had, they would not have looked under Habie's toys. What Wole was up to he had not told us.

Guardian: 18 October 1965
Nigerian police seek playwright
By Walter Schwarz
Wole Soyinka, Nigeria's foremost playwright, is wanted by the police concerning a 'pirate broadcast' which was made from the Western Region broadcasting station on Friday.

A man carrying a gun entered the Ibadan studio as a pre-recorded broadcast by Chief Akointola, leader of the Nigerian Democratic Party, who was returned to power after Monday's disputed election, was due to go on the air. The intruder substituted his own tape, of which about a minute was broadcast.

It said: 'this is the voice, the true voice, of the people of Western Nigeria.' It called on Chief Akintola to 'get out and take with you your band of renegades who have lost all sense of shame' and added that the Progressive Alliance, the party of Alhaji Adegbenro, who has proclaimed an interim government of his own, 'is the lawfully elected government of Western Nigeria.'

Wole Soyinka, 33, is the author of the play *The Road*, which had its première in London during last month's Commonwealth Arts Festival.

Wole was caught and arrested. To ensure he got a fair trial, Amnesty International sent John Mortimer out as legal observer. Mortimer came to stay with us. I drove him to the courthouse in Ibadan, 78 miles away. It was a hilarious trial.

Observer: 21 Nov 1965

Drama and laughter at trial

By Walter Schwarz

Was Wole Soyinka, Nigeria's leading playwright, the gunman who held up the broadcasting station? His trial is in its third week, probably the last. He is charged with stealing, probably with threats of violence, two tapes valued at £2 12s... The Director of Public Prosecutions, Mr Tajudeen Oki, admitted yesterday that the evidence of identity was 'divided' and that his men, while trying to break down the accused's identity while questioning staff at Ibadan University, had had 'difficulties all the way.'

As the evidence unfolded, it began to look more and more like a situation in a Soyinka play. The studio engineer who confessed that the gunman made him feel so 'near to death' that he couldn't remember how long the nightmare incident lasted, the acting head of programmes who was said to be trying to edge himself safely behind the studio engineer, the Revd Olumide, Controller of Programmes, whom the defence counsel asked to 'pray for us' – all might have been characters in *The Road*.

131

High drama mingling with the lovable buffoonery of unimportant men is Soyinka's speciality.

But as judgment day approaches there is no more laughter.

Everybody knew the gunman had broadcast the truth. Nobody would testify against Wole, who was acquitted. Mortimer was impressed that in the land of corrupt politicians lawyers were still lawyers and judges would not convict without proof of identity.

In his amusing memoirs *Clinging to the Wreckage* (Weidenfeld 1982), Mortimer says he stayed with a 'British writer' whom he does not name, no doubt to be sure that Dorothy doesn't sue him for libel. After describing our household as 'reassuring as it presented the usual North London scene of drying nappies, plastic knickers, chewed bikkipegs swinging from the sides of cots, crumpled copies of the *The Manchester Guardian* and paperback Hemingways ripped from the shelves and stamped on by an apparently intoxicated three-year-old,' Mortimer tells this story about his un-named hostess driving him into town.

> She was a flamboyant driver and we screeched through the curiously deserted streets of Lagos, still subject to rioting and sudden death, until we were stopped by an enormous policeman, a Hausa, perhaps, from the north, hung with every conceivable armament and brandishing a riot stick. He asked for my hostess's driving licence and, when it was clear it had run out six months previously, he told us both to follow him to the station... However, instead of docilely accompanying the huge officer, my hostess leapt from the driving seat and attacked him with her dangerously sharp fingernails, brilliantly coloured by chipped varnish. After one swift claw from the roused *Guardian*-reader, the police officer turned tail and ran into the darkness, his revolver thudding against his side, wailing with uncontrollable fear as though pursued by evil spirits. We heard no more of the matter and so I left Nigeria with increased respect for our legal system and a new awareness of the almost invincible power of the middle class housewife.

I have questioned Dorothy and she says Mortimer's account is exaggerated. 'The stupid policeman was being a nuisance so I just slapped him.' I remain puzzled. My wife can be sharp with her tongue but does not slap even her dogs.

Upwardly mobile, we moved to a small flat in the fashionable Ikoyi suburb where our garden backed onto the lagoon. Here the sea breeze mitigates the humid climate and with our servants and nanny we lived well. Through a friend in the navy we acquired a boat – neither a yacht nor a speedboat but a ponderous naval craft with an outboard engine too powerful for it, so that at full throttle the bow lifted up and swerved alarmingly.

Dorothy joined the polo club and rode round the perimeter track in the company of dashing cavalry officers from the north. (Southerners, men of the forest, don't ride). Because of the heat she went out riding before breakfast.

I was woken by Dorothy wearing her breeches. She said she had seen soldiers outside Government House. It was January 15, 1966.

I had never experienced a military coup so I didn't know what to do. The radio said the civilian government had been abolished throughout the federation and the army was taking over under its chief, General Ironsi. I went to police headquarters, joined a small crowd. Army officers with grim faces passed in and out.

There was a bustle and I saw Ironsi coming out. I had never met him. I pushed my way through.

'How is it going, sir?'

'Very badly indeed.'

He strode away. Ironsi was a straight-talking soldier and I remain grateful to him for this scoop. Clearly he was not the author of the coup. I could not file the story because the cable office was barricaded by soldiers, telephone lines were blocked, the airport closed and the frontiers sealed. This was standard practice for coups but I didn't know that.

A Commonwealth conference had brought several foreign correspondents to Lagos. Some managed to fly out in time, aware of the coup and expecting the clamp-down – including the *Guardian's* Patrick Keatley. 'What an idiot – flying out and missing the story,' I thought. Back home, Patrick had his front-page coup story – leaving me impotent.

Six foreign correspondents were left incommunicado in Lagos. We pooled our information, but how could we get it out? The BBC's Angus McDermid, an old hand at coups, scoured the Lagos docklands looking for a ham radio, found one and talked to a ham in a village near Southampton.

'This is Angus McDermid of the BBC,' Angus intoned in his dignified BBC English. 'I want you to telephone the BBC at Bush House, London...' The radio ham in Southampton interrupted: 'I haven't got a telephone.'

Angus (unperturbed): 'Well, go to the nearest telephone, tell the BBC to set up a daily call from your radio to me in Lagos...'

It worked. We reporters got together every evening, wrote a joint story and gave it to Angus to transmit on the ham radio. Although there was only one pool story, each of us was given his own by-line.

I was the best informed because I lived here. Dorothy and I were friends with some of the ministers and civil servants involved in the drama. On the day after the coup the senior surviving cabinet minister, Alhaji Dipcharima, was made interim prime minister and recorded a statement. In the evening, as it was broadcast, Dipcharima was our dinner guest. He probably felt safer hidden away with us: in a nearby street two senior officers who had tried to flee from the perpetrators of the coup were lying dead. We tuned in to listen to Dipcharima's statement. Highlife music in the background: in the excitement the studio engineer had failed to wipe the tape.

The cable office reopened. I was free to write and my news was good news. In Lagos and the whole of the south the new regime was wildly popular, so I, in turn, was popular with the regime. The coup leaders – a group of majors – had failed to establish control. Dipcharima, unable to rule because Nigeria's key politicians were dead, handed over power to General Ironsi, who had had nothing to do with the coup. My bullish pieces were reprinted in the government's news service and quoted on the radio.

Guardian: 22 January 1966
It has been a dream of a coup. 'Bang, bang – you're dead!' – an infantile aggression fantasy... The fantasy was that one night the

soldiers would come. They would shoot Chief Akintola, whose electioneering seemed to epitomise the worst in the regime. They would shoot the Sardauna of Sokoto, the Northern premier who seemed unfairly powerful because the British had left him with a region bigger than the others put together... One morning they would all be gone – all the 300-odd Ministers, Federal and Regional, those with portfolios as well as those with only sinecures... On the whole it was a remarkably bloodless coup, and it was wildly popular.

Days later we found out what had happened. Four army majors staged the coup at night. In the north, the dashing Major Nzeogwu, chief instructor at the military academy, held a night exercise as a cover to kill the imperious Sardauna, his chief wife and his bodyguard. His colleagues in the west killed Chief Akintola, the champion election-rigger. In Lagos the federal prime minister, the gentle but ineffective Tafawa Balewa, the finance Minister and several top army officers were also shot dead. Ironsi escaped because he went to two parties that night.

Post-coup euphoria didn't last. The well-meaning Ironsi, a soldier who knew little of politics, now needed to tackle the intractable tribal rivalries of 55 million Nigerians. No wonder he floundered. He promised a new constitution but that proved too difficult. He issued a decree abolishing Nigeria's federal structure – but that led to anti-southern riots in the north. 30,000 Ibos were killed. Over a million fled from the north back to their homelands in the eastern region. Ironsi climbed down, explaining his decree was only a stopgap measure to help his military governors to govern. The seeds of Nigeria's disintegration had been sown and they were soon to sprout in the secession of the oil-rich eastern region, calling itself Biafra, and civil war. As I reported these ominous developments my articles were no longer popular with the faltering regime.

Deported by Nigeria, imprisoned in Biafra

Dorothy has taken the children to London for a holiday with their beloved nanny, Esther. Alone in the house, I do what many Nigerians and many expatriates do in this primal age of pre-Aids exuberance: I call on a pretty Ibo girl whom I have admired for a while. I bring Abigail over. We are in bed. It is mid-afternoon.

A knocking at the front door. I cover Abigail up and go to the door. A policeman stands outside, with five others in a straggly line behind him.

'Mr Walter Schwarz? We have come to take you to the airport. It is the order of the minister of the interior. You are being deported. Pack your bags, sir, please.'

I am, for once, speechless. I usher the men into the living room where they sit on chairs ranged round the walls, shuffling their feet. They have not done this before.

In the bedroom Abigail understands; she gets dressed and walks through the sitting room to the front door, passing silently between the two rows of seated coppers. None of them acknowledge that they have noticed her existence. The presence of Abigail, and her silent departure, is a part of Lagos life not worthy of comment.

My instinct is to play for time. I remember that the press officer at the British High Commission has advised me to leave my passport with him, to give me breathing space in case I should be deported. I have ignored the advice and the passport is here with me. But now I am short of luggage because Dorothy has taken the suitcases. I ask the senior policeman if I may telephone a friend to get some suitcases sent over. He agrees. I call our British friends, Jeremy and Pat Lang, who live in a posh area where most of the diplomats live, including the Brits. I tell Pat I am being deported and ask her to send over some suitcases.

The luggage arrives and I start packing. I slip my passport into one of the Langs' suitcases. I ring Pat again. 'You sent me too many, so I'm sending one back. You might want to have a peep inside, Pat, and maybe pay a visit to your good friends down the road.'

I tell the police that I can't leave for the airport because my passport is with the High Commission. It is Saturday. The High Commission will not be open until Monday. I am under open arrest. The officer is helpful, almost apologetic, lets me drive around with him sitting in the back to say goodbye to friends.

I am the first resident British correspondent to be deported from a Commonwealth country. A question is asked in the House of Commons. The Nigerian High Commissioner in London is making inquiries. At the British High Commission I retrieve my passport and am told that the Nigerian Government must buy my ticket. It does. All this takes time and it is Wednesday before I finally leave Nigeria. At Heathrow I give interviews, a celebrity. In the BBC news clip Dorothy looks glamorous in headscarf and sunglasses, Habie looks bewildered and baby Ben, dressed in Nigerian robes, is the star.

What went wrong? It was Nigeria, not me. As post-coup euphoria evaporated the old tribal tensions had re-appeared. The good General Ironsi wanted to keep Nigeria united but when the north erupted and the West fulminated, he fell back on people he trusted – fellow Ibos. As the situation deteriorated everyone was a suspect, especially the Brits. The British High Commissioner had travelled in the north just before the murderous anti-Ibo riots: was he stirring up trouble because the British, as ever, prefer a divided Nigeria under the domination of the conservative north? Paranoia had set in. Was Schwarz, too, conspiring with northerners known to be his friends?

In London Geoffrey Crowther, editor of the *Economist*, went to see the Nigerian High Commissioner to ask why his correspondent, Schwarz, had been deported. He was told of 'reports' that just after the coup Schwarz was in Rome, where the ex-Minister Dipcharima, known to be Schwarz's friend and now regarded as a conspirator for the Muslim north, had taken refuge. I hadn't been to Rome for nine years!

Or had I? Of course! After the coup, when communications were fragile, the *Observer* had asked me to fly to London at their expense to write an uncensored front-page report. The Nigeria Airways plane made a stopover – in Rome. I walked into the transit lounge with my typewriter and went on writing my story, watched, no doubt, by fourth-rate spies on board to whom it never occurred that if they had asked me what I was typing I would have been delighted to let them read it.

137

My father, heavily afflicted with Parkinson's, had died aged 73. For him I felt more nostalgia and gratitude than deep grief. He had saved us from Hitler, established us comfortably in Manchester and brought us to even greater ease in northwest London. He had seen Vic and me married, both to beautiful girls, and Marlene married to the eminent historian Eric Hobsbawm. Father died a month too soon to see my first dispatches in the *Guardian*, the paper he had revered.

Mother moved to a flat and we sold our house in the Garden Suburb to buy my parental home in that leafy no-man's land between Golders Green and Hampstead. We had no financial worries as long as retainer payments continued to arrive in my bank account. With a heavy heart I wrote to tell *Newsweek, Neue Zurcher Zeitung* and others that, sadly, I didn't live in Nigeria any more. The payments stopped. I needed a job. Starting at the top, I asked the *Guardian* for one, promising Alistair Hetherington to be his faithful correspondent anywhere in the world.

Alistair started by telling me there were no vacancies and he hadn't any money, which is standard *Guardian*-editor talk. He hadn't met me before and this must be his way of sizing me up. He looked shrewd and sounded Scottish; stern but benevolent, he said little but his soft voice and kind eyes put me at ease. He seemed to be thinking. A silence. Out of the blue he asked: 'Have you ever written any leaders?'

Yes, I remembered with a lucky flash of inspiration, I used to write leaders at *West Africa* magazine. I felt sure I had written at least two. Alistair said he would like to have a foreign leader writer and, since I know the Middle East and Africa, would I like the job? I would.

Ordinary *Guardian* journalists work at desks in open-plan floors. Leader-writers share a special office of their own – a rarefied relic of the Cross Street corridor. We lead the life of gentlemen. We don't have to be in the office until after lunch for our conference with the editor. If we're writing a leader the editor needs to have it by 7pm so that he can approve it and alter it if he wishes, since every leader is theoretically his. Often we're not writing and can, if we wish, go home. Nobody in the office has time to notice us, least of all the editor who is our only boss.

My expertise was in demand, with Nigeria disintegrating into civil war and Israel – well, is Israel ever out of the news, is it ever not in need of gentle admonishment expressed with sadness and deep understanding? On these two topics I was an *haut vulgarisateur* again, explaining and analysing as I had always done, plus a word of sympathetic advice at the end.

But I didn't enjoy this privileged existence. I was, as I had been at Oxford, out of my depth. Between 3 pm and 7 pm I had to produce 600 wise words, telling the rulers of countries I'd barely heard of – Laos, Uruguay, Vanuatu, Grenada – what to do. How do I get the facts? There was no Google, no BBC-news-on-line, no Uruguay government website, no blogger in any of these exotic places. Only a single Reuters cable with the news I had to pontificate on. For background there was our library of battered cardboard folders containing browned old cuttings. I prayed that our devoted and intelligent lady librarians would find the folder I needed – they nearly always did – and that it would contain useful facts. Often it did not.

The truth is, I was shamefully ignorant. Immersed in the dramas of Israel and Nigeria, I had barely noticed the rest of the turning world. At leader-writers' conference, stormy waves of argument washed back and forth about Ireland and Vietnam, the hot topics of the day, leaving me silent, often inattentive. Nor was I an ideologue. Geoffrey Taylor is mistaken, in his admirable history of the *Guardian*, in including me in the 'phalanx of left-wing leader-writers – Jonathan Steele, Richard Gott, Walter Schwarz, John Palmer' – confronting the more centrist Hetherington. I may have been left of my Tory father and brother, but my sixth form master had described me accurately, if disparagingly, as a liberal of the old school. I have remained so.

Harford Thomas, my kind old boss at the *Oxford Mail*, was now the deputy editor. Alistair was away, Harford was in charge and I was floundering: I could not frame my argument about some shadowy faraway government that needed to be sagely chastised.

The 7pm deadline passed: Harford was waiting and I was still stuck. Glancing at his watch, he came over to my desk and said look, Walter, a leader needs only three parts: state the problem, state the alternatives and conclude what should be done; I can give you 20 minutes. It worked. What a nice man.

Alistair was a nice man, too, when he allowed me a month off on full pay to finish my book, *Nigeria*, for which Pall Mall Press and Praeger were waiting. It was difficult to write during a civil war which could be the making of a new Nigeria or lead to its disintegration. When it came out the book had as good reviews as *The Arabs in Israel.* Kingsley Martin said in his *New Statesman* that I had 'accomplished a difficult and complicated task with great skill' and the *Times Literary Supplement* said sniffily that 'Mr Schwartz (sic) is without doubt the best of today's ephemeral commentators on the Nigeria scene.'

Alistair was a keen hill walker, so was I and so was my brother-in-law Eric Hobsbawm. No, the three of us did not go hiking together but there is a connection. Alistair understood my passion and agreed to my saving up my days-off so that once a month I could take four or five days at a stretch to go to North Wales, where Eric and Marlene had a leased cottage that they allowed us to use.

The cottage is in the Croesor valley, near Penrhyndeudraeth, just under Knicht mountain, in sight of Snowdon. After a few months the Hobsbawms moved out of the village, a little way down the valley, to Parc Farm. This ancient estate has a medieval stone gatehouse with walls three feet thick – just one room down and one room up, outside loo, no bathroom – known as Gatws Parc. The lease of this austere and beautiful gatehouse became vacant, and for the next 22 years Gatws was our mountain retreat, loved by all the family and many friends. Dorothy and the children spent whole summers there, washing bodies and clothes in the stream and sometimes not washing at all.

In term-time Dorothy was still Eric's history student at Birkbeck, so I went to Gatws without her. I bought an old Ford delivery van and after work, winter and summer, I would scoop Habie and Ben out of their beds, tuck them up in the van and drive to Wales. We would arrive at 3am, light the fire, take a walk on moonlit slopes, and go to bed.

Home life in our leafy no-man's-land between Hampstead and Golders Green was enriched by the presence, in the other half of our semi-detached house, of Sigmund and Muriel Nissell. Siggie was the second violin, and unofficial manager, of the Amadeus string quartet, the foremost ensemble in Europe. When the quartet met for rehearsals in their ground floor living room I would squat outside, just out of sight below the window, to imbibe the heavenly sound and gain insight from the musical problems and arguments that arose.

The Nissels, with their children Daniel and Clare, were genial and hospitable neighbours. We went to their parties and on July 20, 1969, we sat with them before their TV for hours, waiting for the moment when Neil Armstrong in his clumsy spacesuit would grope his way down the steps to become the first man on the moon.

Now my family was in crisis: Ben was seriously ill and Dorothy was heavily pregnant. In hot weather Ben, aged four, had become so listless that we took him to the doctor who noticed bruises forming instantly wherever he was touched. He had the rare and alarming blood disease called *thrombocytopenia ideopatica*. Blood clots are formed that can result in massive bleeding; the treatment is by steroid injections which may or may not work.

For five weeks Ben was in his ward at the Royal Free Hospital in Hampstead, pale and thin but not in pain, surrounded by toys. When a visitor asked him what he would do when he grew up, he replied casually that he wouldn't be growing up because he was going to die.

Dorothy went into the Wimpole Street maternity clinic and after work I shuttled between the two hospitals bearing flowers for Dorothy and toys for Ben. I was so tired that while waiting for her contractions to start I stretched out on the next bed and slept. It was August 14, 1969. I was awake when Tanya emerged, as beautiful as her sisters and brother even though she caused a moment of anxiety because she was born with her umbilical cord wrapped round her neck. Soon Ben recovered, with no ill effects.

From Nigeria old friends came to visit, to criticise my editorials, to chat, to commiserate on my deportation. Allison Ayida and Ahmed Yoda, permanent secretaries in two of the ministries, and Godfrey Eneli, another top official, came to dinner. We admired these brilliant civil servants who had kept this vast country from falling apart, managing a smooth transition when Ironsi was murdered and replaced in a counter-coup by a young northerner, Colonel Yakubu Gowon. We felt that these men had saved Nigeria.

Dinner talk over *hors d'oeuvre* and main course wafted back and forth about the tragi-comic scandals of the Nigeria we all loved. And then the dessert. Eneli said: 'Walter, since you left we've had no decent reporting. You know the place. Why don't you come and see for yourself?'

'Don't be daft, Godfrey, you know I'm *persona non grata.*'

'Oh no, that isn't a problem. We've fixed all that for you.'

Next morning I told Alistair that I was free to go back to Nigeria which was on the brink of disintegration, probably civil war and I needed to go. He agreed at once. I aimed to visit all the regions, including the east which had started calling itself Biafra.

Since Biafra had become the rogue state, inviting its Ibos home from other parts of the federation in apparent preparation for secession, I needed to make contact with the rebel regime of Colonel Ojukwu. Luckily Chinua Achebe, Nigeria's best-known novelist, an old friend, was in London as Ojukwu's roving emissary. Chinua had dinner at our house the night before I left. He was delighted that I was coming to Biafra, which desperately needed friends. There were no postal or telephone links with Biafra, so I made him promise, as soon as he got back, to alert Ojukwu's officials that I was coming, and arrange a meeting with the rebel leader.

17 June 1967 Ikoyi Hotel, Lagos

Darling... Lagos is terribly the same. They are planning a war but don't quite know how to set about it, which is to their credit... Within four hours of arrival I'd been to a party with the Akinyeles, a top-drawer Yoruba affair in which nobody offered me a drink, had an hour's chat chez lui with Anthony Enahoro (who is now

142

Infomation and Labour Minister) and was downing beer at the Cuban Embassy with Wole while being entertained by Malian strip dancers. I stay here until Thursday, then go North for a week and then come back here before seeking 'oriental' pastures new. No-one knows what will happen but something must.

Guardian: 26 June 1967

Lagos – 'The war starts on Monday morning.' That is the weekend whisper in Ambassadors' parlours and the Island Club, where non-information flows even more freely than Star beer.

Anyway as I write it is still, in the frugal cablese of a veteran colleague, 'unballoon.' If it has not gone up by the time you read this, you can be sure a new date will be going the rounds.

Meanwhile, there is a Shakespearean leisure about the oft-postponed war between the Federal Government and its breakaway Region. The slowly massing federal army publicly and deliberately takes up its position opposite the known camps of the enemy. The sober, bearded, histrionic Colonel Ojukwu talks to visiting journalists in measured prose, while, in the opposing camp, the youthful, idealistic General Gowon confers far into the night with his hawks and doves.

Yet the crisis matters to people. The departure of Ibos has left uncanny gaps everywhere, like that of the Jews from Europe. Now that the Ibos have gone, physically and politically, and the survival of Nigeria is threatened, many people have woken up and thought of themselves as Nigerians for the first time.

I wrote to Dorothy from Lagos airport on my way to Benin, in the midwest, from where I took a bus to the ferry to take me across the Niger into the new Biafra. 'Kisses to the kids. I do hope I can return next week.' As I wrote I did not know that the balloon had gone up.

I crossed the river on the old sixpenny ferry into Biafra. At the police post I offered my passport, the officer looked up at me, back to the passport, and reached for his telephone. He talked in Ibo. He told me to wait. I waited for seven hours. I was not alone. I was in a teeming underworld of detainees. Next to me was a girl of about 12 whose father has been killed in the northern massacres, her sisters raped and murdered.

They told me my 'case' needed to be cleared in Enugu, the state capital, now the capital of Biafra. Suddenly I understood. Ibo police and officials in Lagos had fled here, into the safety of their new country. For them I was *non grata*, citizen of a hostile country, a man who must have been deported for a reason – no doubt plotting on behalf of murderous northerners.

At two in the morning the last ferry had come and the office could be closed. The superintendent drove me away, 70 miles to Enugu. He had been on duty for 30 hours. He fell asleep at the wheel twice but each time refused to let me drive. He was one of the least likeable people I had ever met. He confiscated the licence of a taxi driver merely for being in his way. But it was in my interest to keep up a lively conversation.

At Enugu headquarters I was again a suspect among many. Men, women, boys and girls were propped up against walls, looking as if they have been there for days and nights. I found a seat somewhere.

When nobody was looking I wandered into another room and found a telephone. I still had my old address book. None of my Enugu friends picked up the phone. Feeling like an outraged British taxpayer, I rang the British Deputy High Commission. They sounded beleaguered. They were. A federal relic in a 'country' Britain did not recognise, the Deputy High Commission was hostile territory, tolerated only for convenience. The Brits were unsympathetic. They said they were not surprised I was being held and would have warned me not to come to Biafra at such a time. I rang Ojukwu's headquarters at State House, hoping to reach Chinua. I was told Mr Achebe was still abroad. I couldn't think of anyone else to ask for.

My illicit calls were discovered. After a second night waiting, two detectives came up. 'All right, get your things, we are taking you to your High Commission.'

Dazed with lack of sleep, I didn't notice the route. We stopped before a flag. It wasn't the British one. Have the idiots taken me to the wrong embassy? The gates of Enugu prison opened and we drive beneath the brand new red and yellow flag of Biafra.

144

'I suppose I had better sign for the body,' drawled the prison superintendent. A blank scrap of paper was produced and everybody signed. The superintendent asked me my name: clearly there was neither a warrant nor a detention order. The detectives departed, my belongings were catalogued down to the last British postage stamp, and within minutes I was in my cell.

A night warder smelling of beer snarled through the bars: 'You are Gowon's men. The Hausas killed us before and now they are coming to kill us again. You British are helping them.' All night warders pass by muttering in Ibo what seemed to me sinister remarks accompanied by hollow-sounding laughter.

In the morning I heard the war had started and the battle was raging at Nsukka University. I feared, irrationally, that they would take me there and push me into the firing line as a captured mercenary. General Gowon's printed code of conduct to his troops urged restraint in victory – except towards mercenaries.

All the other inmates on my corridor were condemned murderers, yet there was a surprising amount of laughter and song, mainly hymns. We conversed along the corridor though we couldn't see one another. They talked continuously of their 'trouble' and urged me with some success to take mine philosophically.

A claustrophobic with a horror of low tunnels and cramped caves, I had always assumed that being locked in a cell four paces by five would turn my hair white. It didn't. Crisis and danger counteract phobia.

New arrivals all the time. It was the first week of the war: people were rounded up. All were thrashed.

I had the unique luxury of a cell to myself in the best corridor – death row. Even a bed. I appreciated this privacy when, on day four, the door burst open and they put a couple of highway robbers in with me. They stayed for three days.

After starting on African prison diet – cassava meal and watery, peppery soup eaten by paddling the fingers in it – I graduated to an Afro-European mix more to my taste than its equivalent in an English prison would have been. It was served on my cell floor in dainty, flowered china plates. The biggest luxury, shared only with

145

condemned murderers, was weak tea with every meal. I rejected the matching floral teacup in favour of the much bigger prison mug.

Washing water was brought to my cell. After five days the superintendent said I could request books from the prison library. I read Shakespeare which took me away from there. I thought that ordinary life with my family was paradise and wondered why I never appreciated it.

Two days after the books arrived they were taken away. The superintendent's superior, the deputy director of prisons, had disallowed them. He had no doubt been turned away from lodgings by colour-conscious London landladies. I spent hours plotting imaginary revenge.

Black thoughts. I was in a condemned cell, so would I be hanged? There were no gallows here in Enugu – only in Port Harcourt down on the coast. So, I reasoned, if they take me away, down the Onitsha road on which I came – a road I knew well from the old days – a right turn to Nsukka would mean they're taking me to the battlefront. A left turn, 20 miles further on, meant Port Harcourt and the gallows. I thought, for no reason, that it would be worse if they take me away at night.

On the eleventh night, at two in the morning, I was woken up by three men with double-barrelled shotguns at my cell door. They took me back to the reception room, collected my belongings, signed something and drove me away. I was so glad to be out that I felt no fear, only apprehension.

'Where are we going?'

'To headquarters.' They said nothing else. But we didn't go to the police station. We drove out of town. On the Onitsha road.

It was wartime and there were roadblocks. The men said: 'We are police officers with a prisoner. Open the gates.'

The Nsukka turning. We drove straight on. My mood lightened. The Port Harcourt turning. We drove straight on. I was daring to be optimistic. Were they really going to put me on the ferry across the Niger, back to freedom?

146

What got me out I still do not know. There had been questions about me in the House of Commons. Two editorials in the *Guardian* explained to Ojukwu why holding on to Schwarz would not be in his best interests. Dorothy had lobbied every Biafran she knew, laid siege to the Biafran delegation's office in Kensington. Wole came to the house to commiserate with her. Perhaps Chinua Achebe finally got back to Ojukwu's headquarters and said Schwarz was OK.

At Benin in the midwest region the British Deputy High Commission passed on the news of my release and put me in a hire-car to Lagos. In the car I typed my story for the *Guardian*. In Lagos I handed it in at the cable office.

> *Guardian:* 20 July 1967.
> Biafra, fighting for its life as Federal forces advance on two fronts, remembered to disgorge me from its vast underworld of suspects and detainees. My 13 days as an involuntary observer from below – 11 of them in an Enugu prison cell – ended as alarmingly as they had begun. At 2 o'clock in the morning.

Just after filing my story I was telephoned from London by the *Evening Standard* and I gave them an interview. That night at the cable office my telegram to the *Guardian* was so popular with the staff – everyone had to read it – that it didn't get transmitted for five hours, missing the *Guardian*'s deadline. So my prison story appeared in my old paper a day before it appeared in my new one.

Right and wrong about Biafra

The war dragged on for 30 months with the deaths of a million civilians, mainly by starvation under blockade, and 100,000 soldiers. Back in the leader writers' room, I was now more than ever the Biafra man – the war-stained veteran, the expert. Controversy mounted on the rights and wrongs of the war, with Harold Wilson's government arming the federal side and, later in the war, France supporting Biafra. I wrote analytical features on the war as well as leaders. Like most other newspapers we supported the federal government, which had strengthened its case by dividing Nigeria into 12 new states – thereby neutralising the traditional domination of the north which had been Biafra's grievance. And Biafra, predominantly Ibo, had the fatal weakness that the oil on which it proposed to live was in coastal areas peopled by non-Ibo minorities who didn't want to be Biafrans.

Guardian: 16 August 1967 (leader)

If we must now back one side, the federal one is the right choice. Now that the North is split, Northern domination looms much less large than before. True, 12 million Biafrans would be alright on their own. But what about the other 35 million Nigerians? Without a Federal Government, strong and rich enough to stay in control, what is now Nigeria would probably degenerate into decades of war and chaos. From that the whole of Africa would be the losers.

Meanwhile in London I was seeing friends old and new from both sides of the conflict. Chief Enahoro, now serving as the top federal propagandist, took me out to lunch and said: 'Walter, I want you to know that if you continue to support our case we will make it worth your while. I can arrange a substantial monthly payment.' I, like a young virgin after her first encounter with a predatory male, rushed into Alistair's office and told him all. He was unimpressed; he told me to forget it.

Biafra's propagandists were after me too. Frederick Forsyth had been a BBC reporter in Nigeria's eastern region, had not distinguished himself as an objective journalist and, when the Region became Biafra, he had become one of Colonel Ojukwu's propagandists. In a pub near Regents Park Freddy took me through the Biafran arguments, which of course I knew already. I felt sorry for him – a failed journalist – and as I left I asked in a patronising way what he was up to these days. He said he was writing a novel. Oh yes (still patronising), what about? 'It's about some people trying to kill De Gaulle.' I wished him luck. Like everybody else I loved *The Day of the Jackal*, the film even more.

Freddy Forsyth didn't sway me but Kenneth Dike did. West Africa's foremost historian, a former vice-chancellor of Ibadan University, he had broken new ground in telling the African story as Africans experienced it, not the European colonialists. Over several lunches and suppers (we were friends from the old days)

Ken, an Ibo, finally convinced me that after holding out for a year against all odds despite appalling suffering, Biafra had won the right to its independence.

Once again I went to see Alistair. I said the time had come to change our line: the Biafrans had held out for a whole year longer than anyone had expected; we should urge the British Government to stop arming Lagos and recognise Biafra, as France and other countries had done. Alistair gave me that same penetrating look that he had given me in my interview for a job. At last he said I was right and invited me to write our first pro-Biafra leader.

> *Guardian:* 13 January 1968
>
> Biafra's continued resistance against overwhelming military, economic and political odds has been a surprise not only to General Gowon; it has confounded most of the experts... How can the war be stopped? The only effective pressure can come from those who supply the arms to keep it going... British interest has always been in stability so that commerce may flourish and oil may flow. The prospects for that now seem worse if the war drags on than if an autonomous Biafra is allowed to exist.

> *Guardian:* 3 June 1968
>
> British policy has been based on wrong premises and Mr Wilson must find the strength to change it. It is no argument that other countries will continue to supply Lagos with arms. In the face of growing sympathy with Biafra in Africa, the Russians would probably also stop, as the Czechs have already done. Once the Federal Government feels compelled to seek a genuinely negotiated solution, it will not be difficult to find one.

A braver protest against the federal war machine had been made by Wole Soyinka when he tried to prevent the war with one-man shuttle-diplomacy. Accused of aiding the secessionists, Wole was arrested by the federal government and spent the entire war in prison. His book *The Man Died,* describing his imprisonment, was banned in Nigeria. It was deeply ironic that one of Nigeria's foremost patriots was locked up in the war which, in the end, cemented the country's unity.

The *Guardian*'s new pro-Biafra line offended not only the Wilson government but also the majority of Africa experts, including my friend Colin Legum, the doyen of them all. Colin, an emotional man, was furious with me and after demolishing my arguments over the phone did not speak to me again until the war was over.

The *Guardian* and I were wrong to support Biafra; Colin and the other Africa experts were right. I had switched sides because Biafra had held out longer than anyone had expected amid appalling loss of life and starvation. I had not understood that Biafra's long stand owed more to the incompetence of the front-line federal officers than to Biafra's iron will. Apart from Dorothy's polo club friends I had never known any Nigerian officers.

As it turned out Nigeria, with its new multi-state structure, was a viable and promising federation in which the war had generated a new patriotism. Biafra on the other hand was never a realistic proposition. The oil on which it pinned its hopes did not lie in the Ibo heartland but in coastal areas inhabited by non-Ibos who opposed secession – a reality that had been obscured in the fog of war. I apologised to Colin. I ought to have apologised to Alistair but the truth dawned slowly: there was no single appropriate moment. Newspapers move day by day from one agenda to another; we were now preoccupied with the Soviets, Vietnam and Ireland. Biafra had passed into history.

Tired of leader-writing, I wanted to go abroad and be a foreign correspondent – a real one this time, on the staff of a newspaper. Neither the *Guardian* nor the *Observer* had a staffer in Israel and I began negotiations for me to go, shared by the two papers. Finally it was agreed. Poor Dorothy had just graduated with distinction at Birkbeck and had won a much sought-after fellowship at the Institute of Education. This was her chance to become a qualified teacher for life. She decided instead to come with me to Israel. I went ahead to establish a base for us.

Chapter six:
Trying to be objective in Jerusalem

American Colony Hotel, Jerusalem

11 April 1970

Darling one,

Shabbat Shalom. It's lovely to be here, in fact so exciting I've hardly slept for two nights. Israelis are much nicer than I remembered them: perhaps they have mellowed as well as me in twelve years. Less strident, more sophisticated, friendlier and more sociable than people in Europe.

As you may have seen in the paper, I decided to skip the days of grace and plunge straight in. Been here four days so far: two *Guardian* stories, a CBC circuit lined up for tomorrow, and an *Observer* Foreign News Service piece going off tonight.

This is a dream hotel, on the Arab side of town, all flowers and lawns and cool courtyards and thick stone walls and humus for breakfast, lunch and dinner. At £2.15 B&B I can afford to stay here indefinitely, and they have a dream two-room suite overlooking a flowered garden which we could move into temporarily if we have not found a flat...

You're going to find the place so stimulating and beautiful that I doubt if you'll mind deferring your course to be here. As for me, I'm in terrific spirits; hadn't realised how much I missed being a proper journalist again, with every day a challenge. This is the favourite journalists' hotel, and the toughest and most seasoned colleagues here keep me in my place.

I had come back here at a high point in Israeli morale. Three years after the Six-Day war had unified Jerusalem under Israel's flag and added the West Bank, the Gaza Strip, and the Golan Heights to the territory it controlled, the Israelis were relaxed and confident. Three years later the Yom Kippur war was to begin a series of reverses.

I, too, was pleased with myself. No longer a freelancer, I was staff correspondent covering a country that was never out of the news for more than 48 hours, familiar to me yet with a new character, a deeply controversial story that challenged my objectivity in every piece I filed.

Whose side was I on? Officials in Israel's foreign ministry and press office wanted to know and feared the worst. While researching Israeli Arabs for my book 12 years earlier I was known for having Arab friends, and had attracted attention. I was reminded of this by an official who was friendly enough to add that I was suspect in another way: a Jew writing for Britain's two main bleeding-heart newspapers is in danger of leaning over backwards.

I thought of myself as impartial. Like most other correspondents who had no particular axe to grind, I was blown this way and that by events. Israel gets under your skin.

> 13 April 1970
> Darling... Remember Freddie Chassnick, the genial Austria-born photographer with two cute little boys? One of them, aged 20, was killed at the Suez Canal two days ago. I've just been to the funeral at the military cemetery on Mount Herzl. I was alone at the back of the crowd and cried. It's not going to be easy being an objective journalist round here. One goes around being earnest and impartial and wonders why people freeze up on you. I think I got my answer today.

The exception among us impartial correspondents was the BBC's Mike Elkins, who told the Israeli story day by day in heroic tones as if the Six-Day-War were still on. We disapproved of Mike, but with his high-level Israeli contacts he kept us all in awe.

Stories with an anti-Israel tone were usually about the Israelis 'creating facts' by building Jewish settlements on Arab lands, often disguising this as a military necessity. But criticising Israel is easy because whatever you want to say has already been said, better than you can say it, by Israeli dissidents.

> *Guardian:* 11 April 1970
> Israelis protest at Premier Meir's house
> Walter Schwarz, Jerusalem
> More than 100 critics of Prime Minister's Golda Meir's policies towards the Arabs demonstrated at her home in West Jerusalem

152

today. Eight got into her garden and were arrested; three others were taken to hospital after clashing with the police.

The protest... was organised by the Israeli New Left... to condemn last week's decision to settle 250 Jewish families near the Tomb of the Patriarch at Hebron. Another target was the refusal of the Israeli Government to allow Dr Nahum Goldman, President of the Word Jewish Congress, to visit Cairo. 'Goldman to Paris. Golda to an old peoples home', proclaimed a banner seized by army reservists.

I drove to Hebron to see for myself.

Guardian: 25 April 1970

Israel seals off sacred site.

Eight hundred sun-baked acres, rocky but softened and humanised by terraced vineyards, villas and olive groves, have apparently been included in Israel's policy of 'creating facts' in the occupied West Bank area. The area is the north-west extremity of Hebron, and the Mayor has been told that from next Wednesday it will be closed off 'for military purposes.' Among these, he assumes, will eventually be the construction of houses for the 250 Israeli families which the Cabinet has decided to allow to settle in Hebron.

A Ministry of Defence spokesman said he could not confirm or deny the Mayor's suspicion. The 'main' purpose was to create 'a military presence to secure the security of Jewish access to Hebron from Jerusalem in the north and Beersheva in the west.'

Security and settlement have scarcely been separate since the first settlement in Israel in 1911. The new 'fact' promises to be the most controversial since the annexation of East Jerusalem.

I dictated my stories over the telephone to the *Guardian* copy-takers – a skilful, long-suffering, idiosyncratic breed. It was not uncommon for them, when a piece was long, to interrupt in a querulous tone with: 'Is there much more of this?' And of course they got things wrong. I dictated a long feature about Israeli plans for the future of Jerusalem in which I referred three times to Israel's 'creating facts'. Each time this appeared in the paper as 'creating flats'. It did not matter much because that is what the Israelis were doing.

The American Colony Hotel was a good base for being objective. Owned by foreigners, it was, and still is, a place where Jews and Arabs comfortably meet, a haunt for foreign correspondents, high-ranking officials of the United Nations, diplomats and, no doubt, spies.

Dorothy arrived with Ben, aged six, and Tanya, aged one, while Habie stayed with her grandparents in London to finish her school term. For six weeks the four of us lived in our garden flat at the hotel. When I wasn't on a story we drove down to the Dead Sea, visited my relatives, Emil and Erica Shomroni, in Rehovot, or went househunting. Dorothy was on the lookout for horses.

Dorothy, now an experienced traveller, had a relaxed, African-style regime for the children, in which they looked after themselves and each other. They were often barefoot, incurring the disapproval of Israelis who are conventional and don't often mind their own business.

'Your child isn't wearing shoes,' a woman on the street informs me.

'Oh that's all right,' I say. 'I've got plenty more children at home.'

At dinner in the hotel dining room the children would sit up with us as long as they wanted, then Ben would drag baby Tanya up the wide stone steps to their bedroom. Sometimes Ben found his sister too heavy because she was asleep, gave up and left her on a stair. Other diners were horrified. Over many years our rule was that as long as the children didn't bother us – after dark was grown-up time – they could stay up as long as they liked, often until they collapsed in a heap and were eventually picked up and put to bed.

Our nonchalance did not trouble the owner-manager, Horatio Vester, a member of the hotel's American founding family. He and his English wife, Val, became our friends and remained so long after we left the hotel. In our next home we held fortnightly Shakespeare readings in which the Vesters were stars, a man from the British Council came up from Tel Aviv, Israeli friends joined in and the children banged drums and blew trumpets at (mostly) the appropriate moments. Twenty-five years later Val, a widow of 86, came to my retirement party.

We found a small house with a garden for rent on the windswept slopes where Jerusalem ends in a cul-de-sac and Bethlehem begins. With two Arab horses we could explore the Judean Desert, with the Moab hills and a blue sliver of the Dead Sea in the far background. We could look across another slope towards Tsur Baka, the epitome of an Arab village, draped round a hilltop with a slim mosque at the summit. Every day the Tsur Baka shepherd brought his flock across the border that had been obliterated by the Six Day War, to graze on vacant lots. The sheep came nibbling right into our staid suburb of Arnona, to the quiet displeasure of housewives who complained about the smell, but really about its lowering the tone.

Next to us on the ridge was Kibbutz Ramat Rachel: a quick canter through its neat apple orchards and we looked down from United Nations Hill to the twin domes of Aksa and Omar; at night from our house we could see the square, classical outlines of the Israeli Knesset, floodlit.

The kibbutz welcomed Habie and Ben into its school and our horses into a vacant cowshed. They changed Habie's name to Aviva and both kids were speaking Hebrew in three months, imbibing kibbutz values which we admired.

From Arab friends Dorothy had acquired two spirited Arab mares, Sherkiya and Yohara. Sherkiya had a problem: as a young foal she had been shackled by her right back leg, which had become sore, so now she would kick viciously if anyone tried to touch the fetlock. She made no exception for the vet or for the blacksmith: the only way Sherkiya could be shod was for the vet to give her a total anaesthetic.

The operation was performed on our landlady's well-groomed lawn surrounded by her beloved flowerbeds which we had been instructed to water and weed. Afterwards Dorothy had to go out, leaving me alone with the unconscious mare. I was telephoning a story to the *Guardian* when I heard the sound of stamping horse's hooves. Through the window I saw Sherkiya, awake, staggering round and round the lawn and the flowerbeds. I told the copytaker: 'Sorry we have to have a break: there's a horse running round the garden.' It took an hour to calm Sherkiya and resume my dictation. It took weeks for the garden to recover.

A month later, left in sole charge of Sherkiya again, I was bringing her half a bucketful of oats in her stable when suddenly, for no reason, I was sure that she would let me pick up her fetlock. I was right. Sherkiya's problem was solved. Dorothy taught me to ride, making me go round in circles at the trot to improve my seat. She said feeling secure on a calm horse ambling down a track was not enough. At last I was comfortable in the saddle and thought I could ride.

But alas, Sherkyia had another problem. In her early life she had been under-nourished, and had come to us in a state of unnatural calm. Now, after many half-buckets of oats over several weeks, I took her for a long ride through orchards and orange groves, sampling fruit from the trees, enjoying the views up towards the hills and down towards the sea, visiting villages and settlements. We turned for home and I put the mare into a canter. But that was not fast enough for the new Sherkyia, homeward bound. Her canter became a gallop and I could not stop her. We streaked across two roads with traffic.

Home at last, I suffered Dorothy's amusement and with a new humility I resumed my training in her improvised manege in our sloping field.

In a bunker on the Canal
I make my life sound leisurely and luxurious but two days rarely passed without news, attacks, counter-attacks, controversies, peace plans, war plans.

Israel still held Egypt's Sinai Peninsula which it had captured in the Six Day War and its troops were dug in along the Suez Canal with the Egyptians entrenched on the other bank and sending over shells every day, killing an average of five Israeli soldiers a month. Tension was heightened by the presence of Soviet airmen flying Egyptian fighters overhead.

from Walter Schwarz, Kantara

As I arrived they were loading someone onto a helicopter with nasty shrapnel wounds on his head and chest. But if you stay alert, move smartly, do as you're told and never stick your head over the top, you will probably survive on the Canal front. My escorting officer, who had slept all the way from Jerusalem in the back of my car, opened an eye in what is left of Kantara and suggested: take it fast along here, they can see this bit of road from the other side.

The position itself is well bunkered up so if you don't stick your head over the top the Egyptians cannot see you any more than you can see them. The bunkers feel cosy even to a chronic claustrophobic like myself. The low arched roof, the narrowness, the hum of generators, the crackle of radios and the unheroic camaraderie all help to make it feel like a submarine, except that people keep coming in and out. I wanted to stay the night, but the commander disallowed it because my car was out in the open. His concern was not for the car, he said, but if it was hit it would become a torch for a couple of hours.

Through a telescope hidden among sandbags you can see across the lazy water to their part of ruined Kantara and their heaps of sandbags. They too keep their heads down and nothing is seen to move. How do the Israelis, famed for their mobility and modernity, stand the tedium of trench warfare as static and old-fashioned as the Western Front in 1916? They are too busy for boredom. The Egyptians help in this by making sure that no day is like another in what comes across the water. Not that there is much to do except building up mounds of sandbags, improving bunkers, changing guards. It is part of the Israeli way of doing things to rush around being busy.

A lieutenant in his first fortnight at the front said he found it exhilarating and his face showed that he meant it. He is a *kibbutznik* – the Israeli version of the 'boy from a good home' who is reckoned to make the better soldier, anywhere. Living uncomfortably and unpredictably has always been part of the kibbutz ethos.

The doctor, a reservist who holds court in a bunker of his own, said morale was incomparably higher than when he did his service in 1954. He had come here armed with psychology on how to deal with trench depression. 'When I try to use it the boys laugh at me.' Nobody has to stay for long out here at a stretch, and these men are pampered with the best food, drink, film shows and lectures the Army has to offer. In a debate held while the commander was out (he does not approve of 'politics' in his bunker) there was total agreement that the line was being held not for the defence of Sinai but of Israel. There was also agreement that there would be another war. The only argument was whether it would be a local war or a world war.

We moved to a small farmhouse at Beit Zait, a semi-collective community (*moshav*) in the Jezreel valley West of Jerusalem. The owners wanted to spend a year or two abroad.

Beit Zait was prosperous, relaxed and friendly. Habie found the village school hospitable; classes started each day with singing the teacher's favourite folk or love song: after that an hour of Bible study. The school organised village fêtes and celebrations, with costumes hand-made by parents. Ben at his school got into a naughty set and was often not seen at home until bedtime. Three-year-old Tanya, though she was more serious and rarely smiled, told us she loved her first nursery school where the teachers were experts at starting small kids off with Hebrew.

Our new home had stabling in a disused chicken shed, plenty of village-grown fodder and wonderful rides in the hills across the farms, right up to the outskirts of Jerusalem.

I installed a telephone in a garden shed which became my office, where I could dictate articles to the dreaded copy-takers. All dispatches from Israel had to be passed by the censor, but in an unspoken understanding I was tolerated as a correspondent who knew the rules: the censor was only concerned with military matters, stories about Israeli Arabs and about Jewish immigration – and even these could usually be cleared over the phone.

In the world of horses Dorothy had met Vivian Dinitz, whose young daughter Tamar was a keen rider and the whole family enjoyed lazy Sabbath-day lunches in our garden. This was lucky for me because Simcha Dinitz was director-general of the prime minister's office and one of Golda Meir's advisors. Simcha trusted me and gave me off-the-record briefings in his office – so meaty that I could write with authority during the various crises that arose, about the government's attitude to the Russians, the Americans, the Egyptians and everyone else.

On those days I knew I had the best job in the world. The prime minister's office was at our end of Jerusalem, just up the road. In the morning I ride round the orange groves. After lunch, drive the 20 minutes to Simcha's office, get briefed, come home, write my exclusive inside story and dictate it before supper. I felt I could afford to look down on ordinary mortals who hung around the government press office waiting for official handouts. The feeling was irrational of course, because there were surely other privileged correspondents, especially American ones.

We still had Arab friends, some left over from when I was writing *The Arabs in Israel*, and some new ones. The closest was Atallah Mansour, a refugee in 1948 who had returned to his home in Nazareth, learnt Hebrew and become the first Arab to join the staff of *Haaretz*, Israel's serious, liberal daily newspaper. Atallah and Evelyn were often our companions in Jerusalem and Nazareth; in a crisis Atallah would help me give an objective account by translating Arab broadcasts and treating me to his own mix of scepticism and sympathy for both sides. As a Christian Arab with a sense of humour he could see the flaws in every camp and helped me enjoy the funny side of Israelis and Arabs. Atallah was brave and, against the odds, optimistic.

Please Daddy, read us some Bible

Letter from Jerusalem

Guardian: 27 March 1972.

'Please, daddy, read us some bible – please?' is not what many seven-year-old boys ask. Ben does, although he has had no religion from me. Nine-year old Habie joins in the pleading. Living in Israel gives our family a sense of our ancestry.

Much of the credit goes to the *New English Bible*, which leaves out neither the gruesome bits nor the sexy bits and tells the story in plain English. For pace (if you skip the genealogies and

159

prescriptions for offerings), suspense and gore it beats most things on the children's bookshelves.

Living near Jerusalem helps too. Where Rachel died at the side of the road is three miles from Arnona, our first home here, which was next to kibbutz Ramat Rahel. We looked down at the Dead Sea from the top of the 'hill country' which Joshua conquered so ruthlessly.

Beersheba ('not Beersheba, daddy – beer-sheva') is not an outlandish name: the kids go to a Hebrew school and know it means Seven Wells. It's the big dusty, makeshift town we pass through on our way to Eilat. We stop there for falafel (meat cakes wrapped in flat Arab bread). Jericho we pass on our way down for a swim and a picnic at the Dead Sea: we stop there for oranges sweeter than the Israeli ones. At Hebron we buy the slender blue vases and goblets made by the famous glass blowers, and the unrivalled grapes.

The old language is as alive as the old places. 'Do not call me Naomi, call me Mara.' The kids explain that Naomi means sweet and Mara means bitter. 'Don't say Reuben, daddy – Re-uven.' Of course they got it dinned into them at school. At Manchester Grammar School 'scripture' lessons were a time for larking about. Here scripture is told as a true, local story, still unfinished.

Not just the kids: there is no people like the Israelis for living in the past. The finals of the annual Bible quiz are broadcast live and have as high a rating as a Cup Final. General Dayan caused much embarrassment in New York when he declared that Hebron was as much his home as Tel Aviv. He was being undiplomatic as usual, for he was taken to imply expansionism. But Dayan is neither a 'religious' Israeli nor an expansionist. He meant it quite literally: Jews should be allowed to live in Hebron as they used to, close to the tomb of Abraham, Isaac, and Jacob and their wives, Sarah, Rivka, and Leah. The Arab mayor of occupied Hebron, Sheikh Ja'aberi, said he agreed with Dayan: he didn't see a problem about having Jews living in Hebron again.

Horsing around Israel

'You remind me of the pioneer days,' said an Israeli. He was in a jeep, I on a horse, and we had met on a track that meanders down from the Jerusalem hills to the Tel Aviv plain. He sounded wistful. That is why I remember him – because he was untypical. You have to go round Israel on a horse to find out just how far it has travelled from its pioneer days. I had a practical purpose: Rebecca had to be taken home from Jerusalem to her owner near Tel Aviv but she had refused to enter a horsebox. So I took three days on a trip you can do in an hour and a half by car.

'We used to keep horses and ride down the hill to the Dead Sea,' said a member of Ramat Rahel kibbutz. 'But we got rid of them.'

'Why?' The answering shrug was deeply Israeli. 'Because we don't need them.'

Collective settlements were the last precarious strongholds of the horse. At Afikim, near the Sea of Galilee, one of the oldest and richest of the *kibbutzim*, 11 horses survived in the shadow of the plywood factory, fed after a fashion by an old man who loved them. He begged for scraps from the communal kitchen and stole bits and pieces from the cowsheds. It happened that Rebecca had been reared at Afikim. I now understood why she ate potato peel with such relish.

Riding for three days with only what can be tied to a saddle, one finds out about the hospitality of a land. The modern Israeli villager turned out to be as unforthcoming to strangers as farmers are anywhere. I stopped a housewife on her way from the village supermarket to ask where I might find water for my horse. She replied in the interrogative Jewish manner: 'Do I have a bucket?' Sometimes I was moved on like a medieval vagabond.

Kibbutzim are different. Like monasteries they are equipped for hospitality. There is always a vacant hut belonging to someone who is away on a course, visiting a dying mother in Yugoslavia, or serving with the reserves. Ride into a kibbutz and ask the first man you see if you and your horse can stay the night. Never beat about the bush with Israelis. He will explain that he has to check with the secretary but you know it will be all right. The room is found and you eat with everyone else in the dining room. No charge.

Rebecca's owner was an immigrant from England. He ran a posh English-style riding school near Tel Aviv. Exit grandfather's work horse; enter the riding-pony of the affluent society.

161

Many of our Israeli friends were either *kibbitzniks,* former *kibbutzniks,* wistful would-be *kibbutzniks* or failed *kibbutzniks* with the fierce hostility of renegades. What had happened to the *kibbutzim?* The *Observer* wanted to know so I spent three weeks visiting a score of settlements from tiny to enormous, from idealistic to materialistic, from poor to affluent. There were 225 *kibbutzim* and more were being established at frontier posts and strategic points in the occupied territories.

Kibbutzniks in the early days were pioneer farmers and brave guardians of Israel's perilous borders. Many had become affluent, running factories, employing cheap Arab labour. Veteran settlements by the Sea of Galilee had replaced their corrugated iron shacks and now looked on weekdays like sedate garden suburbs, on the Sabbath like genteel country clubs. Driving into Dagania or Kinneret, you passed through avenues of tall fir trees. A giant sawmill and plywood factory overshadow the entrance to Afikim; you have to park your car here because only bicycles are allowed among the pampered lawns and flower beds where the members live.

Was Afikim still a kibbutz? Astonishingly it was. It still gave to each according to his needs, whether he ran the factory, minded the chickens or was too old to do either. Most *kibbutzim* still reared and educated their children in common, owned no property, ate their main meals together and took decisions by the direct democracy of the weekly general meeting.

Of course *kibbutzniks* worried that affluence may have stifled the idealism of the founders. The communal children's house had disappeared in 24 settlements where the children were now brought up at home. And the brave frontier mystique of the original outposts had been overtaken in an Israel that depended for its security on Phantom jets. Perhaps the deepest transformation was that austerity had ceased to be an ideal in a consumer society.

Hijack

The phone rings. It's the *Guardian* foreign desk. 'How long will it take you to get to Tel Aviv airport?' Only forty minutes, because I live just off the Tel Aviv road and the airport is on the near side of town. 'There seems to be a hijack.'

Three Arab guerrillas of the Black September group, one of them reported to be a woman, had hijacked a Belgian Boeing 707 to Tel Aviv and were threatening to blow it up with its 90 passengers and crew unless 100 Arab guerrillas in Israeli prisons were freed before dawn. The airport was sealed off. General Dayan and other ministers could be seen in a huddle on the tarmac. The radio said Mrs Meir had summoned the rest of the cabinet for an emergency meeting.

I drove round the perimeter to where I could see the Boeing and sat in my car all night, twiddling the knobs on my radio to stay informed and to pass the time. Searching idly up and down the FM frequencies I was astonished to find myself listening to the conversation between the hijackers and the control tower. A tense male voice from the aircraft – the captain's – was imposing a deadline of 5.30am for the arrival of the released prisoners. A cooler voice from the control tower promised to pass the message on to the highest authorities. The Israelis were playing for time.

An hour later the hijackers were asking for the plane to be refuelled for a flight to Cairo. Then I heard the Israeli strategy unfolding: they agreed to refuel the aircraft and promised that a favourable decision about the prisoners was 'imminent'.

After another hour they told the hijackers: 'There is a problem on your plane. The two rear wheels are damaged and a tyre is flat.' The Israelis, aware that the crew of a Boeing 707 cannot see out of the back, had crept up, deflated the tyres and drained the undercarriage's hydraulic fluid. This put the hijackers at so big a disadvantage that in their negotiations with General Dayan and his colleagues the question of liberating 103 prisoners got pushed into the background.

21.35: Captain Levy: 'They are asking for fuel and I am in control of the flight. It is our only alternative. I am quite serious, our only alternative is to leave here. Otherwise I am quite sure the plane will be exploded.'

22.00 Control: 'We will have an answer in a few minutes' time.'

163

23.00 Control: 'We are definitely positive that you cannot take off with the situation of the aircraft as it is now. Please let the gentlemen know that we are prepared for any other arrangement to be made for the freeing of the prisoners. I am waiting for your answer'.

23.30 Captain Levy: 'The tyres are flat and we have no hydraulic fluid. If the repairs are not carried out in time they will blow up the plane.'

02.00 Control: 'I would suggest that you talk over with your gentlemen again. We are going to send a technical crew to the aircraft. There will be tractors and quite a number of people – between seven and ten.'

02.45 Control: 'The working party is being grouped to come to the aircraft.'

After another hour eight 'mechanics' arrived in bulging white overalls, carrying hydraulic equipment and a spare wheel. Once in position the commandos brought out their weapons and stormed the plane. Two male hijackers were killed, two passengers and two wives of Arab prisoners who had accompanied the hijackers were injured.

Back in the airport building, in the confusion after the rescue, amid shouts, laughter and tears of relief, someone shouted that I was wanted on the telephone. It was the BBC, live. There was such pandemonium that I could not hear a word. I dived under a table, clutching the telephone, and a live interview with The World at One went ahead, with me screaming: 'Speak up – I can't hear you.'

An interview that failed

General Moshe Dayan, Minister of Defence, hero of the Six Day War, often mentioned and quoted in my despatches, was the most glamorous of Israelis with his eye patch and outspokenness and quiet, earthy humour. I was granted an interview. But it was a disaster. It happened like this.

Dorothy and I were children of the swinging sixties and many friends smoked hash: so did Dorothy but I was not interested, quite satisfied with beer and wine. On the day of the Dayan interview I came home in mid-afternoon to change. Dorothy was entertaining friends, drinking tea and eating homemade cakes: two trays of cookies with nuts and raisins looking delicious. I sat down with them for a few minutes and ate a cake. Being a greedy person, I then had three more. Nobody had told me they were hash cakes.

I arrived at Dayan's office stoned for the first and only time in my life. I remember nothing about the interview except that it was brief, that I was laughing the whole time, that no article appeared in the *Guardian*, that I was still laughing when I got home and, I am told, laughed all night.

Not always so objective

I have claimed earlier that my reporting from Israel was objective. As a middle-of-the-road liberal I tended to support the mild-mannered government of Golda Meir and her mundane and un-aggressive defence minister. But on one occasion I was not objective. I am ashamed to this day about my interview with a member of Menachem Begin's *Gahal* party, the extreme nationalist, expansionist heirs of the *Herut* party whose members were later to form the *Likud* alliance which brought Menahem Begin to power in 1977.

In my time, Golda Meir's and Dayan's time, such views were extremist. I was shocked and sickened by what I heard: the steely xenophobia and cool conviction that Israel must include all its biblical lands, that the Palestinians were not a nation and should be driven out, to be forcibly absorbed into other Arab countries.

These views were so distasteful, so unlikely ever to be put into practice, so likely to disgust *Guardian* readers, that I scrapped the interview. That was worse than pro-Israel bias: it was an error of political judgment, because some of these attitudes were later to become government policy. As I write now, Begin is dead and his successor, Ariel Sharon, is in the third year of a coma. But Begin's political heirs are still in office, and views I found so outlandish have become mainstream. I could have sounded an early warning.

Israel right or Israel wrong? The answer is as elusive now, as I write, as it was in the 1970s, and indeed ever since the birth of Israel in 1948. I am pro-Israel because of the Holocaust, because of the Israeli narrative of re-possessing their (our) ancient homeland from which Arabs (conveniently) fled in the 1948 war. I am pro-Israel because of my Israeli relatives and friends who try to forgive my long friendships with local Arabs.

Today, after the building of Israel's 'security' wall which locks Arabs into ghettos, after the blitz on Gaza's captive, helpless population, after the return to office of the pro-expansionist Binjamin Netanyahu, after the inhumane blockade of Gaza, I am afraid for Israel's future. When urged to take risks for peace Israelis traditionally retort that it's all right for people living safely abroad (like me): if they ever take the wrong risk Israel would cease to exist. But in the long run there is no safety in creeping expansionism and refusal to come to terms with Palestinian nationalism, which will always be backed by wider Arab nationalism and, beyond that, outrage and militancy in the rest of the world.

Like other pro-Israelis I did not see the Palestinians as a 'real' nation, believing the Israeli narrative that in 1948 the refugees had fled because Arab governments had told them to, promising a return in triumph after Israel's anticipated annihilation. I learnt better from Benny Morris, the Israeli historian who showed in his book '1948' that ethnic cleansing was an integral part of the Israeli war effort, that many Arabs were chased out, their villages demolished so that they could never return, while some, perhaps many, were killed on the spot. I understand, belatedly, that the Palestinians are indeed a nation, not less so because powerful empires – the Turks, the British, and now the Israelis backed by the Americans – have prevented them from having an independent state of their own.

I hope, somewhat desperately, that international opinion and American pressure can find a way of coaxing, pressurising and perhaps ultimately forcing Israel to abandon its expansionism, overcome its chronic paranoia and pursue peace based on compromise. The odds are unfavourable and nobody can rule out a catastrophic end.

Chapter seven:
War correspondent

We were still living in Israel when the *Guardian* wanted me to be a war correspondent. Together with Harold Jackson I was to cover India's campaign for the liberation of East Pakistan, now to be called Bangladesh, a war in which 200,000 people were killed, nine million became refugees, many thousands of Bangladeshi women were raped and millions were left hungry. Every dimension of this epic conflict was beyond my experience, beyond my imagination. But first I had to get to the war.

21 December 1971

Walter Schwarz in Bombay

The battle we saw was our own against Indian bureaucracy, which shuddered and bent under the strain but never broke. At the front, history was being made hour by hour, but in Delhi our accreditation papers had first to be processed in duplicate. Some people got through by perseverance and luck to places like Sylhet where Gurkhas slipped into the Pakistani trenches in the night, threw away their rifles and got to work with their kukris. In the dark the correspondents saw a Pakistani brigadier with his surrender written out on the back of an envelope trying to find someone to give it to.

Between us and the officials it was the younger photographers, especially the French and the Italians, desperate to get their action shots, who caused most trouble. 'They don't want us to see what is happening out there, that's what it is,' shouted a French television man at the Hilli sector. He looked all of 22 and he was white with anger. 'They're butchering one another and they don't want us to photograph it.'

Of course the French and Italians had nothing of India in their cultural heritage. They would shout and bang on tables, then plead and grovel and finally they would make a dash for it towards the shooting - without the proper authority! We British applied cultural perspective, used tact, flattery, and even veiled threats of giving the war a bad press if we were not allowed to see it. Neither approach made the slightest difference. The truth, I suspect, was that the brigadier, a man of old-world military courtesy, finally lost patience and had the lot of us cleared off his battlefield.

Transformations from luxury to discomfort were chastening to the soul. At the Great Eastern Hotel, Calcutta, white-haired old room bearers loiter outside your door waiting to be rung for, and three waiters hover over the succulent curries on your table. Then it's two days with no food at all, sleeping on tabletops without blankets, trekking endlessly, Dante in Inferno, in search of ever-receding gunfire…

An Indian major said in Dacca: 'What beats me is how they expect us to hold on to this place, when they got hold of women and (he lowered his voice) rogered them and then killed them.' The vocabulary of this war belongs to 1940. Air force types, straight from Biggin Hill, talk of good shows and bad, and taking a 'shufti' at things. One of the army's intelligence chiefs is called Clarence Proudfoot.

How can India, mired in poverty, afford to go to war? The same way as it goes on existing, too big and too amorphous to really feel anything until it is all over. Even those nine million refugees, which was what the war was all about, are no more than the population increase in a single year.

At last I got to see the war, and I found the Indian officers determined to do it like gentlemen.

Guardian: 15 December 1971
Up the line to glory
Two Pakistani captains were captured in the assault on Hilli this weekend. One shot himself with his own automatic rifle. The other sat drinking and chatting with his captors in the officers' mess until 2am next morning.

The dead captain 'must have been depressed because they have had a very rough time and fought very hard,' said Brigadier Farhet Bhatti. 'You see, we are really the same people. We're trying hard for a quick finish so that we don't have to kill them.'

We were sitting, late at night, over rum and hot water at the brigadier's forward HQ, which had just been set up in a deserted Pakistani police post. It was the day after the big Indian

168

breakthrough at Hilli and we were thirty miles inside Bangladesh. The front line was receding rapidly to the south east, towards Bogra, the Bramaputra river, and Dacca. No-one fired during the night, but soon after dawn today field guns opened up from Brigade HQ at a couple of tanks which, in spite of all the odds, were still making a stand.

The brigadier twirled his ample moustache between sips of punch and recalled sadly that he and the brigadier he was fighting against – Atta Mahommed Malik – had been at military academy together, at Terradhon near New Delhi, 26 years ago.

The breakthrough at Hilli has been crucial. This seedy railway town was a natural salient into enemy territory from which the Indians threatened to cut East Pakistan in half. That is why the Pakistanis defended it so heavily and held out grimly for a whole week... For both sides, all roads now lead to Dacca...

'How hard it was you can tell by the casualties,' said a major, being indiscreet because casualties aren't mentioned much. He thought one Pakistani battalion had been 'virtually wiped out' in the assault and another 'very badly cut up...'

How many Indians died at Dangbara? The colonel who had led the assault would only say: 'we were attacking. They were very well dug in, so you can draw your own conclusions.' Last night Hindus among the Indian dead were still being burned on pyres of logs...

That the opposing sides had been 'the same people' had been a ludicrous over-simplification. What the brigadier had in mind was not the people but the Army officers who are fighting an orthodox, methodical war with few extraneous factors to make the old text books obsolete.

The Pakistanis fought at Hilli until they were outflanked and almost encircled. When they decided to leave they lost no time. They left no vehicles, except four light American tanks which had been hit or bogged down in the damp corners of the rice fields. But they did leave their ammunition and its quantity showed they had prepared for a much longer stand...

The Indians are moving their infantry first, using their Russian PT26 and the bigger T55 at long range for fire support against well dug in positions...'We clear mines with people and not until someone loses a leg or a jeep gets blown up do we know where they are,' said a Colonel...

Before breakfast this morning the Brigadier and most of his staff had already moved forward and as I drove back to Hilli column after column of fresh troops were coming up through the gap.

The Israel-Arab theatre is too small for orthodox warfare, while India-Pakistan is much too big... On the eastern front all the military aces are in India's hand but the colossal distances involved give the campaigns an eighteenth-century air of immobility, even when everything moves as fast as possible. And there is an old-fashioned feeling of remoteness in forward areas...

For me, three days with the Indian troops was long enough to be impressed. As one might expect at the front, there is no euphoria – that seems to be the preserve of briefing officers and high officials in Delhi. Discipline is smooth and relaxed. Orders are given in soft voices and received without obsequiousness.

I saw hundreds of jeeps, trucks and mobile guns moving over the rutted tracks – with not a single broken-down vehicle. Men on foot moved in correctly spaced-out single file, carrying spades and pickaxes as well as their arms and heavy bedding packs. In new positions they dig themselves in swiftly, fanning out in all-round defence, even when there is no known danger of counter-attack. Everything goes according to the book.

The officers are a delight to listen to. At Hilli base camp a Sikh Brigadier, tall and fleshy, emerges from his jeep, benignly swinging a swagger stick, a blazing scarlet sash on his green turban. Further forward all badges of rank and unit flashes are removed, as the book says they should be. Shouting across the static, officers talk to each other in English, to the men in the appropriate Indian language.

There is no doubt the Indians are welcome in Bangladesh. The brown-skinned, diminutive Bengalis filter out from their tiny villages, waving and smiling at passing vehicles... The Brigadier told me that the villagers had volunteered to find ways through the minefields during the assault.

Passing through Delhi on my way back from the front, I had a mission of my own: to see if I and the family would like our next posting to be India, where the *Guardian* had no staff correspondent. We felt we had been in Israel long enough: I was writing the same story over and over. I wrote to Dorothy that the world of horses looked even more promising in Delhi than in Jerusalem, that our family life would be exotic and comfortable, and that for me, covering the whole subcontinent, including Pakistan and the brand new Bangladesh, would be the biggest challenge yet.

Chapter eight:
Trying to be optimistic in India

'Well now, let's see, there's a riot in Bihar. Worth a quick trip?'

'Perhaps. But floods in Bangladesh could be more dramatic.'

'But then, Bhutto's in trouble again: might do something drastic at any moment. Could drive up to 'Pindi and have a look. Good chance to take the car out of India and renew its customs licence.'

'Well, yes, but going out of town would mean missing the foreign ministry briefing – it seems they might have something to say for once.'

This is the morning conference in my 'office' – the little spare bedroom of our flat in New Delhi. Nobody is here except me. I am talking to myself. I have too many possibilities: I can hop on an airplane to anywhere on the subcontinent – Pakistan, Bangladesh, Sri-Lanka – or I can stay in town all week. I can't consult the foreign editor because it's 4am in London and anyway it takes four hours for a call to get through to London and by that time my line is likely to be down. My route to a commonsense solution is talking to people with common sense, even if I have to dream them up.

Unreality was a constant feature of our life in India which was luxurious, adventurous, amusing and exotic while my reporting was mostly about droughts, riots, floods, famines, failed reforms, targets not achieved, people rioting, people in prison. In the street outside our garden flat in the affluent Rattendon Road a huge drainage pipe lay for some weeks, waiting to be installed underground. Every night a family of eight settled down to sleep in it. Tanya, aged four, asked why we couldn't invite the people in to sleep on our dining room floor. We never gave her an adequate reply. In India you need every hour to change your perspective on human life.

India is a fragrant land where women adorn their already bright saris with flowers, streets smell of jasmine and saffron, people offer garlands to Lord Krishna and to their pot-bellied politicians and throw marigolds to each other during festivals. But you will walk on beaches strewn with excrement because they serve as communal toilets. No land offers starker contrasts at every corner between beauty and squalor, opulence and destitution, subtle dignity and abject servility. If there is a valid generalisation about all Indian castes and classes it is they share a gentleness in manners, a softness in speech, an alertness to other people. Not only their history but also their national character enables them to operate the largest democracy in the world.

We had rented the ground floor in the home of the Sikh writer Patwant Singh. Habie in her diary remembers it as a

> stunning home – space, light, a garden in which you could swim during the monsoon just by going out onto the lawn and laughing yourself silly, parrots flying over lovely plants, snake charmers coming to the house and spreading snakes all over the lawn which literally danced for us. Magical things happened – Venu the bearer taking me on his bike at 6.45am to the riding school, where I'd mount my beautiful pony Onyx. After every ride at the military-run school, you had to pat your pony's neck three times as the instructor chanted, 'Make Machaorsiz, One One Two!' it took me a year to realise he was saying, 'Make much of your horses, one, one-two.'

I had driven out to India through Greece, Turkey, Iran and Afghanistan, over the Khyber Pass into Pakistan. This was common sense. Importing a car in the conventional way would have incurred import duty equal to the value of the car, and the only Indian car on the market was the rattling monstrosity they called Ambassador. My new tax-free Peugeot estate car was allowed in for six months on a tourist document. So I loaded it with what seemed to me essential including a kitchen cooker, and revisited much of the route to Turkey I had taken with Dorothy and Tio 20 years earlier. Some roads were better. Dorothy was too pregnant for this trip so I went alone.

I drove up the hippy trail through Kabul, where I stayed for a few days to write a piece that the *Guardian* called 'Cop-out up the

Khyber.' 70,000 'travellers' a year were passing through Kabul, sleeping six to a room at the Peace Hotel, the 'Holiday Inn', Sigi's, or in courtyards.

Guardian: 21 July 1972

They look alike, in unwashed jeans, long Afghan shirts, carrying shoulder bags or rucksacks. They all patronise the same hotels at around 10p a bed or camp out at 5p. Underneath their disguise most are not freaks at all. It would need a modern Chaucer to describe, and chronicle the adventures of this annual pilgrimage to the East. Their route is well-established: hitchhiking to Istanbul, then, when hitchhiking gets too hard, by bus and train to Ankara, Teheran, Herat, Kabul, and beyond.

Most of the travellers are students seeing the world. 'You can really live in this place for a dollar a day,' said a nice American boy who only smokes hash to be sociable. He was with a nice girl and their worst adventure was in a remote railway station in Turkey, 'where the people seemed to decide they were going to take our girls from us.' He was too modest to tell what happened next, but the girl indicated that he had been a hero.

Some are compulsive travellers who have been on the road for years. These include fugitives on fake passports and philosophers. An American with two girls in tow, one British, said he had spent two years in the bush in East Africa, indulging his passion for living on wild fruit. 'Boy, I never felt better.'

Then there are solid middle-class citizens, mostly Germans, taking a few months off to let their hair down and give up washing for a while. They travel in beat-up Volkswagens, giving themselves away by their expensive camping gear.

At the 'freaks clinic' Floyd McLung, a seven-foot, bearded American, was handing out tetramycin tablets for tummy troubles and bandages for sore feet and stab wounds. His clinic and the adjoining 'tea house' dispensed free tea and spiritual advice ('please do not smoke hashish here') and McLung also offered the 'house of peace' (his own home) for anyone interested in becoming a Christian.

Having brought my car into India as a tourist on a six-month permit, I have to drive it out periodically across the border into

Pakistan. The five-hour drive up the Grand Trunk Road through Amritsar is famous for its ambling cows, jaywalkers and sudden crowds at prayer or celebration. I stop for tea and spicy samosas at roadside snack stalls but I never try the 'English wine' that is advertised on shop fronts (what is it, fake whisky?)

Crossing the border back into India, I am often chatted up by young men who hang about asking for news and gossip from the other side – obviously baby spies learning their trade. I don't know if it is legal to keep re-importing my tourist's car and never dare ask: I just hold my breath every time. Once the Sikh customs man shook his turbaned head and said ominously: 'I know what you are doing,' but waved me through all the same.

Indira Gandhi and her ministers and officials were in excellent spirits after their army's brilliant victory over Pakistan. But under the surface their gigantic country, never free from a famine here, a flood there, a riot somewhere else, was as impossible to govern as it was for me to adequately cover.

The Indian newspapers helped – such a treat after Israel where everything was in Hebrew except the blandly loyal *Jerusalem Post*. Each morning the *Times of India*, the *Hindustan Times*, the *Indian Express* from Bombay and the *Statesman* from Calcutta were delivered to my door, all written in mellifluous, sometimes a little archaic, English. This luxury stopped me learning Hindi which I soon regretted and still regret. Hindi is easier than Hebrew; had I learnt this *lingua franca* of northern India, which is understood in much of Pakistan too, I would have written richer pieces and enjoyed my travels even more.

I started in an upbeat, positive mood, wanting to write about development projects that worked. I took my optimism to Rajastan's 'green revolution' – the Chambal Valley irrigation scheme where all the planning errors of the past were to be corrected. The land was being drained and scattered holdings consolidated into viable units under the dedicated management of a British agricultural engineer, a German project manager from FAO and an Indian civil servant. The first model farms were already under cultivation and 157 more farmers had signed on for the package deal. The change was 'spectacular,' I reported.

> 22 January 1973
> Fanatics of the green revolution
> Driving across the region, with newly irrigated land on only one side of the track, is like seeing a film with half the screen in technicolour. They were growing the 'new' wheat. The new dam had brought in electricity and the nearby town had a boom atmosphere. I had to reach the village of Bichri by bullock cart, but found it clean, freshly painted in white, the children well-fed, new strands of wheat. The man installing the irrigation pipes, Mahresh Narain, told me: 'These people are like a god to me, giving them water is like a prayer.'

So could this green patch in Rajastan look forward to a bumper harvest? Unfortunately not. There was a national shortage of fertiliser: state-run factories had not produced their quotas because of strikes and power cuts, the state of Rajastan was getting only half its requirement, the Kota region only a fifth. 'Perhaps next year, or the year after,' I concluded ruefully, 'there will be neither a drought nor a fertiliser shortage and this part of India will have won its food battle.'

But the battle was not won. I was sucked away from the faltering green revolution by a succession of disasters. Whatever the government planned, something always spoilt it. If not droughts, floods or riots, it could be inflation which caused famine. India suffered badly from the sudden rise in oil prices after Israel's Yom Kippur War of 1973, which made food unaffordable for the poor because the official ration system broke down. Market prices went up faster than the level of government subsidies. Now it made sense for a farmer to hold onto his grain, or to send it off in trucks that bribe their way through interstate road blocks to where the stuff would fetch prices commensurate with the soaring cost of fertiliser and diesel fuel.

I can still feel the nausea in my stomach as I watched a group of emaciated women, with children too hungry to cry, finally reaching the front of a queue at the relief centre and being turned away because they did not have a card issued by the village headman. Thousands had already died in the Cooch Behar district of West Bengal. I saw plenty of food on sale in the market but people had no money to buy even the meagre ration, at subsidised prices, of 1lb of rice or wheat a week per head.

Observer: 13 October 1974
They die of hunger within sight of food
Walter Schwarz
Cooch Behar – Starvation is spreading with the geometrical progression of a plague in this district and three others in the State of West Bengal. There is rice to be bought in the market, within sight of people dying of hunger. They cannot afford to buy even the meagre ration at subsidised prices of 1lb of rice a week per head.

In the ex-princely state of Cooch Behar, now a district with 1,500,000 people, at the most conservative estimate, more than 1,000 have starved to death in the last two months... People have become so weak that hundreds more are now dying every day in the four districts of Cooch Behar, Bankura, Purulia and Jalpaiguri...

Everywhere there are people, especially small children and old people, so emaciated that they could scarcely survive even if substantial relief were expected in the coming weeks. But no relief is in sight and next month, when cold weather is added to hunger, the death toll in this state will inevitably run into several thousands.

The immediate cause of the famine – the worst since the great Bengal Famine of 1943 – is not outright lack of food, but that the poor have no money to buy it. The West Bengal government had no funds for more than token relief, while the central Government in New Delhi has not yet accorded the situation any special priority...

As I drove into Punibari village, my car nearly ran over a corpse on the highway. The man's naked body, with an empty begging bowl by its side, might have come out of Belsen...

The headman of this village of 14,000 people said he knew of 80 who had starved to death in the last two months. He said hundreds would die in the coming fortnight. Like many other officials, he was resigned rather than angry, though he said the volunteers who hand out the free gruel supplies got 70 paise (about 4p) a head a day but spent only 30 paise... The free gruel is a watery mixture of broken wheat mixed with bran and pulses, without spice. Only people with cards issued by the village authorities can get even this.

Those without cards are forcibly turned away and leave, moaning or weeping, to die. Across the road from a distribution van I saw a man collapse on the roadway, motionless except for the tongue working in and out... People are roaming about everywhere, looking for wives, husbands and children.

The basic failure of the State government is that it did not procure enough rice for distribution. Out of a million tons that came onto the market this year it planned to purchase only half – and in the event it managed to buy only 160,000 tons, leaving the rest to find its way to the inflated open market. The deficit should have been made up from the central Government's pool, but there is famine in Assam, Orissa, Maharashtra and other States too.

No relief is in sight. When the winter rice crop comes in there seems no prospect of the indolent and corrupt State government procuring more for its distribution system. And next spring's wheat crop in the surplus states of the 'green revolution' is expected to suffer badly from the shortage of fertilisers and power for irrigation pumps. Foreign relief experts say next year's famine may be more severe than this year's because of the world-wide grain shortage.

Many thousands of children and old people could be saved by a massive foreign relief operation, like that mounted in the 1968 flood here or in the 1970 influx of refugees from Bangladesh. Powdered milk on a massive scale, and clothes and blankets for the winter, would be obvious measures.

The *Observer* led the paper with my story which concluded that many thousands of children and old people could be saved by a massive relief operation 'but Cooch Bihar has not yet attracted world attention.' The foreign editor cabled me to say he had been overwhelmed by readers asking how and where to send help.

As I write now, India has been transformed by a technical and commercial revolution and a new middle class is prospering. Yet the poor are still hungry: the World Bank estimated in 2008 that one in three Indians – more than 450 million – still lived below the poverty line.

I had come from one woman prime minister to another. Golda Meir and Indira Gandhi were dispiritingly similar: both doughty patriots, rigid in ideology, neither interested in uttering quotable sayings. Mrs Gandhi's India did not prosper. Still locked into the socialist dogmas of her father, Nehru, her administration was bogged down in its labyrinthine officialdom which could not cope with the crises that overtook it.

She was ill at ease with journalists and in my only interview she stalled every political question. At the end, desperate for something to write, I asked what she did for relaxation. 'I need neither hobbies nor vacations because my work is my relaxation.'

Relaxed or not, things got worse and worse for her.

Guardian: 1 April 1974.

Inflation makes corruption too expensive

Like a cornered queen, Mrs Gandhi retreats, square by square, until she will have to strike out boldly, perhaps desperately, to survive. Rioting students, opposition parties jumping on the bandwagon, grain producers at home and oil producers abroad have all moved against her... India looks, as it often does, like a hungry land on the brink of revolution. The appearance is usually deceptive. Always stronger than its challengers, the system has always survived – with its unshakeable alliances between big business, big farmers and paternal politicians in Gandhi caps with pot bellies. Corruption is made tolerable by broad good intentions, a wide share-out of spoils, and, for some at least of the poor, slow and steady progress in spite of everything.

In the end Mrs Gandhi did strike out boldly, in the Emergency she imposed in 1975, but I had left India by then for Paris. I would have hated working under press restrictions.

My interview with Mrs Gandhi, scheduled long in advance, had me delay flying to Bangladesh to cover a catastrophic flood, although other Delhi-based correspondents had gone there. I received a telegram from the foreign editor that read: GREATEST INTEREST HERE BANGLADESH FLOODS. That was the nearest the dear,

179

gentlemanly *Guardian* ever got to telling me to get off my bottom. I took the next plane.

Five years without trial

Mary Tyler was grateful to me for writing about her when she was abandoned for five years without trial in Indian prisons after being arrested with her Indian husband, a Naxalite revolutionary. And I am grateful to her for introducing me to the perennial Indian nightmare in which thousands of men, women and children linger without trial and with no effective rights. A British citizen living in this limbo opened a door for me into the routine suffering of the locals.

> *Guardian:* 15 October 1973
>
> Jamshedpur – 'I have nothing against the prison staff – they only obey orders. My complaint is against the Government of India for keeping us locked up year after year without trial. It makes a mockery of their democracy.'
>
> This complaint was conveyed to me from the central gaol here this week by Mary Tyler, the 30-year-old British ex-schoolteacher who became a Naxalite (Maoist) revolutionary and has spent the past three years and five months in Indian prisons...
>
> She talked to me indirectly through Indian reporters because the local authorities had permission to allow only Indians in. The interview was held in a room just outside the prison, and there I was able to see her and be seen by her.
>
> 'If they made up their minds and gave us life sentences I could settle down and write books or something,' she said. 'But what they are doing is holding us indefinitely. This is against the spirit of Indian law which I fully respect...
>
> In her brief court appearances she has evaded photographers ('Do you think I'm a film star?') and taken every opportunity of drawing attention to the much worse fate of the Indian Naxalites and many others who are merely suspects, but still languish in gaol without trial.
>
> In her own case, her complaint about the law's delays is not entirely fair. She has been offered the chance of a relatively quick separate trial, with the implied prospect of deportation. However, she has refused to 'abandon' her Indian colleagues, who include

180

her husband, and fears that in a separate trial she might be obliged to incriminate them...

Mary Tyler is good-looking in an austere way. Her blonde hair is neatly tied in plaits behind, while in front, between the parting, she wears the vermillion marks of a Hindu wife. She wears black spectacles and a sari...

Under prison law Europeans are entitled to special food and clothes. But she has refused. At first she even refused such privileges as a toothbrush, but has lately relented and allowed British High Commission officials, who visit her occasionally, to buy her coffee and shampoo. Since she was moved from a much worse prison at Hazaribagh, she had put on more than 10lbs in weight...

Mary Tyler is the daughter of a former London dockworker who is now Port Superintendent at Tilbury. After graduating at King's College, London on a scholarship she taught at Willesden High School.

She met Amalendu Sen in a chance meeting on a train in Germany – and found they shared the same views. She travelled overland to India and married Sen in Calcutta.

According to the prosecution, she and 51 others were arrested in a jungle at the triple border between Bihar, West Bengal and Orissa, in possession of hand grenades, sticks of dynamite, picric acid, carbines, rifles and sten guns...

Talking to Indian reporters, Mary has stuck resolutely to her political views... The Naxalites are now divided and many are disillusioned – yet they are far from extinct. Across the West Bengal border in Bangladesh, hardly a week passes without a raid on a police post attributed to Naxalites.

Few students of the Indian scene regard the country as ripe for violent revolution, for all its discontents and frustrations... However, the tradition of revolt is long and honourable in both parts of Bengal and Mary Tyler is probably right in her prediction that 'a new wave' will come. Meanwhile, the fate of the thousands of failed revolutionaries in Indian gaols gets little publicity in India or abroad. In this respect the appearance in their midst of a blonde and eminently serious Englishwoman has come as a godsend.

Civil rights researchers estimated that there were 32,000 political prisoners in India – 20,000 of them in West Bengal alone. Only a small minority were detained under emergency laws designed for them. Most were charged with specific crimes ranging from theft to conspiracy or murder, and are listed as 'under-trials' (a huge army of people come under this).

An association for the protection of democratic rights was run by a retired eye specialist in his former waiting room. Dr A K Bhose's new 'patients' were young men who had been warned that they may be picked up at any time, and distraught or despairing relatives of people 'inside' – often held without trial for years.

The Indian press – perhaps the freest and most professional in any developing country – devoted a lot of space to the democratic niceties of parliamentary procedures but did not write much about political prisoners. This was partly because so many political prisoners were suspected Naxalite rebels who were no longer news. The press, rich in fine writing, was poor in investigative reporting.

After patient efforts by British diplomats and other well-wishers – and three pieces from me – Mary Tyler's plight was finally noticed by Mrs Gandhi; charges against her were withdrawn, she was released and deported. She has told her story with characteristic modesty, compassion and idealism in her moving memoir, *My Years in an Indian Prison* (Gollancz 1977).

Covering Pakistan was convenient because of that car I had to drive out at least every six months. But mostly the crises came suddenly and I had to fly. If the six months were nearly up (I now confess this for the first time) I was not above telling the foreign editor that things were quiet in India but getting really interesting in Pakistan.

But then again, things in Pakistan are never quiet. In losing its eastern provinces, now called Bangladesh, the country had lost its *raison d'etre* as the home of the subcontinent's Muslims. The new president, Zulfikar Ali Bhutto, told the nation: 'We have to pick up the pieces, very small pieces, but we will make a new Pakistan, a prosperous and progressive Pakistan.'

I admired Bhutto, wrote well of him while also quoting his enemies in full. He was ruthless, never at home with democracy, but he seemed to me to be playing a difficult hand with dexterity. Sometimes at my hotel in Rawalpindi I would suddenly get a call to be at State House in an hour to see him. He offered me whisky and was affable and persuasive.

Guardian: December 2, 1974.

Quiet death of democracy.

Pakistan's experiment in parliamentary democracy is being quietly abandoned and in candid moments Bhutto admits that it has failed. When I asked him about it last week, tactfully recalling that democracy was hardly flourishing in India and Bangladesh these days, he said he pinned his hopes on economic progress to satisfy people's wants.

It was a depressing answer because its tone was paternalistic and reactionary. Mr Bhutto's temperamental impatience with opposition is undoubtedly a major cause of the failure of the democratic experiment, yet up to now his system has held up very well. Pakistan even enjoyed an economic miracle after the loss of her eastern wing.

Back in Delhi the children flourished in our leafy suburb with their nanny and servants, horse rides, itinerant entertainers with snakes and monkeys and travellers from Rajastan selling dresses sparkling with mirrors.

Zoë Sarojini was born in the British High Commission's well-equipped clinic on 5 December 1972. She was as beautiful as her sisters and brother. Sarojini the nanny, Anthony the cook, Venu the bearer and all the rest of us called her *Babiji* (honoured baby). In the Lodhi Garden just behind our home, in the shade of the massive stone tomb of the Mogul Emperor Mohammed Shah, Babiji let go of my hand and took her first solo steps.

Habie went to English school, favoured by expatriates of many nations. Ben, disinclined to discipline, was deemed more suitable for the American school where he was free enough but learnt little. Dorothy spent much time at the polo club and the barracks where army grooms looked after her horse. A favourite companion was the Italian Ambassador who was a horseman of the top rank, though hardly better than some of the army officers.

Delhi friends

The BBC's Mark Tully and his family lived quite near us. Exuberant, enjoying India more than any other foreign correspondent, Mark was willing to share his knowledge, his contacts, and his enthusiasm. Mark thought of India, where he had been born and raised, as his home. That was hard for his wife Margaret and his children who, like the rest of us, thought of 'home' as England.

Our closest friends were Indian, especially Abu the cartoonist, an outwardly lugubrious guy like most cartoonists, and his beautiful and brilliant wife Sarojini and their little daughters Aysha and Janaki. In London Abu had been drawing cartoons for the *Observer* and the *Guardian* until he and Sarojini decided to go back to India where they felt they belonged. Their friends Sonny and Maggie Thomas and their children became our friends. Sonny was our family doctor too. He refused to take from us more than the minimal fee he charged local people.

Anthony cooked only Indian food for us. So did the cooks at the lavish and cosmopolitan dinner parties given by John Bissell, founder of the Fab-India clothing store and his wife Bim who was the lynchpin of expatriate social life. Also in our circle were Norman Reynolds who worked for the World Bank and his wife Pamela and their kids: we all took weekends up in the hill station at Manali.

Taking a rest from famines, floods and riots, I wanted to be in step with progress. So I went to cover the launch of India's first indigenous car, the Maruti, whose proud designer and maker was Mrs Gandhi's son Sanjay.

It looked like a cross between a small Morris, a small Fiat and a small Renault but Sanjay, who had been on a course at Rolls Royce, assured me it was unique.

Guardian: 3 November 1972

Mr Gandhi's motor

Nothing like the Maruti has ever happened in India where governments have always felt that motorcars are a wickedness that people ought not to want even if the country could afford them. There are only three shoddily produced, over-priced models made here under licence. The least unpopular is a lumbering version of a long forgotten Morris Oxford called the Ambassador.

Mr Gandhi is short, slightly built, unassuming but remarkably self-confident for 25. He was not put out when I sat in the display car, pressed the clutch pedal and felt it go limp as the linkage broke. 'You can't avoid that stiffness in a pre-production car and it's only the cable that went.' He gave quiet orders for repairs. From tomorrow the car will be safe on a revolving platform and nobody will be able to sit in it...

Eight years later Sanjay Gandhi was piloting a new aircraft of the Delhi Flying club, and while performing a loop over his own office, lost control, crashed and was killed.

My articles went by cable, at the mercy of unseen operators who punched the text onto tape. Those unassuming ill-paid people never let me down. An hour after filing my report on murderous riots in Bihar I braved the evening curfew to go back to the post office to make sure my cable had gone and that the sent text was tolerably accurate. The man behind the desk called out to the operator who emerged from his cramped and stifling workroom with the despatched text, word perfect, in his hand and said: 'Very fair, Mr Walter Schwarz, a very objective account. Thank you, sir.'

Driving South

In Delhi we had a charming, handsome driver. Satish's only fault was that he often reported this and that wrong with the car which I had never noticed but I always felt I ought to have fixed, at the price Satish quoted as minimal. For our holiday we decided to have Satish drive us down the length of India to Ootacamund, the famous hill station the British called Ooty, in the Nilgiris hills straddling Kerala and Tamilnadu – a 12-day round trip of 3,500 miles. Sonny Thomas had a house there and Abu's family lived in Trivandrum. We all planned to meet in both places.

The road was tarred all the way with plenty of filling stations and rest houses, but people living along it thought of it as a village lane. They slept on it, held wedding feasts on it, dried out their grain on it, drove their animals along and across it. Towns in Northern India looked as if they would have been pleasant fifty years earlier when the population suited their size. Ubiquitous family planning signs showed an insipid couple with two featureless children under the caption: Two is Enough. You could not move for children.

At a fork the road to Mysore branched right, but a man was painting a sign 'To Mysore' with an arrow pointing left. It was a beautiful arrow, bright red and ornate with a wiggly tail. People standing around confirmed that Mysore was to the right, but nobody told the man. He was old but his hand was steady, an artist. He knew the way to Mysore, of course, but arrows were not in his culture, except that they looked better pointing left. A little earlier we had come to a fork with sign which said 'To Bangalore,' and that arrow, also in red, also beautiful, pointed both ways at once.

Monkeys gambolled across the road with babies slung underneath. Spotted deer wandered about where the road passed through a game reserve and from time to time we squelched over a snake. An elephant and his boy driver were piling up logs by the roadside: the elephant worked systematically more or less on his own, while the boy, in gaudy bush shirt, sat on top listening to pop music on his transistor radio.

The south was statelier, the towns cleaner. Bangalore was splendidly laid out with parks and avenues and policemen who moved you on briskly – not yet the polluted, traffic-jammed nightmare it has since become. Then on through Mysore, all temples and palaces, and up hairpin bends to the uncannily English atmosphere of the Nilgiris hills where even the drizzle was British.

Two English ladies in macs and tweeds, each leading a well brushed Labrador, walked up the hill to Spencer's, bought Wensleydale cheese, some Rose's lime juice and a bar of Pears soap. They browsed a little in Higginbotham's bookshop before walking

186

back to Charing Cross. Could this be India? The resort of Ootacamund, the queen of British hill stations, used to be called Snooty Ooty. It hadn't changed much. The British had gone, except for a few retired colonels and tea planters, widows and sturdy old maids making do on their pensions – enough for a servant or two even if they can no longer afford the club, which was now half-empty. The toffs were Indian now: tycoons who had come up for the motor racing; the Maharajah of Baroda was up at his summer Palace. Ooty had not changed because its nature was not foreign to India. Golf, tombola and billiards, tweeds and sports coats, Labradors and rambler roses were as upper-class Indian as they used to be middle-class British.

Twelve miles down the road was Wellington Barracks, home of the Madras Regiment since well before independence. The regiment still bashed the same old squares, and in the officers mess I saw a proud new oil painting labelled *The Glorious Conquest of Seringapatan*, showing Indian soldiers in tartan kilts storming a rebellious castle on behalf of the East India Company in 1790. 'What we instil here is regimental pride,' the commandant, Colonel Bedi, told me. He said that in his opinion what the British gave to India was no longer British. 'It's all become universal, like the English language.'

I decided to take Ben, aged nine, for a holiday to Australia where we had friends. Ben was a bright, affectionate, naughty eight-year-old with a flair for music. He had learnt to play the recorder with enthusiasm and, lately, to be better at chess than his parents. In great excitement the two of us set off late in the evening for the airport.

But alas! The customs officer noticed that I had a tourist's car on my passport and would not let me out of India without it. I demanded to see the senior officer but even he would not let us go. We returned home at two in the morning. Unable to sleep we sat on the veranda playing chess until breakfast. He beat me as usual but I claimed he was distracting me by his bad habit, between moves, of standing on his head.

I was lucky to have been detained in Delhi because that day, September 7, 1972, India exploded its first nuclear device which it called Smiling Buddha. Bleary-eyed I concocted a late and somewhat inadequate news report that India had become the first developing country to join the 'big five' nuclear nations and that Mrs Gandhi said it was nothing to get excited about and was only for scientific purposes.

Three years in India was enough. Dorothy hoped that our luxurious lifestyle would make the children grow up self-confident, like old-style aristocrats. But I thought they were too over-privileged for the real world. We overheard Habie, aged 12, tell one of the servants to go to another room to fetch her handkerchief. We were driving in the countryside, had stopped for a picnic lunch and were immediately surrounded by wide-eyed children watching every mouthful. It was time to go.

Ben, Tanya, Habie, Zoe, captured by Abu

What next? When I told the *Guardian* I wanted to leave, they had nothing in mind for me except returning to the office and waiting for something to turn up. Could I do better on my own? Had my *Guardian* days come to a natural end?

At that point the foreign editor, Ian Wright, hearing that I was thinking of leaving the paper, suggested Paris. Out of the blue.

Chapter nine:

Paris, the dream posting

Paris! The city I had fallen in love with when I was 17. I dreamed then that I would be a journalist but never that I would be Paris correspondent of the *Guardian*, the newspaper my father revered.

Ian Wright, a sociable foreign editor who loved visiting his correspondents, had stayed with us in Israel and India, benevolently bemused by the more outlandish aspects of our lifestyle; he and Lydia had become family friends and have remained so. He told me many years later that sending me to Paris had been his idea, not the editor's. Alistair Hetherington was in his final days as editor: a staff election had been won by Peter Preston. I remembered Peter from my leader-writing days as the colleague with an awkward gait who came round the office every day intoning 'alms for the love of Allah!' – begging for scraps of gossip for the daily diary he had to write. Ian now recalls that he and Peter discussed my appointment at length: I got the job not for my fine prose or cultural eminence, but because I had a sounder record than two rivals for filing stories on time. In my second week in Paris I spent three days shadowing a communist candidate in his local election campaign and Peter, not normally outgoing, sent me a cable: 'A smashing start.'

Paris correspondents file three or four news stories and a feature or two a week about everything and anything from high politics to low scandal. We must cover France's recurring strikes and demonstrations, colourful corruption in the government and the police, murderous Corsican separatists, the rantings of histrionic and self-important 'new' philosophers, new trendy films, new books, new exhibitions, new museums. An election is always coming up nationally, locally or in an important city, and some 'intellectual' (a prestigious species which does not flourish in Britain) always has something outrageous to say.

190

We are tacitly expected to emphasise, subtly, the Frenchness of the French, their quirks from the latest food fads to the chronic discontents of winegrowers. *Vive la différence!* I tried to avoid the condescending cliché of calling everything 'Gallic' but the label slipped into my copy all the same.

And often we are on airplanes because foreign editors use Paris as a jumping-off point to places where there is an overnight crisis but no staff correspondent – an earthquake in Italy, Franco dying in Madrid, the Pope suddenly dead, possibly murdered, in Rome, a civil war in Tchad.

And of course the jaunts, the freebies. The King of Morocco invites us by private jet to his palace for dinner, to hear his latest pronouncement against the Polisario rebels in Western Sahara. When we arrive he is too busy to see us so we have two days in Rabat as his guests. President Houghpouet-Boigny of the Ivory Coast wants us to be his guests for as long as we like, living in luxury at Yamasukouri – the new capital he built at outrageous expense to flatter his glory. And UNESCO has its seat in Paris, offering free trips to China, Poland, Egypt...

In addition to all that I was soon to cover West Germany from my Paris base, a 'fireman' racing up the motorway from our conveniently placed home near Compiègne whenever there was a German crisis, a scandal, a peace demo or a terrorist outrage. Now I had to describe, with suitable tongue-in-cheek detachment, the very different quirks and idiosyncrasies of the West Germans.

Arriving from India I was struck by the triviality of 'news' in Europe. Back there: famine, floods, wars, rebellions. Over here: a dispute over the common agricultural policy, a scandal over a gift of diamonds from an African emperor to the French president, a strike by prostitutes.

I found France torpid, ill at ease, bored, mildly disgusted by Giscard d'Estaing's haughty presidential manner which barely concealed a reactionary, repressive and corrupt regime. Giscard thought of himself as a moderniser: he brought down the voting age of from 21 to 18, built the TGV express trains, projected France full-tilt into nuclear energy, introduced new-fangled computers to the telephone system (way ahead of Britain) and completed the futuristic Pompidou arts centre.

All that might have carried more conviction if the late seventies had not been a period of recession and soaring unemployment. Giscard and his coterie of remote and arrogant ministers had few solutions and did not appear to care. The right had been in power for 20 years. A French friend, a teacher in Compiègne where we lived, told me he had lost interest in politics because alternation of power had ceased to work and the regime had become more and more monarchical.

Six years later all this was swept away when the big moment arrived, my big story: Francois Mitterrand's election triumph on 8 May 1981. Our Compiègne friends sped down the motorway into Paris and we danced in the streets in the rain. France had woken up. This was a watershed more historic than the victory of New Labour in 1997 because Mitterrand not only ended the long decades of right-wing rule but brought in a coalition of socialists and communists: unprecedented and unpredictable.

> *Guardian:* 30 May 1981
> Mitterrand's adventure begins
> …This is the wind blowing through France, a heady rush of air. Nobody on the Left, or the Right, knows whether Socialist economics will work, whether Mr Mitterrand is serious about socialism (many of his supporters hope he isn't), whether the Communists will spoil the whole show…
>
> Young people are more optimistic, and that goes for the young at heart. Television and radio are less biased and less pompous. Policemen are not throwing their weight about quite as much… It is an adventure and everyone knows it can end badly, but almost everyone seems prepared to give it a chance.

Where should we live? Any dreams I may have had of a vibrant apartment in the Latin Quarter were scotched quickly by Dorothy who wanted to live in the country and breed horses. She had already bred Shahjahan in a field near our gatehouse cottage in Snowdonia. Shah, well-bred, good-natured but spirited, was to live with us for 29 years until his death, loving and loved by all the family. I gave way to Dorothy and was grateful because we had, for nearly ten years, a country life full of adventure and misadventure about which I wrote some of my best pieces.

We lived successively in three chateaux. Not because we were rich or snobbish, though we did like big houses, but because we needed a hectare or two of land for the horses. In France farms are sold without land; houses with land tend to be chateaux which can be surprisingly cheap. Mostly they aren't real chateaux, just imposing country houses we would call manor houses.

We saw an advertisement in the *International Herald Tribune* by a group describing themselves as 'creative people' who were jointly renting a chateau near Compiègne in which there was room for more tenants. English speakers were welcome. Horses, too, because the stables were empty. This group of five youngish males considered that Anglo-Saxons, especially with horses, would add class to their chateau.

The Chateau de Blincourt, as Dorothy later fictionalised it in a gruesome novella –

> ...floats above the wheat fields of Oise looking like a medieval castle but it was never real. It was built in the fake Gothic of the 1840s by Louis Philippe for a bastard son whose wife was pregnant. The hunting was superb but the wife died in childbirth and the royal bastard sold up and moved to Peru. His father had paid the architect at knockdown prices and the architect then screwed the carpenters. The lavatory seats were mahogany but the fresh pine shutters warped within a year. No-one ever founded a family beneath the Blincourt roof, uncaring owners let its fabric decay and it became a rented chateau, surrounded by 11 hectares of neglected park, fields of nettles, matted shrubberies, roses with thorned arms reaching upwards, choked by the mummified corpses of last season's weeds. An ivory-wreathed folly stands drunkenly aslant its atoll, its Greek statue long since toppled and smashed. The stables were early 19th century, with small cream tiles and six boxes lined with mahogany planks...

The real-life chateau and its estate were prettier than in Dorothy's satire, though both were indeed run down. The haughty and avaricious madame who was our landlady had cut down the old chestnut trees that lined the avenue, then refused to pay the contractor who left in a huff, leaving chestnut corpses lying about, unsightly but useful as jumps for the horses.

Ben showing off at Blincourt

Our co-tenants were dreamers, rebels against city life. Hervé, the leader, wanted to make films if only he had any money or any ideas. Marcel actually worked in films but dreamed of being a country gentleman and insisted on the grandest bedroom. Denis was a commercial traveller on *chomage* on the grand scale of those days, drawing a dole of 90 percent of former earnings for three years. We never discovered what Arne, from Sweden, did for a living. Dorothy suspected he was a pornographer.

Our share of the chateau was a stately bedroom, use of kitchen and living rooms, the stables and the groom's flat above the stables where we housed our four children: Habie (13), Ben (9), Tanya (7) and Zoë (2). The stables were magnificent but the cramped flat upstairs, thrown together by putting up a partition in the loft, was

194

built at a time when more money was spent on horses' accommodation than on grooms'.

The kids liked living apart from their parents up a spiral staircase. Nor would they be sleeping by themselves. Venu, our houseboy from Delhi, had come to better himself in Europe. We took him on as a general help while he learnt French and until he could strike out on his own (which he did: he became an embassy chauffeur and soon got married). Bringing over our Indian servant further increased our prestige with the aspiring artists who were snobs under the skin. In truth Venu had become more family friend than servant.

Richly accommodated in cream-tiled boxes below the children were Yanka, an elderly Lipizzaner, her colt Benjamin, Kismet (Anglo Arab) and Oriana, an Anglo-Arab brought over from North Wales with her colt Shah.

In that first golden summer at Blincourt everyone liked our charming and beautiful children and loved our horses: we have a picture of Marcel coaxing the little colt Benjamin up the terrace steps. We enjoyed this downmarket chateau life, the flowerbeds, the sophisticated food and wine, and our companions were never boring. But summer gave way to a winter of discontent and a spring of open dissent.

Our *chatelains* were excellent cooks but argued at length about who would go shopping, who would cook and how much people would pay. We had meals fit for gourmets – at nearly midnight by which time our children had gone to bed with bread and jam.

They adored our horses but objected to their dung. They opposed our fencing off a paddock because fences are anti-libertarian. They had elegant dogs they never trained and didn't always feed. They staged elaborate picnics with piped music on the lawn but never ventured outside the grounds. They were romantic and left wing but wouldn't let the farmers' children into the grounds to play. They installed flipper machines in the living room and a nightclub in the cellar.

The kitchen and other common rooms of the chateau were in a perpetual state of dirt and disrepair because these romantics could never agree among themselves how to share out the chores. I suggested in my British way that jobs could be listed and each man could put himself down for one. That's silly, they said, the first to arrive home from Paris would always choose the softest job. We were left cleaning the eight toilets and carrying out the rubbish ourselves until, in protest, we stopped. The rubbish remained, until there were 40 bags of it, crawling with worms.

French romantics can live indefinitely on ideas and visions. Horses yes, fences no. They wanted rural life but objected to our cock crowing at 4am. We objected to their drunken guests carousing all night. It was time to move.

The 16th century Chateau de Neuville-Ferrières, in the remote Normandy village of that name, was for sale, the price was low and, as a horse breeder, Dorothy qualified for a cheap loan from the Crédit Agricole. We did not buy the whole chateau – a portion was sold off to the mayor's son – but we had our own space at last.

Our semi-detached mansion of honey-coloured stone was beautiful in parts, spoiled in others by cheap renovation and brick walls covered in cement. The magnificent staircase curved like the one in *Gone with the Wind*: we never lived up to its grandeur but the kids loved sliding down the banister. The cellars could have stored three thousand bottles. Once again the stables were the best part: a range of solid 16th century outbuildings around a sweeping grassed courtyard. We owned a hectare of paddock, a mature vegetable garden, a reed-fringed pond and in addition Dorothy rented two adjacent fields of ten hectares for the current price: 100kg of butter – which worked out at £50 a year. Neufchatel-en-Bray is two hours by train from Paris, where I rented a tiny flat near the *Les Halles* market and I became a weekend commuter between two worlds.

Not one of the children in our village of 450 souls had been to Paris and many hadn't even been to Dieppe or Rouen. Old ladies with baskets of live rabbits and geese came up to the weekly market bringing fruit, mushrooms and the famous Neufchatel cheese made in their homes. It would take a modern Zola to describe these peasants' fanaticism about land and money. In winter before breakfast the children would stumble in darkness through our neighbour's yard to collect churns of fresh milk; he had a yard light but was too mean to switch it on.

We entered enthusiastically into the life of Neuville Ferrières, took part in village festivals giving the children rides on our horses, became friends with Monsieur Le Bas, the school inspector and council secretary who effectively ran the village. We grew vegetables, kept ducks around the pond and a pair of rabbits in a wire enclosure. But apart from M Le Bas we didn't get close to the villagers. In rural Normandy you are a stranger for a generation, even if you are French.

We were prone to mishaps. We bought a goat at the market which turned out to be dry, chewed through her rope and destroyed a neighbour's rose garden for which we paid compensation, after which she made do on our own vegetables. We laboured with pitchforks to make hay for the horses; it rained and rained and the hay was spoiled. We kept ducks around the pond; all their babies were eaten by water rats.

Determined to live the life and kill my ducks with my own hands, I asked with feigned nonchalance: how do you do it around here? (trying to imply that I knew how they do it elsewhere).

'We hang them'

'Hang them? Why?'

'Keeps the blood in.'

'How?'

With a shrug: 'Tie a rope round the neck and hang it of course. Your gatepost will do.'

I carried this out to the letter. The poor bird flapped its wings for ages and ages as its neck grew longer and longer and when it finally croaked it resembled a swan. We cooked inexpertly what we hoped was *canard rouennais*, the local speciality, but we wouldn't have enjoyed it even if we hadn't cooked away the blood that was the point of it all.

The rabbits soon had babies. One day we found that the babies had disappeared. We concluded that the rabbits were infanticides and we decided to eat them. Disillusioned with home slaughter, we

197

gave the animals to Mme Brillot, our cleaning lady, to kill and prepare them.

Mme Brillot had been gone a few minutes when Tanya ran indoors yelling: 'stop her, please stop her.' Tanya, precise child, had examined the wire enclosure properly. The doe had ignored our rickety rabbit hutch, dug a nice hole and kept her babies in it snug: they were about ten days old. We sent a child running to Mme Brillot's. Too late. We ate the rabbits out of a casserole with three children holding three baby rabbits on their laps, feeding them with fountain-pen fillers. Only one survived. Jacko became very tame. Playing on the table when he was five months old, he jumped off onto the stone floor and broke his neck. We never kept rabbits again. Tanya, decades later, is still a vegetarian.

We lived this rugged country life for two years. The children were made welcome in local schools and our neighbours were friendly enough on the surface. Tanya invited her best school-friend for tea; the invitation was accepted, Tanya waited under the weeping ash tree, her dolls and teddies seated on cushions, and waited, and waited. Her friend never came. We rang her mother who said she never allowed her children to visit strangers' houses. And that welcoming school of hers soon showed its limitations. Tanya had to write an essay on a visit to the moon and came home with all the imaginative bits crossed out in red pencil as 'irrelevant'.

One evening, at supper, a knocking at the front door. Four young men, about 18. Their spokesman, Antoine, said they were from Neufchatel, the nearby town, they had heard that we were cool and could they camp in our grounds? Instantly, without consulting the family, I said yes. Just what we needed to break out of our isolation. After four days it was clear that three of the youths were druggy layabouts but Antoine was the opposite: he lent a hand in everything, fixed what was broken, offered advice on gardening and cynical local wisdom, though he was a stranger from the provincial capital, Rouen. Antoine despised bourgeois niceties and the children grew to love him because he was a free spirit. He joined the family, moved with us to our next chateau where he lived in the gatehouse at the end of the avenue until we left France and then he often came to stay in England where he played much the same role. He became a skilled decorator, working only for people he liked and never paying taxes.

Dorothy's horse-breeding business was barely breaking even. I was lonely in my Paris flat and tired of the weekly train journey. Still, we persevered in Neuville-Ferrières – until trouble arrived. It was the night of the second round of the 1978 general election. Such nights are tense for a foreign correspondent who has only minutes after the result is announced to file his front-page story. I was in my Paris office, waiting by the telephone. I had a story ready in case the opposition won, another for a government win. I had arranged for a friend in Agence France Presse to telephone the result a minute or two before it was broadcast. At last, the telephone rang.

'Oui?'

But it was Dorothy.

'The house is on fire.'

'Call the fire brigade!' I slammed down the phone. The election result, a surprise win for the government against the union of the left, came two minutes later.

The stove had exploded, the kitchen was alight. The firemen insisted the whole family evacuate the house, though the children were in nightclothes on that cold March night. The whole village turned out to watch the spectacle. Not one of them invited the shivering children into their house. We decided that our Normandy days were over, we would sell out and move nearer to Paris.

Le Chateau de Vaugenlieu, near Compiègne, is an 18th Century hunting lodge, built on the cheap on top of a coal quarry by a prince for his mistress: a handsome L-shaped mansion behind a flower-lined avenue, with gardens, potager, a sturdy shed that could serve for stables, and a lodge by the gate. If you dig below six inches you strike coal.

We were only an hour from Paris so I could give up my town flat; I had a sofa in my Paris office where I could spend any night I pleased. The children settled in the fine village school, the local township school and the lycée at Compiègne.

Beyond our fences was a 1,000-hectare intensive goose farm which provided a background of noise and a smell, both of which one can get used to, but the goose farmer became a formidable foe. He had wanted to buy the chateau for himself and now wanted us out. He killed our cat as soon as it crossed into his field and killed its successor and three cats after that. He chopped down 25 trees on our side of the divide because they were in the way for a fence he was building. We sued, but he had the only competent lawyer in town so we lost. Everyone said: *que voulez-vous*, the man is rich. One day I found our current cat, alive and well, inside a wooden trap he'd set, baited with fish, right up against the boundary. I released the cat and took the trap to the gendarmes. They shrugged and said '*que voulez-vous*, this is country life.'

We got our revenge on M Demester. As well as geese he kept guinea fowl. One Sunday, when he was out, a flight of thirty birds flew over the wall. Ben had a shotgun. We shot the guinea fowl one by one – they were too stupid to take the hint and fly back home – hurriedly plucked them, stuffed them in the freezer and enjoyed them at leisure.

Here, in spite of the neighbour from hell, we were happy for five years until we left France. Making friends is easier in Oise than in upper Normandy. We met some, like the left-wing, world-weary psychiatrist Jean-Marie Artarit (who didn't think much of Mitterrand, even in those heady first days), and his wife Ghislaine, through the children (they were Habie's friends first). The eminent economist Professor Angus Maddison, whose little daughter Lizie was Zoë's friend, lived in our village. We met others through the horses, like the dashing Belgian baron Jimmy Snoy and his hospitable wife Marie-Noelle – whose elegant chateau was an hour's easy ride away. And then people I interviewed for my colour pieces – farmers, lawyers, village officials – sometimes appreciated my interest, invited us over for a meal and became friends.

Four children became five with the birth, on 30 June 1980, by caesarean section in the Compiègne hospital, of Zachary, a boy as bright and beautiful as his brother and sisters. For the first time I was not present at the birth: Zac arrived ten days late, by which time I had left for China on a UNESCO-funded freebie. Ben presided in my stead, with backup from Antoine, the godfather.

We were on the wrong side of Compiègne, not the posh southern side where the state forest is. So it was a five-hour ride for me – through the ancient forest along its long, straight tracks – when I took the mare Kismet to the stud farm to be coupled with one of their prize stallions. That was the best ride of my life apart from that one from Jerusalem to Tel Aviv.

Around our chateau were sugar-beet fields with wide tracks meant for tractors, ideal for riding. No fences or gates. How privileged we were, only an hour from Paris, riding our horses in any direction, in scenery sometimes so unspoiled that you could shoot a period film in it.

Family portrait as a mural by Michael Fitzjames on the chimney breast at Vaugenlieu: Ben, Walter, Dorothy, Habie, Tanya, Zoë.

From our Paris office

The *Guardian* had a room in the *International Herald Tribune* office in the rue de Berri, right off the Champs Elysées. This was exciting, with *Washington Post* big shots like Jim Hoagland and Flora Lewis hanging round the office and the nearby bars. Space was dreadfully short here – as well as in all other national newspaper offices I have ever known – and soon I had to move.

Starting at the top, I dared to ask *Le Monde* if they could possibly, please, find me a teeny-weeny room. They are as gentlemanly a crowd of journalists as you can find anywhere and *Le Guardian* was a name they respected, so they found me a teeny-weeny room in their busiest corridor. I was thrilled; I could use their cuttings library and from chance encounters with the staff (not many: they were always in a rush and their working day finished as mine began) I imbibed wisdom on the stories of the day. Alas, after five months *Le Monde* had grown so overcrowded that staffers could hardly pass each other in the corridors, let alone sit down, so I had to go.

Someone in the Paris bureau of the Metz-based daily, *Le Républicain Lorrain*, told me they had converted a flat into an office, grandly sited in the rue de l'Echelle, opposite the Palais Royale, a minute's walk to the river and the Louvre. It had a bathroom they didn't use, so they kindly offered to rip out the bath and let *Le Guardian* move in. In place of the bath I imported a sofa on which I could spend the night at busy times or when I wanted a rest from horsy hurly-burly at Chateau Vaugenlieu. They had an Agence France Presse ticker tape that ran all night with French news. Its tick sent me to sleep but sometimes I impressed the *Guardian* foreign desk with stories that cropped up in the middle of the night. Looking out into the night I saw that our street was a pick-up point for young male prostitutes.

I loved waking up in that office, crossing the stately Palais Royale square, buying the morning papers and, at the elegant café where I was a regular, ordering fresh, warm croissants. By the third coffee I had decided what to write about that day. This was a foreign correspondent's life as it ought to be.

What did I write about? Absolutely anything. My story on the prostitutes' strike in Lyon appeared under the headline *Whores de Combat*. The womens' protest against repression, police corruption and political hypocrisy had nationwide support, catching the public mood of cynicism under Giscard's year-old regime. Prostitutes in

202

seven other cities joined the strike, the Lyon women took sanctuary in a church until they were brutally evicted by police with dogs.

12 June 1975

...They wore jeans and headscarves, like other working women. They talked of their children more often than themselves ('what will happen to them when they start sending us off to prison?') They revived the old tear-jerking tale of the street-walker, victim of male chauvinist hypocrisy...

Victims of whom? Of the pimps, said M Poniatowski, the Minister of the Interior who sent police out with dogs to chase the girls out of the churches. He said the pimps had organised the revolt to cut losses through excessive fines. This hardly rang true, as the girls kept repeating that they wanted to be left in peace and not go back to the old brothels that were abolished in 1947. They could not have been that scared of the pimps.

Authority came off badly. Mme Francoise Giroud, the Minister for Womens' Affairs, refused to listen. The priests were sympathetic as well as hospitable: the press of all shades supported the girls; but nobody in the government seemed ready to listen. Then finally, on the day Poniatowski struck, the President's staff put out word that President Giscard d'Estaing had asked for an inquiry in the 'human condition' of the prostitutes. It was too lame and too late.

'Ponia strikes, Giscard consoles,' said the irreverent headline in the *Quotidien de Paris*. The affair caught the government in disarray at an awkward time. By the autumn, half a million school and college leavers will have joined 800,000 already unemployed. Giscard is staking his reputation on building an 'advanced liberal society' but there is an uneasy public suspicion that Giscard talks while Ponia calls out the dogs...

Graver Giscardian scandals were to follow. One Tuesday evening in 1979 I went to the theatre with a friend. Throughout the first act I was restless, uneasy, too distracted to take in the action. In the interval I left my friend, crossed the road to a bar, picked up the telephone and dialled the number for the *Canard Enchainé*, the satirical weekly that breaks a new political scandal or two every Wednesday morning. A female voice said: *'Oui?'*

203

C'est bien le Canard? [Is that the Canard?]
Oui.
Tout va bien? [Everything OK?]
Mais oui, pourquoi?' [Yes, why?]
C'a va. C'est tout. Merci madame. [Nothing. Thanks.]

I hung up, went back to the theatre and enjoyed the rest of the play. If everything was OK at the *Canard* then I was safe.

Three hours earlier, as on every Tuesday afternoon, an advance copy of Wednesday's *Le Canard* had been delivered to my office. It led with the story that Giscard had been receiving gifts of diamonds, worth £100,000 in one instance alone, from the Central African Republic's former tyrant, the Emperor Bokassa. The friendship between Giscard and the mad dictator had been scandalous enough already: Bokassa's grotesquely extravagant coronation as emperor had been financed with French support. And now this.

> 10 October 1979
> Bokassa 'gift' to Giscard
> The normally well-informed satirical weekly, *Le Canard Enchainé*, published a document this morning apparently showing that President Giscard received a personal gift of diamonds in 1973, when he was Minister of Finance.
>   The paper claims that French paratroopers, who carried out the coup which deposed Bokassa last month, went to the Imperial Palace and 'at the point of a their guns' confiscated the Emperor's private papers and took them to the French Embassy...'

After filing the story I could not enjoy the play because I was haunted by a nightmare fantasy in which copies of *Le Canard* were confiscated and the whole issue banned, leaving Schwarz alone in the wide world accusing the President of France of gross corruption. Next day *Le Monde* carried the diamonds story: I was safe. So was Giscard, who rode the scandal, as he always did, by not commenting for weeks. Such arrogance was accepted in France by all political parties and to some extent still is. For the Socialist opposition, Lionel Jospin commented: 'This is not America, nor is it

204

Britain or Holland. There isn't the breeding ground here for a Watergate – not the same puritan spirit.'

When Giscard did react to the diamond story it was with high-handed disdain

> 22 October
>
> Giscard plays a deep game in diamond scandal
>
> The importance of the diamonds is the way they have illuminated the workings of presidential rule in the Fifth Republic. Some of Giscard's African operations turn out to be astonishingly personal, secret, arbitrary and muddled. The Foreign Minister and the Minister of Communications, who are supposed to share responsibility for Africa, often learn in the newspapers about French doings in that continent.
>
> But the real scandal is the official cynicism that allowed Bokassa, a known tyrant, torturer, murderer and profiteer, to be crowned emperor. That fabulous ceremony was paid for by France and the systematic extortion that followed was at the expense of one of the poorest populations of the world.

Frenchness fascinated me, as it does every Brit living in France. Why was life here so different? Was it better over here or over there? I decided to investigate. The town of Compiègne is twinned with Bury St Edmunds in Suffolk, a historic rural town of similar size at a similar distance from the capital, a place I had never been to. Why not attempt a detailed comparison? I would compare like with like – talk in each city to a teacher, a doctor, a pupil, a policeman, a postman, a butcher and see who lived better. The *Guardian* sent a top photographer with me and I enjoyed this self-imposed assignment. My three long articles concluded that the French earned more money and had a higher standard of living, but the British lived better, with a higher quality of life.

> 7 and 9 August, 1979
>
> Coming to terms with change
>
> Constable Nigel Farthing sings in St Mary's Church choir. 'I'm a traditionalist,' he says. He personifies the wayward spirit of Suffolk as well as anyone else. He used to keep a pub but found it

tedious. On his beat, Farthing finds Bury people 'very nice, always ready for a chat…'

The Compiègne beat is tougher for Jean-Louis Delage because, as he explained, 'the French don't take kindly to the police. You check a motorist politely and he's likely to abuse you…'

French prices are 30 percent higher but they are more than offset by higher wages, higher family allowances and lower income tax. Yet the British manage to enjoy life more. The Bury police constable who sings in the church choir has no equivalent in Compiègne – nor has the Bury teacher who writes plays in French for his pupils to perform when he is not playing chamber music with them.

The British play more, laugh more and are less suspicious of their neighbours. Young Britons in a provincial town have more to do. Their teachers, outrageously underpaid by French standards, are closer to their pupils than their status-conscious French counterparts – for whom 1968 is a distant memory.

The lunch menu at the Lycée Pierre d'Ailly is circulated for approval a week in advance. On Monday: mackerel in white wine; roast beef with olives and carrots; Camembert and St Paulin; strawberries. The week's fare maintains that level to the end…

At King Edward VI Comprehensive, an equally ancient and distinguished school, Monday's lunch was rissole or roast followed by tart or prunes. But many people at King Edward VI don't turn up for lunch because there is too much to do. Some go for swimming or indoor tennis… some wander over to the music master's house for lunchtime practice. Many are rehearsing plays. The British find compensation for indifferent food. At the lycée pupils work longer hours because the *baccalaureate* is harder than A Levels. Like their hard-working parents they are earnest and rational. English pupils play more.

The Mitterrand moment

Giscard's nemesis came on 10 May 1981 when Francois Mitterrand, leader of the Socialist-Communist Union of the Left, ousted him in the presidential election. The French left, the centre and the entire youth went wild and danced in the rain. Not with enthusiasm for the introspective and secretive intellectual with a controversial past who had become president, or for the problematic union of socialists and communists: just relief after two decades of unbroken conservative rule culminating in five years of Giscardian hypocrisy, repression and scandal. 'Light has succeeded dark,' Jack Lang told the damp crowd, days before he was appointed minister of culture. Next day's *Le Monde* has the headline The New Taking of the Bastille and the days that followed were pure revolution. Pierre Mauroy, the first socialist prime minister for 23 years, spoke of 'victory for the Republic. It feels like the people of the chateau have gone and the real people can have their say at last.'

> 11 May 1981 (page one lead)
>
> Mitterrand ends 23 years of right rule
>
> ...First public reaction was incredulity – that the left should have won its first election after decades of division, deadlock and frustration. Then the Champagne came out in millions of homes... Newspapers brought out midnight editions while some leading television newscasters, appointed by Mr Giscard, whose supine style had contributed to the mood of popular revolt, tried unsuccessfully to look happy as they reported the events of the night.

I joined a dozen of our French friends in Compiègne and we roared down the Paris motorway in three cars to join ten thousand others in a drunken march down the *grands boulevards* ending in the Place de la Bastille. My friends, including a psychiatrist, a doctor and two teachers, had helped me form my opinions and judgment on French politics.

I gatecrashed Mitterrand's inauguration ceremony in the Elysée Palace's *Salle Des Fetes,* rubbing shoulders with the left's celebrities: our friends said they saw me on the telly. But Mitterrand was cold and aloof, even on that delirious day of victory. The only warm moment in a cool and rational ceremony came when Mitterrand hugged and kissed Pierre Mendez France, the 74-year-old former radical prime minister and said quietly, 'But for you I would not be here today.'

After the euphoria Francois Mitterrand's old self re-emerged: distant, devious and conceited. It had been a proud moment for me (yes, I am boasting now) during the election campaign when we foreign correspondents were chatting at a political rally and the man from *The Times* told me his foreign editor had advised him to read my article on Mitterrand.

6 December 1980

Victory for the least unloved.

...He is too bookish, too convoluted in his wit, too malevolent in his sallies, too remotely rustic in the silent avenues of oaks in his country estate. A man you say 'vous' to and not 'tu', altogether too cerebral to command strong affection... And yet, in challenging 'King Giscard,' Mitterrand has found a new and no doubt historic role. He has become spokesman for many more than Socialists. From judges and professors of political science to ordinary people who think Giscard has carried presidentialism much further than De Gaulle ever did – all think that one-man rule has gone so far that France is going through a *crise de regime*...

Am I proud of my reporting from Paris? My strength was staying alert when talking to people – from my kids' friends, teachers and parents, to the shopkeeper and local farmers who spoke freely without feeling they were being interviewed, so that my reporting was flavoured by the vernacular. Dorothy, more sociable than I, kept our home filled with locals, while Habie, already at secondary school, brought friends home who were as bright and alert as she. And I revelled in the comic differences between the French, the British and, later, the Germans.

Guardian: 19 September 1980

Scratch a Frenchman and find a peasant.

Passionate advocates of liberty, egality and fraternity, they are ruled in haughty and paternalistic fashion by a monarch they elected as president. They carry identity cards, their children wear uniform aprons in nursery school, they expect their police to be racist and their shopkeepers to be rude (but to stay open until after dusk).

They buy and sell their houses through rapacious notaries, have their news read to them by announcers who sound like hysterical wardens in an asylum, and broadcast music by people solemnly identified as Beetov, Mozzarr, Endel and Back.

In French eyes the British are suicidally decadent. But they still have remnants of a civilised society the French never knew, like country buses, milkmen, newspaper deliveries, chatty shopkeepers (until tea-time when they close), friendly policemen, a TV service free from crude political pressure and news read calmly...

A basic paradox about the French is that they try to be more modern than anyone else, going nuclear all the way and dreaming about electronics and aerospace, yet they are peasants at heart. This explains the main bone of contention between Britain and France: the Common Agricultural Policy. The French are more rural, not only in statistics (9.3 percent of them live on the land compared with only 3.1 percent of Britons) but in attitudes. Scratch a Parisian and you find a peasant, not surprisingly since 25 years ago nearly a third of France was rural. This has its good effects, like the talent for good eating and a taste for ecology, although that has not managed to stop the headlong rush to nuclear energy forced through by an authoritarian regime.

Its rural dimension is the France that most British tourists enjoy... but a peasant mentality in jacket, waistcoat and tie can be nasty. In Paris, 'merci' and 's'il vous plait' might as well be Chinese for all the currency they have. An average middle-aged Frenchman seeing another of his kind in the street would assume he was hostile until the opposite was proved. The British assumption is still the other way round. This instinctive suspicion does not affect the young who have a defensive fraternity of their own.

Having had their industrial revolution so much later, the French are superficially more modern and successful with their newer factories, neater housing estates, more streamlined banks and department stores. Their standard of living has outstripped Britain's. But their schools are stuffy and rigid, way behind in sport and art. Women are still treated as inferior in spite of the law. Petty officials summon the public to present themselves, with no question of 'your obedient servant.'

Still, my interests were too narrow. I wish I had written more about the arts, the universities, marginal and extremist political groups. But then I would have had to spend more evenings in town instead of with my family and the horses at the chateau. In India, too, I wish I had more often moved outside the agenda of the day and gone to visit the Naxalite insurgents in West Bengal or Andrah Pradesh. Foreign correspondents are sent out to 'cover' a territory, but of course they mostly only scratch the surface.

As well as me the *Guardian* employed a permanent Paris stringer, Paul Webster. This allowed me to travel. Paul and I shared our office but never became friends. He lived out of town with his French family, hurried into the office to write his story and then hurriedly left. He never seemed to take more than a few minutes on any story, which made me see him as superficial, a hack. In fact Paul, a permanent resident, knew French politics and culture better than I; he was more coldly professional in his methods, eschewing fancy prose, and I think I struck him as silly and pretentious, though he never said so. I had no evidence that he read a single one of my articles. Matters were not helped by our rivalry in freelancing: we both earned good pocket money from the BBC and other broadcasters whose various news services kept ringing up for instant comment on the news of the day. This was easy because we would simply answer questions on the story we were writing anyway for the *Guardian*. Paul will not see my reminiscences: he died in 2004 aged 67.

The Anglo-American Press Association was supposed to include us all so I joined. But I was bored at its lunch lectures by self-important people. I heard that there was another club for all the rest – the Foreign Press Club – which sounded more fun, or at least more cosmopolitan. It was both. The staid and self-righteous Anglo-Americans did not allow their members to join that other club but I joined it all the same, was welcomed as a renegade – their only Brit – and became its secretary. Here was the wide world that I loved (why else be a foreign correspondent?) – Latin Americans who could go to prison for what they wrote but never seemed to care, passionate Spaniards who appeared with more ladies than one at our parties, sinister Soviets who wrote down the names of applicants for membership in black notebooks.

Those Russians must have been low-level KGB. But the Ignatovs were different: Alexander and Helena became our best Paris friends. They chatted freely even on sensitive issues because *glasnost* and *perestroika* were in the air, if not yet enacted. Yao Yun of the Xinhua agency and his wife Tai Lee were our friends too, and invited us to penetrate the fortress that was the Chinese Embassy to learn, among other things, how the Chinese really eat, as opposed to Chinese restaurants. How different those two friendships were. The Ignatovs were Europeans reaching easily across the ideological divide. The Chinese had to shout across from another culture but Yao Yun and Tai Lee radiated enough warmth to cross the barrier. Years later I met Yao Yun in Beijing and the Ignatovs in their Moscow flat: both were extravagantly hospitable.

A dozen foreign press colleagues drove out to Chateau de Vaugenlieu for Habie's 21st birthday party. As we waited for our guests on that hot June afternoon we detected a bad smell: our underground sewage pipe had burst, just under the spot where the guests were to emerge down stone stairs onto the lawn. Malodorous water was seeping up onto the grass. We had five minutes. We dashed over to the stables, tore the tarpaulin from the haystack and spread it over the polluted grass. Some of the guests complemented us on the welcoming 'carpet' we had thought to put down.

The party was a success. One of the burly Russians chatted me up and asked me how much I earned. I thought I could see his KGB notebook bulging in his pocket. Habie fancied a good-looking, witty, mundane Spanish journalist but he turned out to be a priest writing for a leading church newspaper.

What else did I write about? Food, of course. I was invited to a publicity lunch at a fish restaurant, Les Bernadins on the Quai des Tournelles. The young Breton patron, Gilbert le Coze, was a wild-eyed fish fanatic who ran the place with his sister because, he said, you can't be married and run a serious restaurant. Every night after his last customers left, around 3am, he drove to the wholesale market at Rungis, out near Orly airport, to buy the day's fish. A few nights later I went with him.

At 4am he was the first customer: they were unpacking crates as we slithered across the wet floor. Gilbert said: 'You see this mackerel; looks all fresh and shiny? It's been treated with hyperphosphate. Ugh!' He taught me that fish has to be firm but not too smooth – just a bit gummy. I smelled of fish for a full week.

Gilbert moaned that there was hardly any really fresh fish 'because they go out in large boats and freeze it on the spot. Ugh! In five years I will quit. I think I'll try my luck as a travel agent.' Instead of that Le Coze and his sister went to Manhattan where their fish restaurant Le Bernardin was highly esteemed until his early death of a heart attack. He had an obituary in the *New York Times*.

Alas, I was in France when *nouvelle cuisine* came in. This was the fashionable revolt of younger chefs against the butter and rich sauces of their parents. I had hardly noticed this craze for delicate eating until an obscure politician who wanted to cut a figure on the world stage invited four foreign correspondents to lunch at the Hotel Bristol. None of us was interested in this man, whose name I have forgotten, but we looked forward to the lunch. Our faces fell, and fell again, and again, when dish after tiny, dainty dish appeared, each tastefully decorated with edible flowers and leaves, each leaving us hungrier than the last.

In Paris there is always novelty. I watched the Pompidou art gallery rise improbably from the ground, looking, as some locals said, like an oil refinery or like a monster with its giant outdoor escalator curling round it. Its British architect Richard Rogers told me he hoped people would ride up and down the moving stairs for the fun of it.

Peter Preston didn't allow me to sink into a routine. In my first year, 1975, the old Spanish dictator Franco was dying and took a long time over it – and I kept flying to Madrid to catch the moment. When it came I missed it and arrived just in time for the funeral.

22 November 1975 (page 1)

Madrid – The middle classes turned out in large numbers today to file past General Franco's open coffin of mahogany and gold at the rate of about one a second. His navy blue uniform of Commander-in-Chief, decorated with ribbons and campaign medals, discreetly hid the emaciation of his body after his five-week ordeal while his doctors kept him alive.

Many men as well as women wept uncontrollably as they approached and passed. Some crossed themselves, some merely bowed, several gave a smart Fascist salute, and others just blew kisses. But a considerable minority did nothing at all – just strode past with no acknowledgement, as if they had come from a sense of history on this second day of the post-Franco era...

As I left that jostling overcrowded square in Madrid a fat woman kept pushing me from behind while someone else blocked my way forward. Of course they were stealing my wallet, which had a lot of money in it. But I am a lucky man: four days later I got it back, with all the money. The thieves had robbed many others, stuffed all the wallets into a rucksack and then got caught with the swag.

Racing to West Germany

Preston rang up out of the blue: since I was reputed to speak German and we had no staff correspondent in Bonn, perhaps...? Eager to please, I said that from where I lived near Compiègne the motorway went straight up north towards Lille and Brussels with a branch to Bonn. Peter said, 'Yes, I've been looking at the map...'

I got to know the motorway well, racing to Bonn, the West German capital in the days of east-west partition, whenever its government tottered or when Baader-Meinhoff terrorists murdered a banker or were caught and brought to trial or died infamously in prison.

I liked Bonn for its provincial atmosphere, courteous officials and waiters who asked if you have enjoyed your meal (imagine a Paris waiter asking that?). In my articles I loved making fun of the sedate and ponderous West German ethos. Any embarrassment at being a British journalist called Schwarz was outweighed by the prestige of the *Guardian*. The West German government ran a comfortable press centre where you could file, eat and drink well, attend press conferences and exchange wisdom and gossip with colleagues and rivals.

My childhood German came back quickly enough to add *vox-pop* to my stories. I discovered that everyday household words learnt in childhood (needle and thread, knife and fork, river and mountain, brother and sister…) are very much more numerous than grown-up words which in any case are often international, such as democracy, president, minister, revolution…

A Sunday walk in the municipal woods outside Bonn inspired my first *Letter From Germany*. The walk turned out to be a marked-out course with knee jerks and arm bends, programmed by diagrams, equipment laid out at 22 points and instructions for proceeding at a trot from one point to the next. A woman doing it with her family summed up the national mood for me: 'First we had the *Fresswelle* (eating spree), then it was the *Reisewelle* (travel spree), now it's the *Trimmdichwelle* (keep-fit-and-lose-weight-spree)'. After France this Germany was in another world: meticulously organised and spotlessly maintained, where people conformed and participated and – for all their economic successes – constantly analysed and criticised themselves.

The big story in Germany, which was to change my life, was the peace movement and, at its heart, the Greens. The Americans had started to deploy medium-range Pershing nuclear missiles in Western Europe, especially West Germany, as a counterweight against Soviet SS20 missiles. Millions of West Germans were appalled: they felt that this was the end of deterrence and the start of preparations for a nuclear war in which Europe would be annihilated, leaving America safe.

24 October 1983

Million Germans march for peace

With a million people on the streets in four cities, Mr Willy Brandt on the rostrum and an 87-mile human chain from Stuttgart to the nearest Pershing missile base, the West German peace movement richly exceeded its own expectations.

The longest human chain in history had been organised in 23 sections. They hoped for 150,000 human links, or one every 30 inches. They got 200,000 (one for every 21.2 inches), enabling the

214

thin, brave line through the country to curve and coil along the whole road, offering up balloons and songs.

Covering these demonstrations I kept meeting angry, militant activists, mostly women, who irritated me because they seemed to have no business here: the Greens. What had missiles to do with clean air and healthy living (global warming was not yet a front-line issue)? Eventually these women converted me to their passionate belief that it was all the same struggle for human values and a return to sanity. I began to write regularly about the Greens – the only British correspondent to do so – which they appreciated and I became their friend.

Our big day: in the federal elections of 6 March 1983 the Greens got 5.6 percent of the vote, scraping over the proportional representation barrier and thereby winning 27 seats. On the day the new session opened the 27 Green MPs walked in a triumphal procession through Bonn to the Bundestag. I, their special friend in the world's press, marched with them.

Within months the Green Party leadership was entirely taken over by six of these feisty women who were as feminist as they were Green. Their group photograph adorned my piece in *Guardian Women*.

> 27 April 1984
>
> Men are parasites because they get most of the money while women do most of the work, Green women MPs told the West German Bundestag recently. One of the women, Ms Gaby Potthast, explained that this situation can only end 'when you, my fine gentlemen, are paid just what you need for yourselves in order to live, and then of course given enough time off to wash your underclothes and do the shopping, and when we women are given enough money to decide freely how, when and with whom and without whom we shall live.'
>
> This came in the Bundestag debate on women's unemployment – a term the Greens consider a macabre misnomer. 'Just imagine, if men worked a 12 or 16-hour day on their own households without pay, would they talk about men's unemployment?'

Twenty years later in my retirement, I wrote occasional pieces for the *Guardian* environment pages whose editor, John Vidal, liked them and wanted more. One day I asked John why he thought so highly of me. 'It's because you were the first,' he said. 'The first to write about the Greens.'

A foreign correspondent is little noticed in Paris which is a self-sufficient and self-satisfied city, unlike Bonn, Delhi or Jerusalem. I was no exception, apart from the odd radio interview when Britishness was in the news. But I did get that one angry piece, in French, into *Le Monde*.

I was cross with the French for their refusal to engage in the missile controversy. They had a 'Socialist' government, yet neither Mitterrand nor anyone else, not even the left-leaning press, ever even considered the case against the missiles. What angered me most was that the French media – even *Le Monde* – referred to the protestors as *pacifistes*. At a reception I met André Fontaine, editor-in-chief of *Le Monde*. Emboldened by wine, I aired my grievance with feeling. Since I was not important, Fontaine soon walked away. Eight paces later he turned his head 180 degrees and snapped: *'Faites-moi un papier'* (Do me a piece).

Absent France appeared in *Le Monde* in French and a few days later in the *Guardian* in English.

> Why is France absent from the great nuclear debate? It is considered a matter of life and death in West Germany, Britain, Holland, Belgium, Italy, Spain and Greece. It is beginning to torment the United States. It divides families, puts powerful political leaders on the defensive, mobilises the youth and causes the church to re-examine its conscience and take a stand...
>
> In France, and in France alone, the peace movement's followers are known as 'pacifists.' Nothing betrays France's intellectual isolation on nuclear matters as much as this distortion. Is it not known in France that these movements and people who agree with them include distinguished soldiers and high-ranking public officials? Eleven ex-NATO generals of eight countries recently issued a joint statement that Cruise and Pershing II are 'first-strike weapons which constitute an appropriate fuse to trigger off nuclear war in Europe...'

After my piece appeared I never detected any change of tone, in *Le Monde* or elsewhere in France.

Peter Preston wrote me a careful letter suggesting it was time I came home. After nearly ten years in France I was no longer fizzing, as he put it. He was right. A foreign correspondent too long in a post loses the capacity to be surprised and fails to go after stories that don't strike him as all that new. Peter came over, we had lunch, at which he said: 'Walter, I've been thinking about your re-entry, what you might do ... don't laugh – religious affairs? I seem to remember that in India you went quite deeply into such things.' I didn't laugh. But that is another story.

We left France but France is still with us. Ben married Fréderique, his lycée sweetheart, and they live in Paris – a French family enlarged and blessed with Chloe, Max and Noé. Our own Habie and Tanya remain bilingual and even young Zac bravely speaks French, of sorts, to anyone French. Antoine still comes over. We all feel more than a little bit French, and better off for it.

Chapter ten:
God and other stories

Seventeen years as foreign correspondent, the job I loved, were over. There was no time for lamentation. We had to sell the Chateau de Vaugenlieu and find a home in England for a family with five children and two horses, of which one was in foal. We came home with trepidation to Britain under the iron grip of Mrs Thatcher, in the depths of a recession, with dole queues and an epic miners' strike.

Guardian: 27 August 1984

Souvenirs of a belle époque

Don't come back to Thatcher's England, friends from home tell us. 'Stay in France if you can.'

We're going back all the same, from our village in Oise, near the great forest of Compiègne. It's got a shop were many cheeses are sold in fresh hunks, not plastic packs, four kinds of pâté, several gradations of plonk and some good wine.

We're moving across with our five children. They were four when we arrived in France, and the French-born one, when in trouble, says '*quelquebody 'as 'it me on my tete.'*

We move to a village of similar size in Essex. No forest, only a small wood. A shop-cum-post office, mostly packaged stuff, no beer because no licence. There is however a pub. Other British luxuries we look forward to are a milkman bringing proper milk in bottles, a newspaper boy, a decent library and people calling you 'dear' instead of monsieur or madame.

In some ways France feels to a Briton like a developing country. Authoritarian institutions but unreliable law enforcement. Colourful local customs and unspoilt countryside but rudimentary social and commercial life, many local tyrannies and an exhilarating unpredictability about daily life…

We look forward to a music programme on the radio with more music than talk, and TV without dubbed films and grinning, overdressed, condescending speakerines…

Early on my theory was that your average Frenchman, seeing another Frenchman, assumes he's an enemy unless he proves a friend; in Britain it's the other way round. That was eight years ago, before miners' pickets overturned police cars on the Humber Bridge. My theory now looks dated. Also, the young in France – a defensive fraternity because the generation gap is wider there – are friendly and maybe will remain so when they grow up.

I had been unfair on France as many readers pointed out. Much of the malaise we felt was our own fault for being too full of ourselves. Expatriates always grumble, however much they are enjoying themselves.

We were lucky to find Greenacres, a sprawling wooden bungalow half way down a winding track overlooking a pretty reservoir, with six bedrooms, two sitting rooms, seven acres and no neighbours. The ceilings seemed to us ridiculously low after our chateau.

Colchester has a fine girls' high school which charges no fees and welcomed Tanya and Zoë although their English spelling and syntax were exotic. Habie was at the London School of Economics; Ben found a place in Colchester's excellent music school to play his flute and become a musician. We had stables put in at the bottom of the garden so that from the sitting room window we could see both the reservoir and the horses' heads sticking out of their boxes.

Now settled in England that was in the grip of both Thatcherism and recession, I had kinder memories of France.

Guardian: 22 December 1984

Two cheers for Britain

…My article last summer about living with the French was much attacked for being harsh and intolerant. One critic suggested I do a piece on the British when I get back. 'You'll be surprised.'

Well, British Rail is a surprise for a start… I will not be boring about details – guards who don't turn up, leaves on the line, signals failures – because they are too familiar. But when British Rail finally perseveres into Liverpool Street, I have to cope with London Transport. The Paris metro stops at stations: the tube stops between stations…

219

The British have always been cheerful in adversity, but the utter resignation of stranded travellers – the way people actually smile at each other when the train lurches to a halt when it has only just started - strikes me as decadent.

My French friends (I did have a few) were not amused when I wrote that their homeland can feel to an expatriate Brit like a developing country – with its authoritarian institutions, racist police, rudimentary commercial services and adventurous drivers…

The British, I insist, are nicer to live among than the French. People here call you 'love,' even 'darling'. They like helping; they're sorry if they can't and say so. A Parisian shopkeeper who hasn't got what you want is triumphant.

However, those nice British people in shops and stores often don't know what they are selling, or how much it costs or, if it is out of stock, when it might arrive. 'I haven't a clue,' says many a charming shop assistant with joy and pride.

French plumbers and builders are as elusive as British ones, but when they finally turn up they get on with the job frantically fast, so they can go on to the next. In Britain they have tea breaks. They are nice to talk to and the job gets done in the end…

Our five bilingual children have settled down well – partly because we had gone to the trouble of choosing an area with good state schools. This education hassle is absent in France, which has a nation-wide state system as good in one town as another.

We had expected the children to enjoy shorter hours, no school on Saturday morning and less homework. But our 12-year old grammar schoolgirl finds this all a bit frivolous: 'Lessons are so short you can't get down to anything serious.'

Living in the country is less of an adventure in Essex than in Oise. We have found no equivalent, so far, of our French neighbour who killed eight of our cats and cut down 15 of our trees. English farmers seem modern and sophisticated after the narrow, peevish French peasants. Our Essex neighbours sound like the Archers with a better-written script. One writes about his farm in the *Essex County Standard* while his wife writes Mills and Boon novels on her word processor.

The editor had suggested over lunch in Paris that I would be writing about religion but when I arrived in the London office he said a bit testily that he already had a churches correspondent. He probably meant that he had to wait until he could put his religion man in another post, but this he did not say. Peter Preston was an editor of few words.

Without a specific title I became a de-facto feature writer, which was exciting because Richard Gott was a distinguished features editor, a public schoolboy with impeccable manners whose heroes are Che Guevera and Fidel Castro. Richard thought highly of me even though my opinions are many leagues to the right of his.

He sent me up north to look with a fresh eye at the miners' strike, the epic battle between Mrs Thatcher and the union leader Arthur Scargill. I was impressed by the miners' embattled solidarity and although I am no leftie I hoped they would win. They lost.

13 September 1984

Men at the front in Scargill's total war

'The way this strike had educated t'lads politically is beautiful, just beautiful.' Brian Wroe, in his 41 years down Yorkshire pits and six years in the Communist Party, has seen nothing more beautiful.

He was helping out in the Barnsley strike office, organising the soup kitchen, finding out if a missing picket was in hospital or merely arrested.

'A strike used to have old-timers up front: now it's the young lads. I'm right proud of t'lads. It's their fight now: when t'pit closes they've nowhere to go.'

That feeling is evident all over this border country between a Scargill heartland around Barnsley and the scab country across the Notts border, where union officials are shamefaced about being at work and won't be quoted by name.

At Shireoaks colliery, Keith Gilfoyle, aged 24, sounded surprised at his own conversion. 'I used to respect policemen and t'law and that. But these coppers come here from all over t'place and do what t'hell they like: they're on t'other side.'

I flew to Germany to disentangle an acrimonious argument among historians about whether the Holocaust was a perfectly natural and predictable corollary of Stalin's massacres. I made myself read history books in German and my report pleased Richard Gott though it attracted little notice.

Next, Richard wanted me to investigate his notion that moral protest against Thatcherism had given Britain a new version of the old non-conformist conscience. I interview outraged bishops, feminists, trade unionists, Green activists, the all-purpose dissident Tony Benn and my Marxist brother-in-law, Eric Hobsbawm.

Eric said it was Thatcher herself who was the non-conformist because she rejected what most people in Britain believed in – 'the sense of fairness, the sense of noblesse oblige on the part of the upper classes, the sense that ordinary people can deserve something, and above all the sense that the community and state have social responsibilities.'

This assignment resulted in a series of articles and a little book, *The New Dissenters: The Non-conformist Conscience in the Age of Thatcher* (Bedford Square Press 1989) which, as I write, is available from amazon (UK) at a cost of one penny.

I am grateful to Gott for indulging my wish to delve deeper into the Green ideology, which he never claimed to share since his soul is red not green. Having absorbed greenery from those feisty women in West Germany, I became an unofficial environment writer alongside John Vidal. I set out to explore a multitude of emerging 'Green' alternatives to the runaway market economy, and Gott was generous with space. A series of three breathless articles appeared under the heading *The Phoenix Economy*, on decentralised Green initiatives that were supposed to rise from the ashes of Thatcherism.

> 28 January 1985
> The long march of the barefoot economy
> If you can't get a job get to work. Start a business, join a co-operative, help improve your village, your suburb or your home. If you can't help yourself help others: exploit your hobbies and your talents. The grass roots economy exists, is expanding and, according to the new economists and philosophers, destined to become the norm...

I covered meetings of TOES – The Other Economic Summit – timed to clash with the annual G7 meeting of the Group of Seven richest industrial countries, where the grassroots economy was explored and fiercely debated. Green economics was not yet widely known but today the New Economics Foundation, on whose founding committee I served, is a respected and much-quoted authority.

I interviewed Satish Kumar, the charismatic prophet of ecological living who had walked without any money from his native India to Britain via the Soviet Union, to promote peace. Satish, who was editor of *Resurgence* magazine and founder of the pioneering Small School at Hartland, Devon, became our friend. He enlisted my help in realising his dream of establishing a Green university: Schumacher College, in the lordly green fields of Dartington Hall in Devon, where it still flourishes.

Satish had founded Green Books and invited me to expand my Guardian series, *The Phoenix Economy*, into a book. I asked Dorothy, a better writer than I, to be co-author. *Breaking Through - Theory and Practice of Wholistic Living* (Green Books 1987) explored what we optimistically called 'a new world which is breaking through the rigid structures of worn-out thinking, like grass coming up between the cracks of paving stones.' We spelt 'holistic' wrong on purpose to show we were talking about living, not praying.

We found we could write together: Dorothy had a better eye for how people and places looked and could put some of her sardonic asides into her prose but she was weaker, I maintain, on the orderly organisation of an argument. Computers had come in but we could barely manage our new Amstrad and sometimes at night we woke our elder son, Ben, to rouse the evil machine from its latest sulk. Ben had left his music school and took a degree in computer science.

Breaking Through received kindly, somewhat patronising, reviews, acknowledging our sincerity but questioning our confidence that these ideas would break through into the mainstream. The Green movement's leading spokesman, Jonathan Porritt, in the *Guardian*, welcomed our 'admirably lucid and accessible update on what's happening on the green scene' but found us too optimistic. Today, 25 years later, we can claim that we were, in a manner of speaking, right: it is politically incorrect not to be Green in one shade or other.

I was settling happily into my role of environmental feature writer, just reaching that wonderful break-even point when your articles get reaction, feedback and information from readers which leads you on to fresh articles. But now fate caught up with me. The editor called me in. A new post was now available if I wanted it: religious affairs correspondent.

I had not the slightest idea what this job involved, having never read a single article by the current churches correspondent, Martyn Halsall, a poet based in Manchester. I asked Peter Preston for 24 hours to think about it. Colleagues advised me to take the job because religion was becoming more prominent in world affairs. I imagined that as a seasoned international correspondent I would operate worldwide, a 'fireman' dashing out to murderous Muslim fanatics, scheming cardinals, Tibetan mystics and surely, somewhere, a miracle. So I said yes.

The job proved less glamorous and less cosmopolitan than that, although I did accompany the Archbishop of Canterbury on a theologically hazardous visit to Rome and to the embattled Christians of war-torn southern Sudan. I did tour eastern Europe after the fall of communism to examine the condition of its soul, and I went to America to poke gentle fun at rabble-rousing, millionaire evangelists, and politely challenge the Catholic Church on its doctrinal embarrassments and paedophile scandals.

In South Carolina I did my best to be serious at Bob Jones University, the unpolluted spring of American fundamentalism.

7 April 1987

On campus, boys and girls must at all times remain at least six inches apart. The thickly-carpeted 'social hall' looks at first sight like a furniture store: scores of spotless divans have been provided for seemly, supervised dating. Off campus, dating is allowed only with a chaperone... No dating is allowed between races, with or without a chaperone, for the precise biblical reason that God

224

separated the races and will reunite them in his own time at the Second Coming...

The men among the 5,000 students all wear ties and none of the women wear jeans or slacks... The campus atmosphere is like a cult; the same inner-group feeling of exclusiveness, the sense of esoteric knowledge, of exaltation and self-absorption...

Those foreign assignments were my treats. Day to day I needed to immerse myself in the tortured intrigues and doctrinal battles inside the Church of England, in which the *Guardian* was not much interested but felt it ought to report because the Church was part of the establishment.

I liked talking to bishops and vicars, who were more friendly, or at least more polite, than politicians. I enjoyed reviewing controversial theology books because what God does or does not do concerns us all and is therefore a good story, whether he or she exists or not. My problem was that church news was difficult to disentangle, hard work for which I needed to be rewarded by my stories appearing in full, at the top of the page, where I had been used to seeing them for two and a half decades. Alas! I now found my hard-won reports at the bottom of an inside page, often heavily cut.

My compensation was my Saturday column, *Face to Faith*, which I could write or commission anyone else to write. I liked to feel that this made me a more powerful journalist than I had ever been, because no editor or subeditor stood between me and the published article. True, few readers and fewer colleagues ever read *Face to Faith* but it had a following, as the correspondence showed.

Updating God

I became immersed in the re-appearance at that time of an old controversy: does faith depend on the literal truth of miracles? A trendy vicar was arguing that it did not. David Jenkins, the Bishop of Durham, was making similar suggestions in a more academic and circumspect way. I agreed. I am not a believer, but my head was full of 'deep ecology' and other forms of spiritual environmentalism and I was dazzled by what little I understood of quantum physics, which had apparently abolished the distinction between the observer and the observed and questioned the solidity of matter.

18 March 1986

Face to faith.

Can God be brought up to date? The recurring dream is as old as religion itself. John Robinson, Bishop of Woolwich, dreamed it aloud in *Honest to God*, in the 60s. Don Cupitt dreamed it more recently in his *Sea of Faith*... The week before last Sir Richard Acland, a brave but lonely critic of the old-fashioned God, dreamed it again in a lecture... The moral message is urgent because God, modernised, is no longer omnipotent, but stands re-defined as the central order of things and events.

A boring, uninspiring God? Not if you see him in a Beethoven symphony, in 3,000 years of recorded religious experience, in the total inability of scientific man to explain the mind, never mind the soul, in the way modern physics is returning to its origins in metaphysics. What makes scientists tick if not their faith in an ordered universe?

A modern God will need a modern church. Its bishops will include nuclear physicists to teach us about the new frontiers that have made atoms unimportant, demoted the status of matter itself and questioned the distinction between observer and observed. Other bishops will be psychologists. Revealed scriptures will include Bach oratorios. Theology will be an empirical science, constructing its theories on the raw material of religious experience...

Modern religion will have no dogma, only theories valid until they are disproved... Its faith: the belief that life has meaning and therefore the world is worth saving. Any volunteers?

Unfortunately, there were. I received dozens of letters. One suggested I hold a public meeting to 'establish our presence'. I was appalled. I replied instantly and firmly that I was a journalist, not an activist, godly or ungodly. But I stuck with the campaign: this was a political story too, because the Bishop of Durham was as fierce a critic of Thatcherism as of literalist religion. I went to Durham to take soundings in his diocese and interview the Bishop in his palace, Auckland Castle. We got on well; David Jenkins appreciated having an ally in the *Guardian* although he was worried lest I get him into more trouble.

And when news was quiet, there was always my column for airing my thoughts on God and his urgent need to be Green.

> 7 March 1988
> Face to faith
> ...Religion needs to be reinvented in every age. In this age a religion which does not speak cogently of peace, human brotherhood and ecology is dated indeed. Conservative religion is false religion, while true religion is subversive.

Thirteen guest contributions to my *Face to Faith* debate about miracles were published as a book, with my introduction – *Updating God* (Marshall Pickering 1988). As I write, four used copies are available from amazon at £2.75.

The big story of those years was women priests. Should they be allowed in the Church of England for the first time in its 450-year history? The *Guardian*, in so far as it cared at all, was in favour (has it not always been the most feminist of British dailies?) and so was I. For months before the synod vote on 11 November 1992, I was wooed by the pro-lobby – mostly bright, lively young women who were nice to me because they saw me as an ally, and also the anti-lobby, mostly unmarried priests, high-church, musty and slightly smelly.

I was at a Christmas party given by a group of smellies. Emboldened by drink, I stood up before my hosts, waved my forefinger at them and said: 'I have a question. Can you imagine Jesus standing here in this room, waving his finger at us like this and saying: 'No women priests'?' I thought that was a good sally but it fell flat: they said I was obviously ignorant of the theology which made such an occurrence entirely plausible.

> 12 November 1992 (page one lead)
> Synod accepts women priests.
> Women deacons cheered, hugged each other and sang hymns yesterday outside Church House, Westminster, after the Church

of England, by two votes from its House of Laity, agreed to admit women to the priesthood…

In search of more exotic copy, I set out to explore the cults – Moonies, Scientologists, Children of God, Hari Krishna. Some of these sects had matured and become less sinister than the anti-cult organisations set up to rescue their young victims. Those anti-cult fanatics tried to 'deprogram' young converts, often using draconian and dangerous methods.

My tolerant approach pleased Britain's foremost expert on cults, Professor Eileen Barker at the London School of Economics who was neutral on the matter and even had cult friends. She asked me to serve on the board of INFORM, an NGO she had just set up with Home Office support to give information about cults to prospective converts, victims, renegades and distraught parents. Eileen and her group were vilified in the tabloid press as being soft on cults, even secret members!

Eileen became a family friend and she arranged for me to be the first journalist to visit the Children of God, whose reputation was that they sexually abused children. This American cult really did have a sordid history in the US but in a remote village in Leicestershire I found some of the healthiest, happiest families I had ever seen – as Eileen knew I would. To tease her, and the reader, I began my piece in mock-tabloid-exposé style.

> 19 March 1993
>
> Children of a lusty god
>
> This week I penetrated the secret home of the Children of God, denounced by the media around the world as a wicked sex cult led by a pervert who made beautiful young girls sell their bodies to get new members, and encourage sex with children to 'glorify God.'
>
> Villagers do not know who lives in the remote house in Leicestershire, where I was led after promising not to reveal its address. Even the vicar does not know the cult is in his village…
>
> I heard the whispered confessions of nine-year-olds and life stories of the leaders, who are called shepherds. I was shocked by what I found.

- The 12-bedroom house, containing 10 adults and 30 children, from babies to teenagers, was spotlessly clean and tidy! As I entered I saw gumboots neatly stacked.
- The children are NOT allowed to watch violent TV programmes! I thought with sadness of my own 12-year-old who watches mostly that... Instead I saw a group of five teenagers with guitars and the latest gear rehearse a rock song. The lyric went: What did Jesus do without a pair of tight designer jeans? What did Jesus do without a Sony Walkman? He tried to teach us how to give...
- Apart from the music there was no other noise! Except quacking geese and children playing – without fighting or quarrelling. They played without expensive toys. In a dormitory I saw a notice: 'It pleases God that children should be respectful to their elders.'
- Sex is NOT allowed for anyone under 16 and FORBIDDEN between anyone over 21 and anyone under. Gideon, 42, told me: 'sex is about two percent of our lives. I wish we could manage more...'
- All the kids seemed as confident that they will fight off their enemies as nine-year-old Martin was, when he overheard gloomy grown-up talk, and said decisively: 'We're not a cult. We're the good guys.'

I did the religion job for ten years – three years too many – until I retired. With women priests safely over the hurdle and environmental reporting in John Vidal's brilliant hands, I became bored, grew lazy and began to be reproached behind my back for being 'semi-detached', as the editor himself reportedly put it.

I often stayed at home beside our pretty reservoir, enjoying our rural family life, covering church news by telephone interviews and uploading my stories on our Amstrad. I congratulated myself that on the news editor's screen my story would look exactly the same as if I had filed it from within the office. On a typical summer afternoon I would be in the vegetable garden, where I could not hear the telephone. One of the children would yell 'Dad – news desk!' I would run at full speed into the house, agree to do the story they wanted, make a phone call or two, write the copy, upload it and go back to weeding.

Peter Preston had rightly brought me home from Paris because I no longer 'fizzed' there. He didn't now move me from religion, even though I had grown semi-detached. Preston was not a communicator. In my ten years as religion correspondent he never once called me into his office to discuss the job and explore ways, perhaps, of widening its scope to make better use of my experience and talents. I don't think Peter was much interested in religion.

It was my own fault of course. I dislike offices, which was why I had wanted to be a foreign correspondent in the first place. Offices make me look at my watch and think of the countryside. I am bored by committees, though I am sociable enough in a pub. Crucially, I never attended the *Guardian* morning editorial conference. For eight years I did not even know that I was entitled to attend, assuming it was only for departmental heads. Nobody told me. If I had been one of the boys, and come up with bright ideas, Preston might perhaps have thought to broaden my range, or even move me beyond religion into new excitement. Yes, my own fault. I wish I had been more clubbable.

Back at Greenacres our horsy family thrived. Dorothy transferred her enthusiasm from breeding horses to training German shepherd dogs. She started teaching creative writing for adults at Colchester's excellent adult education institute (it has deteriorated since then under the weight of funding cuts). Dorothy is popular with her students and as I write, 26 years later, her classes still have waiting lists. She wrote her own stories too, as she has always done and still does, some of which were published or broadcast on Radio 4. Her collection *Simple Stories About Women* (Iron Press) came out in 1988.

Habie took a first in linguistics at the London School of Economics and went on to make films with the BBC. Tanya thrived at the girls' grammar school where she organised debates with the boys' grammar school and found tall and handsome Tom. She went on to Bristol to do medicine, hated it and transferred to anthropology at Cambridge. Her much-praised PhD thesis was published as a book: *Ethiopian Jewish Immigrants: The Homeland Postponed* (Curzon 2001).

Ben, no longer an aspiring flautist, was learning computer science at King's College, London, but his mind was on Frédérique, his sweetheart from his Compiègne lycée. Their two-stage wedding, at the *mairie* in Compiègne and at Greenacres in a summer marquee, was a life-enhancing Anglo-French event, expertly filmed by Habie.

Zoë was a rising star at the Girls High, getting top marks, predicted as a certainty for Oxbridge, popular enough to be the favourite for the upcoming head girl election. She was a stylish rider and was often out early, grooming Najem, the horse she loved. At the piano she played Chopin with more insight and feeling than technique.

Little Zaco had hated moving from France when he was four years old. He kept on tying chairs and tables together with string, which we interpreted as his silent plea for continuity. At last he learnt how to be English, just as I had done half a century earlier, fell in with English school life and soon had five little friends so close that the group is still together as adults.

In London I stayed one night a week with my mother, aged 90, in her flat in St John's Wood and cooked supper for her. She remained a hospitable, gentle Viennese lady to the last. She died in 1995, the year I retired.

Living lightly

I have called myself a lucky boy, and I felt lucky again when I retired. Instead of putting up my slippered feet I was at work with Dorothy on a book that was to take us to Australia, India, the USA, Canada and Japan. In *Living Lightly, Travels in Post-Consumer Society* (1998 Jon Carpenter Publishing) we set out to portray happy pioneers of a simpler, 'greener' life.

In Seattle we stayed among fanatics of 'voluntary simplicity' – middle class eccentrics who bought everything second-hand and read *Tightwad Gazette*, *Penny Pincher Times* and *Use Less Stuff Report*. In New England we were guests at a farm practising 'community-supported agriculture' in which customers pay in advance for what they want grown.

In Tennessee we researched The Farm, the famous hippy community that had survived from the 1970s and matured into more or less sustainable adulthood. The Farm's story began in 1971 with an exodus of biblical resonance by 270 hippie students travelling out of San Francisco in a ragged convoy of decrepit buses known as The Caravan, in search of the promised land. A bearded prophet led them out – Stephen Gaskin, their charismatic, new age, LSD-tripping philosophy lecturer whose 'sermons' preached revolt against authority, against war, against violence, for love, for going back to the land, for hard work and, as the movement matured, for giving up hard drugs. That was a revolution – hippies who wanted to work, live frugally and renounce drugs, drink, meat, and even coffee.

The first generation of children grew up like an extended family. The Farm attracted 10,000 visitors a day during the mid-seventies, ten times its average population. By 1983 its numbers had grown to 1,500. That was the year of the debacle. Debts could no longer be paid. Then the 'changeover' after which only people who could make their own living could stay.

We found a community of 220 people on 900 acres, an oasis of peace and space. The original caravans with their peeling slogans ('*Out to Save the World*') are immobile and rusting with potted flowers on the bonnets. The Farm runs an eco-village training centre. We had to work for our keep, washing dishes, cleaning floors, weeding crops. It was humbling to be scolded for sloppy cleaning by a girl scarcely older than our daughters.

In Canada we stayed on a 'co-housing' estate built by people who wanted to live together while still enjoying the privacy of their own homes. We were guests of a family living self-sufficiently on a Welsh mountain farm. We stayed with townspeople living co-operatively in Chicago, Utrecht and Maleny in Queensland, Australia. We experienced permaculture in its purest form at Crystal Waters, Australia, and cooperative farming in India. We investigated, somewhat tongue-in-cheek but still with admiration and affection, the big new-age Findhorn community in Scotland and the even larger 'City of Dreams' in Auroville, South India.

Again Dorothy and I worked well together. For me it could be disconcerting to arrive somewhere and NOT be feted and spoiled as the *Guardian* correspondent. Dorothy rose better than I to the challenge of working for our keep and conducting interviews as well. She learnt to be a reporter and in the writing, as before, we were complementary in our talents.

Living Lightly came out in 1998 to good reviews but the book proved too long, insufficiently angled for a big market. I suppose we should have been less self-indulgent, but we had so many stories to tell – some funny, some inspiring, some just pathetic.

Chapter eleven:
Losing Zoë

At Greenacres the children do their homework on the long dining room table in front of the picture windows that look over the lawn, the vegetables, the stables and fields, all the way down to the reservoir. Habie, our film-maker, has left home; she comes back to shoot a video of little Zaco. It shows him watching his favourite film *Little Big Man*. Zoë, aged 13, canters up on Shah, taps on the window to attract his attention, canters back in a show-off manner. Zoë sits Shah as if she had grown on his back.

Clouds began to gather over this charmed life when Zoë, at 18, unaccountably lost her sparkle and sank into malaise, then depression and mental instability. Her brilliant schoolwork fell away. On the day of the election for head girl, which she was tipped to win, she stayed at home. She became ill with what the doctor said might be glandular fever. Recovered from that, her moods swung between elation and depression. She became promiscuous, talked of leaving home, of killing herself.

We all saw it as a growing-up problem: such a brilliant, funny, popular, loving and beautiful girl could not be deeply flawed. Zoë was admitted to a psychiatric unit and diagnosed with bi-polar affective disorder, which used to be called manic depression. She hated being a patient, seemed to recover by an act of will and settled back into precarious normality. She passed her exams, went to Bristol University where she chose, unexpectedly, to study religion. She grew manic again, failed to study, became disorderly and was sent down although the dean of students was sympathetic and offered to keep her place open.

Back home she was silent, morose. The psychiatrist advised us to leave her alone in her room but one evening Dorothy looked in on her all the same. Zoë told her she had taken a massive overdose of anti malarial quinine. We rushed her to hospital and had her stomach pumped out – with my formal agreement which was required by law.

Zoë recovered, used her charisma to get a tough job selling insurance on-site to building workers, which she could not sustain (who could?). She met Kingsley from Nigeria who became her partner and persuaded her to go back to college. We thought she couldn't manage that but we were wrong: Zoë had friends (she always had so many) who got her into Essex University in spite of her medical history and her record at Bristol. She went on to the London School of Economics, achieved an MSc with distinction in sociology, and told us: 'I've been to the bottom. I'm strong.' We believed her. We blotted out the nightmare episodes. A consultant had muttered that this problem was likely to recur but we did not hear him.

Zoë took on a pioneering job with United Response, a major charity where her intelligence and energy brought in more customers and money than anyone had hoped for. She was a success, even when, as we know in retrospect, she was becoming manic again. Her plans for her future became irrational, her outbursts of temper physically violent. Yet she willed us to believe in her. She brainwashed us. 'Zoë is Zoë,' we said, and so did her brothers and sisters and friends. If we questioned her, let alone criticised, she would march out and slam the door. The glass panel in our kitchen door still has a crack.

So, brainwashed, we didn't think of manic depression when she punched Habie in a quarrel (Zoë was very strong) and, in another quarrel, bit through Zac's sweater and into his chest. Or when she almost killed her mother and best friend by crashing into a barrier on a busy motorway in heavy rain at 85mph. Zoë is Zoë…

She began smoking pot as more than a recreational drug, and we later found from her diaries that she was taking cocaine as well, even while trying to build up a business of her own, a desperate attempt at self-medication. When her life began to disintegrate, she went to Morocco for an indefinite stay.

'Over the top' was how we all described her emails – deliriously happy in Morocco with a new lover she planned to marry. 'To the best parents, best brothers and sisters in the world,' she wrote, inviting us for a holiday, which she lovingly planned in meticulous detail.

Almost as soon as we arrived at Essaouira, she turned against us. In high mania, anyone who potentially brings you down is an enemy – and who is more back-to-earth than mum and dad? She acted crazy, haranguing the entire hotel with an exalted spirituality mingled with obscene abuse. We had to sign a section committing our daughter to the secure mental hospital in Marrakech. There, they treated her (we checked it out) in exactly the same way they would have done anywhere else, with the same drugs to bring her 'down'. With help from the British consul, we got her home after only 12 days in hospital.

Ten days later, the depression we now expected set in, worsening by the day. Zoë became a hollow, silent woman. Colchester hospital has a state-of-the-art mental-health unit and the specialist in charge visited Zoë at home once a week. She liked him, but as the weeks passed, her depression refused to lift. She sat around all day. We believed, as many friends and relatives told us, that she would 'come out of it in her own time, when she's ready'. We cannot now forgive ourselves for reacting, during some of that time, like normal parents when their unsmiling child is surly and irritable.

On 22nd August 2000 at 11am, Zoë told her mother that she was going to visit a friend. We had repaired her old car, which she had neglected, to give her some independence. Her real destination was a train station on the London line.

Zoë had told her mother, weeks earlier, that suicide was 'not an option'. Once again, we were conniving with her – once more in denial. You cannot accept – it makes no sense – that a young woman who is clever, beautiful, talented, witty and loved should be in such despair that she would end her own life under an express train.

She left this note, meticulously written in neat handwriting:

> To my family and friends. No one is to blame for my death. I love you all but I can't live like this. I'm sorry. Please forgive me. I used to work and see friends a lot, but now I can do neither because I can't function or communicate. I've been in hell for four months and I can't bear the pain any more. Zoë.

Two days after her death, 40 friends and relations came to sit round a bonfire on the lawn. They told tearful stories that we had never heard before, of how Zoë had helped, inspired and empowered timid young people. What if she herself had had better care and attention, if she had not felt so alone?

I believe I have led a charmed and lucky life. But five years after my retirement losing Zoë brought tragedy and grief, and, I hope, a new compassion.

*This account of Zoë's last years is drawn from our article in the *Guardian*, Losing Zoë, 11 December 2002, and Dorothy's book: *Behind a Glass Wall – the Anatomy of a Suicide* (Chipmunkapublishing 2005)

Chapter twelve:
Endgame

It is more than ten years since Zoë died. The children have moved out and tell us that Greenacres is too big for us, although they are happy enough to gather here. We cannot bear to move because of the view over the reservoir and because we have no neighbours although we are only 50 minutes by train from London. The stables and pasture are rented out to the next generation of horsy people. I am properly retired now, content with that because I have always been lazy – energetic only when fired by ambition, a news story, a deadline or hiking in hills.

Walter, Naomi, Aaron

Dorothy's enthusiasm moved on again, from German Shepherds to parrots, of which she has approximately 25, mostly, thank goodness, in an outside aviary. She is, as you might expect, a popular contributor to parrot magazines. She has become famous in the parrot world for 'enrichment' – giving her birds swings, branches, ropes and all manner of toys as compensation for their captivity. In the aviary, at ground level, chickens feed on the seeds and crumbs let fall by the profligate parrots, and lay eggs for us.

To spare myself excessive bird talk I tell Dorothy's parrot friends that I am a parrot husband, not a parrot person. But I have come to love her pair of wise African Greys, Artha and Casper, who perch so discreetly in the kitchen that I hardly know they are there until Casper whistles the opening bar of Beethoven's fifth symphony which I have taught him.

I attend story-readings by Dorothy's creative-writing students whom she has inspired to produce their own anthology. Everyone but me calls her Dot. One grateful class decided to keep going forever on their own, writing and criticising, calling themselves Ellipsis because it means dot-dot-dot.

Tanya graduated from Tom to Niall who is even taller, and the marquee went up again for their wedding. Niall's quiet good nature and common sense have made him a pillar of the family. One day most weeks I take the train to London to be with Aaron, Naomi and Zeb. Habie and Zac live just down the road from them in West Hampstead.

Habie runs her own market research company and writes her reports in French for such posh Parisian clients as L'Oréal. Zac is a headhunted star in public relations, a manager at Shine Communications, where he met his Laura. Ben, a cyber-consultant in Paris, has become a Frenchman: he has that French habit of not replying if you criticise France, as if you had uttered an obscenity. Twice a year he and Fredy come over with Chloë, Max and Noë, all three of whom we love but see too seldom.

On Wednesday evenings I sing in a choir. I listen to classical music on my computer. I take my German Shepherd, Honey, hiking on Essex and Suffolk footpaths, giving shameless preference to walks that lead to a pub. I regret that this land is so flat. I join three male cronies of my age, Ron, John and Jim, for monthly pub lunches without wives. I write my memoirs.

Twice a year I go to Provence, where the Luberon hills are only as demanding as a slow-walking old man can manage.

54th wedding anniversary

Old man in sandals

Montfuron stands in rock and fir on a modest mountain of its own. A stone windmill stands guard, telling of the Middle Ages. Turn right by the dry-stone church into the square, were the *mairie* presides. Stone houses surround the square, each with red-tiled roof and shutters in faded pastel. Look across to the mountains of Digne and Valensole.

The square is empty, as it often is except for the cats. But who is the old man, tall, white-bearded and wispy-haired, who strolls out of the Rue Grande in shorts and sandals? He stops to admire a somnolent black cat, knowing better than to approach it because the Montfuron cats are shy, semi-wild.

He stops again at his friend Francois' little antique store which is also a bar and a tearoom, the only shop in Montfuron. It is six o'clock and Francois is already down in the bar with two or three of his regulars, his cronies. They have squeezed in between antique chairs, vases, crockery and framed pictures and lean against the tiny bar, drinking coffee. Bob is playing against Francois at *quatre-cents-vingt-et-un*, a game of dice that you win entirely by luck so your mind can concentrate on wisecracks and gossip.

The old man suspects that sometimes they gossip about him. Why does this Englishman come here alone, twice every year, spring and autumn, regular as a migrating bird, when he has a wife back in England? To get away from her, Bob might say. Bob is also old; he is here every evening, no doubt to get away from his wife.

But no, Serge might counter, *le vieux anglais* is crazy about hiking in the Luberon hills. Serge, a prosperous wheat farmer, claims to have seen the Englishman as early as 7am, loading his rucksack and boots into his car.

Henri, who has a goatee beard and keeps goats, might add that he's heard Francois, who knows the Englishman better than anyone else, say that the fellow talks a lot about his wife, and in glowing terms. Francois himself may, however, concede that possibly the Englishman comes, in part, to get away from his wife's parrots of whom there are said to be more than 20.

And Francois, pouring himself another pastis, might add in his twangy Provencal growl that his friend Walter the Englishman was a journalist in his day, for ten years the *Guardian* Paris correspondent, and this is obvious because the fellow asks people what they think of Nicolas Sarkozy even though most people in Montfuron don't give a damn one way or the other about the president. And his French is better than any other Brit around here, although Francois, who can play the saxophone and has a musical ear, sometimes detects a faint hint of something else in the Englishman's accent.

A hint of German?

#

Lightning Source UK Ltd.
Milton Keynes UK
02 April 2011

170290UK00001B/17/P